Inventing America's "Worst

Inventing America's "Worst" Family

Eugenics, Islam, and the Fall and Rise of the Tribe of Ishmael

Nathaniel Deutsch

UNIVERSITY OF CALIFORNIA PRESS
Berkeley · Los Angeles · London

University of California Press, one of the most
distinguished university presses in the United States,
enriches lives around the world by advancing
scholarship in the humanities, social sciences, and
natural sciences. Its activities are supported by the UC
Press Foundation and by philanthropic contributions
from individuals and institutions. For more
information, visit www.ucpress.edu.

University of California Press
Berkeley and Los Angeles, California

University of California Press, Ltd.
London, England

Library of Congress Cataloging-in-Publication Data

Deutsch, Nathaniel.
    Inventing America's "worst" family : eugenics, Islam,
and the fall and rise of the tribe of Ishmael / Nathaniel
Deutsch.
        p.   cm.
    Includes bibliographical references (p.   )
and index.
    ISBN 978-0-520-25523-4 (cloth : alk. paper) —
    ISBN 978-0-520-25524-1 (pbk. : alk. paper)
    1. Eugenics—United States—History.
2. Marginality, Social—United States—History.
3. McCulloch, Oscar C. (Oscar Carleton), 1843–1891.
I. Title.
HQ755.5.U5D66   2009
363.9′2—dc22   2008017181

Manufactured in the United States of America

18 17 16 15 14 13 12 11 10 09
10 9 8 7 6 5 4 3 2 1

The paper used in this publication meets the minimum
requirements of ANSI/NISO Z39.48–1992 (R 1997)
(*Permanence of Paper*).

Contents

Illustrations

Foreword

Every so often, a book arrives that fundamentally changes how we think. Marshall Sahlins's *Culture and Practical Reason* reconfigured our understanding of the role of material forms in cultural life. Saskia Sassen's *The Global City* effectively redrew the relationships of metropolitan areas by showing that some cities were more intimately tied to cities in other countries than to those in their own nation-states. William Julius Wilson, in *The Declining Significance of Race,* argued that social class and race were mutually constitutive and that in each historical period, the two had differential import in determining life chances for black Americans; our current thinking regarding the relative import of race versus class in shaping social outcomes has been fundamentally altered by his work. No one would doubt that Sahlins, Wilson, and Sassen have changed the course of anthropology, sociology, and urban geography, respectively.

With the arrival of Nathaniel Deutsch's *Inventing America's "Worst" Family,* we may find ourselves at a similar moment. The book chronicles the topsy-turvy saga of one family—the so-called Tribe of Ishmael—but its impact may be much broader: it could change the way we understand poverty and race relations in the United States.

To see why, one must look at the last three decades of research on race and poverty in America. After the civil rights era, there was unprecedented social scientific interest in understanding the causes of social inequality. The question of interest may be framed as follows: If America truly entered the age of affluence in the postwar era—in no small part by presumably having removed the final barriers to racial subjugation—why then do we continue to find entrenched enclaves of (largely minority) inner-city poor people, who are unable to participate in society in any meaningful way? The answers differ. Some point to the culture of the poor: that is, to the idea that the poor transmit values to their children, such as a lack of respect for the work ethic, in such a way that successive generations reproduce the socioeconomic failure of their predecessors. Others call attention to institutional factors: spatial mismatch patterns and discriminatory labor unions do not fairly or equitably distribute opportunities for work, higher wages, and social mobility. Still others remain convinced that American capital will never integrate black labor in any meaningful way.

But, at their core, researchers generally hold in common that the 1960s civil rights era was a watershed era for race relations—few dispute that America has become a more racially tolerant society or has sought effective means to help its poor populations. Yet all around us we find the existence of entrenched poverty and the effects of racially discriminatory practices. This would lead us to ask, "Have we simply entered another phase of structured inequity and racial disparity, despite certain social and economic advances that have been made?" Perhaps unwittingly, social science has really just bought into popular folk notions of social progress by refusing to consider more critically the staying power of racial hatred in American consciousness. Maybe it is even complicit in maintaining the existence of a poor class of Americans. If social science is implicated in the reproduction of such inequities—and there is no reason to believe a priori that it is exempt—then it may be worth understanding exactly this price of progress.

The contemporary relevance of *Inventing America's "Worst" Family* becomes immediately apparent only a few pages into the text when Deutsch roots the Ishmaels in the efforts of Americans to identify the ideal family and its opposite. As if to presage the 1980s indictment of the black single mother—whom President Ronald Reagan characterized as a "welfare queen"—Deutsch argues that scholars and activists in the late nineteenth and early twentieth centuries turned the white Ishmael family into "the living symbol for all that was wrong with America." The Ishmael "tribe" became the repository of hatred, bigotry, and misunderstanding. And in the process, by specifying the dysfunctional variant in this manner, an idealization of the functional American family emerged.

The Ishmaels were not natural candidates for this role. For the most part, they were southern farmers who until the end of the nineteenth century boasted few remarkable attributes apart from the capacity to work the land. As poverty gripped rural America after the 1870s, such farmers joined European immigrants and emancipated slaves migrating to Midwestern cities in search of opportunity. Those, like the Ishmaels in Indianapolis, who were unable to integrate successfully became the urban dispossessed—an impoverished mix of poorly educated, low-skilled, racially subjugated, and otherwise disadvantaged social groups who could not find work and who had no experience with commerce and city living.

Soon after their arrival, eugenicists, polemicists, reformers, social workers and politicians began portraying such people, and in particular the Ishmaels, as shiftless, morally backward, culturally deficient, and so on. They would be tracked, studied, analyzed, and picked apart in order to identify the causes of their marginal existence. In just a few short years, as Deutsch shows in vivid detail, this surveillance helped transform a relatively commonplace extended family network into "a veritable tribe of savages."

This process was filled with contradictions, and at all points it was both comedic and tragic, with evidence distorted to fit the needs of scholarly ideologues and political blowhards. The fact that the Ishmaels appeared white stymied reformers, who arbitrarily looked for causes of the family's supposed premodern ways wherever they could find them: Perhaps they were nomadic Gypsies, unable to create community and participate in civil society? Perhaps they were Islamic and so at odds with Western mores? These desperate hunches fueled speculation and added to the myth of the Ishmaels, leading eventually to their placement as a public curiosity in the Hall of Science at the World's Fair of 1933. As Deutsch puts it, the Ishmaels had by this point become the "potent symbol for the dangers of unrestricted immigration, the growing epidemic of 'feeblemindedness' and a host of other social problems both real and imagined."

In Deutsch's detective-like rendering of the creation of the Ishmael myth, one sees that, at each moment, the intention of involved parties was serious and purposive. Nothing less than the will to keep America safe, pure, and cohesive in an age of tremendous social upheaval was at stake in the critical (and scientific) scrutiny of the Ishmael tribe. We may do well to pay attention to this myth making, as it reveals a great deal of the machinery for documenting and coming to terms with the existence of the poor in an advanced democracy. The current obsession with the black urban poor in the United States—arguably a modern-day

Tribe of Ishmael—is eerily similar in scope, substance, and tone to the discursive stigmatization of Benjamin Ishmael's children. Just as the myth of the Ishmael tribe was built through the need to determine who was deserving of government and charitable aid—literally, the "deserving poor"—so too does our modern-day apparatus of bureaucratic beneficence run on the basis of creating a distinct class of *un*-deserving. Is it possible to get out of this trap? Must there always be a sacrificial lamb? And, if a family myth could have been created that was so at odds with the available evidence, is it possible that we are committing the same errors—in the name of progress?

Inventing America's "Worst" Family offers us a place to begin this inquiry.

Sudhir Alladi Venkatesh
Columbia University

Acknowledgments

First and foremost, I would like to thank the following members of the Ishmael family and their relatives who generously shared their knowledge and genealogical research with me: Ted Cox, Jean Dalrymple, Carl Ishmael, and Nancy Robinson. Without their help, this book would have been greatly impoverished. I would also like to thank Marjorie Newlin Leaming, former wife of Hugo Leaming, and Dale Chapman, one of his oldest friends, for helping me to understand Leaming and his complex motivations for writing about the Tribe of Ishmael.

A number of other people helped with different aspects of the book. Thanks to Jack Resch of the University of New Hampshire, for sharing his expertise on the Revolutionary War, in general, and the military pension policy, in particular; Graham Hodges of Colgate University for sharing information about Hugo Leaming; and Robert Horton, state archivist of the Minnesota Historical Society, who kindly shared his knowledge of the Tribe of Ishmael with me. Special thanks to Paul Lombardo of the Georgia State University College of Law, who graciously read an earlier version of this book and provided numerous helpful comments.

Over the past few years, I have spent many hours in archives, libraries, historical societies, and courthouses around the country. Invariably, the staffs of these institutions have been helpful. I would particularly like to thank Brian Keough, head, and Amy C. Schindler, curator of manuscripts, M. E. Grenander Department of Special Collections and Archives, State University of New York at Albany; Charles B. Greifenstein, manuscripts librarian, American Philosophical Society; Judith May-Sapko, special collections librarian/archivist, Pickler Library, Truman State

University; Alan January, Indiana State Archive; Edie Olson, president, Family Service of Central Indiana; Frances O'Donnell, curator of archives and manuscripts, Andover-Harvard Theological Library, Harvard Divinity School; Elizabeth Wilkinson, manuscript librarian, and Jesse Lewis, state documents coordinator, Indiana Division, Indiana State Library; Todd Daniels-Howell, director, special collections, and Debra Brookhart, archives specialist, Indiana University–Purdue University Indianapolis Library; Clare Bunce, Cold Spring Harbor Laboratory Archives; the staff of the Cumberland County (Pennsylvania) Historical Society; and the staff of the Nicholas County Courthouse, Carlisle, Kentucky. I would also like to give a special thanks to Valerie-Anne Lutz van Ammers, head of manuscripts processing and library registrar, American Philosophical Society, for her help in navigating what is probably the best eugenics archive in the country.

As always, I enjoyed the support of family and friends while writing this book. Thanks to my parents, Zvi and Suzanna Deutsch; my sister, Yael; my in-laws, Peter and Suzanne Greenberg; my wife, Miriam; and our daughters, Simona and Tamar. Their support and love especially have been invaluable. I would also like to thank my friends Sudhir Venkatesh, Ethan Michaeli, and Benjamin Wurgaft for encouraging me to finish this project. A number of other people played significant roles in bringing this project to fruition. My brother, David, first gave me a copy of Hugo Leaming's essay on the Tribe of Ishmael. Without him, I never would have started the journey that led to this book. Joyce Seltzer read and commented on an earlier draft; without her support in the early stages of this project, I would never have finished it. My colleagues in the Department of Religion at Swarthmore College and in the Department of Religion at Haverford College read and commented on my book during a symposium devoted to it. Swarthmore College granted me a Blanshard Award for Faculty Research that helped support my research trips to Kentucky, Indiana, and Wales. I would like to thank Cordelia Brady for generously allowing me to stay in her cottage in St. Ishmael's, Wales, and for helping me to conduct my research while I was there. I also benefited from my conversations with Jenny Reardon of the University of California, Santa Cruz Sociology Department, who invited me to give a talk on the Ishmaelites. Special thanks to Sudhir Venkatesh for writing the foreword to this book.

Finally, I would like to thank the anonymous readers who commented on my manuscript and the good people at UC Press for believing in this project, including Kalicia Pivirotto and Reed Malcolm, an editor of rare imagination and dedication to his authors and their books.

Introduction

In 1933, forty years after millions of wide-eyed visitors had crowded the midway to watch the hootchy-kootchy dance in the Street of Cairo exhibition, gawk at a model of the Eiffel Tower, and stroll among Samoan, Javanese, and other ethnological villages, the Century of Progress Exposition brought the world's fair back to Chicago. The Columbian Exposition of 1893 had celebrated the achievements of the newly industrialized United States by creating a "living museum of humanity," in which representatives of the world's peoples were literally put on display to illustrate their supposedly hierarchical relationship to one another. For the organizers of the 1893 world's fair, contemporary American culture, exemplified by the suggestively named White City exhibition, occupied the pinnacle of this hierarchy. By 1933, the idea that human groups could be ranked along an evolutionary scale had become both more popular and more controversial, attracting supporters such as the racist ideologue Madison Grant and critics such as Franz Boas, the father of cultural anthropology. Like its predecessor, the Century of Progress Exposition of 1933 sought to naturalize this hierarchy by juxtaposing displays of "primitive" peoples alongside ones that demonstrated the purported superiority of the white American elite. Thus, for example, the fair organizers erected a quaint "Indian Village" in the looming shadow of the General Motors Tower, a modernist temple dedicated to the ascendant American auto industry.[1]

The real Native Americans who inhabited the ersatz tepees of the Indian Village served as reminders of an earlier way of life that had been rendered obsolete by the steam engine, the automobile, and other advances produced by white American civilization. Now vanquished and domesticated on reservations, Native Americans were seen largely as harmless or even ennobled—more deserving of pity than of fear. Elsewhere at the fair, however, in the prominently located Hall of Science building, another supposedly atavistic and far more dangerous "tribe" was being put on display by the eugenics movement.

Unlike the Native Americans of the Indian Village, members of this Midwestern tribe were not physically present at the fair. Had it been possible, the organizers of the exhibit undoubtedly would have included some flesh-and-blood individuals in a simulated version of their "natural" environment, either a run-down slum dwelling or a makeshift "gypsy" caravan.[2] Instead, the prominent eugenicist Harry Laughlin and his colleagues had to make do with photographs and explanatory texts. The evocative name of these modern day "savages" was the Tribe of Ishmael, and according to the Hall of Science exhibition, they were "A Degenerate Family . . . which, despite opportunities, never developed a normal life. Shiftless, begging, wanderers, sound enough in body, their hereditary equipment lacked the basic qualities of intelligence and character on which opportunity could work."[3] Accompanying this ominous caption was an elaborate genealogical tree—a staple of all eugenics displays—and a handful of photographs labeled "Typical Ishmael Portraits" that depicted members of the family, their homes (including that of George Ishmael, described as "the most intelligent of the group"), and the Indianapolis city dump, which several generations of Ishmaels had divided "among themselves peaceably."

Just as the Indian Village stood next to the General Motors Tower, thereby highlighting the gulf between them, the eugenicists had erected a display devoted to "A Superior Family: The Roosevelt Family-Stock" on panels adjoining those dedicated to the Ishmaels. At the head of the Roosevelt family tree stood Jonathan Edwards, the famous Puritan theologian. Official-looking portraits of Theodore Roosevelt and Franklin Delano Roosevelt framed the genealogical tree, along with photographs of lesser-known members of the clan and the legend "Pedigree showing the distribution of inborn qualities in a family which produced two presidents of the United States." The point of the world's fair eugenics exhibition was crystal clear: if the Roosevelts were America's best family, the Ishmaels were its worst.

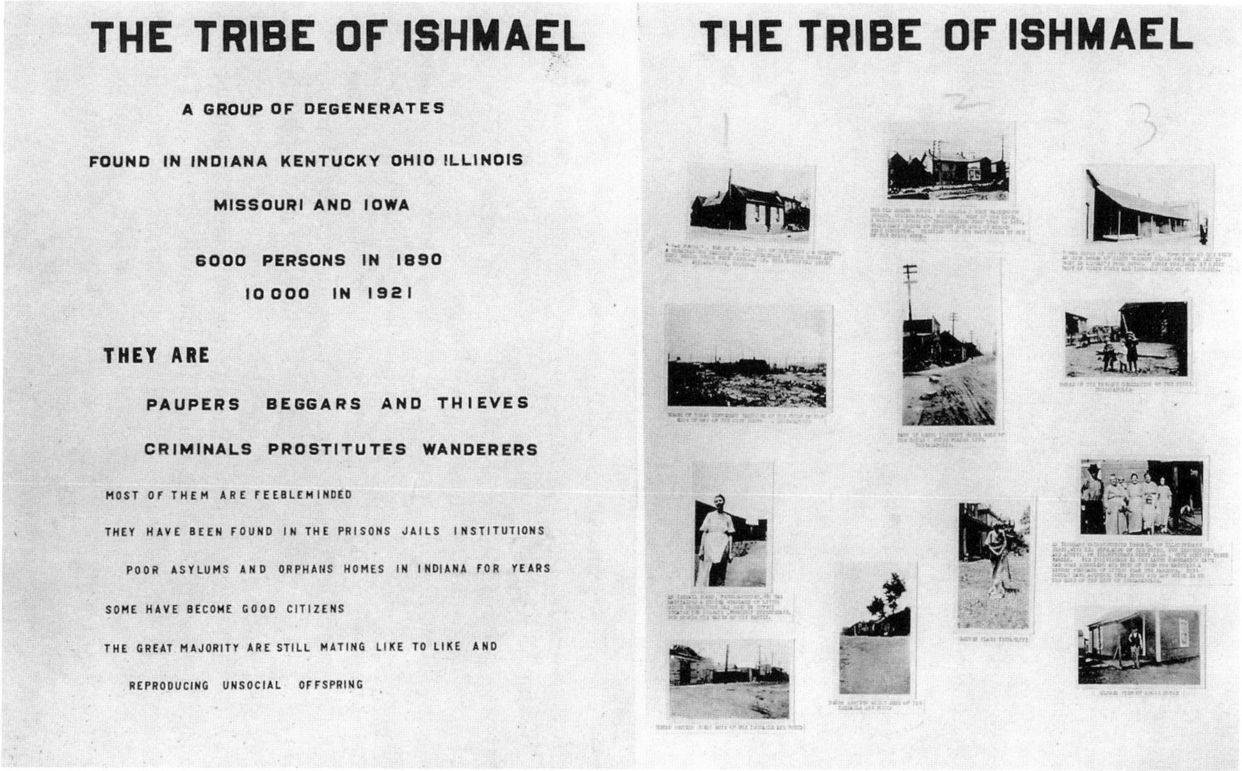

THE TRIBE OF ISHMAEL

THE TRIBE OF ISHMAEL

A GROUP OF DEGENERATES

FOUND IN INDIANA KENTUCKY OHIO ILLINOIS

MISSOURI AND IOWA

6000 PERSONS IN 1890

10000 IN 1921

THEY ARE

PAUPERS   BEGGARS AND THIEVES

CRIMINALS   PROSTITUTES   WANDERERS

MOST OF THEM ARE FEEBLEMINDED

THEY HAVE BEEN FOUND IN THE PRISONS JAILS INSTITUTIONS

POOR ASYLUMS AND ORPHANS HOMES IN INDIANA FOR YEARS

SOME HAVE BECOME GOOD CITIZENS

THE GREAT MAJORITY ARE STILL MATING LIKE TO LIKE AND

REPRODUCING UNSOCIAL OFFSPRING

Figure 1. Tribe of Ishmael display, circa 1921. Displays similar to this one appeared at the Century of Progress Exposition of 1933. (The American Philosophical Society)

In less than two centuries, the Ishmaels went from being an obscure colonial-era family of poor Pennsylvania farmers to being put on display before millions of visitors to the Chicago World's Fair of 1933 as the very image of degeneracy and criminality. Along the way, the Ishmaels had helped to settle the Kentucky frontier and had served in the American Revolution, the War of 1812, and the Civil War. During the economic depression that gripped the nation in the 1870s, members of the Ishmael family, like thousands of other displaced agricultural laborers, made their way to the city, in this case Indianapolis. There, some Ishmaels refused to assimilate into the wage-labor industrial economy and, instead, continued to embrace a lifestyle rooted in their rural, Upland Southern background. It was at this crucial moment in their history that the Ishmaels encountered the man who would turn them into a living symbol for all that was wrong with America, setting them on a path to the Eugenics Records Office, the halls of Congress, and finally, in 1933, the Hall of Science. In many ways stranger than fiction, the true story of the Tribe of Ishmael, as the family first became known in the 1870s, serves as a profoundly unsettling counterhistory of the United States.

The remarkable and complicated man who discovered—or, as I argue, invented—the Tribe of Ishmael was a Congregationalist minister named Oscar McCulloch. A pioneer in the emerging field of hereditarian theory and an important proponent of the Social Gospel, McCulloch helped lay the groundwork for eugenics, scientific charity, and organized social work in the United States.[4] Just as important for the subsequent history of the Tribe of Ishmael, McCulloch was also an armchair Orientalist with a deep fascination for Islam.

In 1878, Oscar McCulloch stumbled upon an extended family living in a hovel in one of Indianapolis's most run-down neighborhoods. Shocked by the wretched scene, McCulloch soon discovered that the family was called the Ishmaels, which he mistakenly assumed was a pejorative pseudonym. A check with local officials revealed that the Ishmaels were at the center of a group of interrelated families notorious in the city for petty crime, wandering, gleaning, and pauperism. McCulloch devoted much of the next decade—indeed, what remained of his short life—to researching and eventually publicizing what he claimed was a veritable tribe of savages living in the heart of darkest Indianapolis.

McCulloch's first challenge in representing the Ishmaels to the public was the absence of obvious physical markers to differentiate this poor white family from its respectable white neighbors. In response, McCulloch created a set of discursive signs to indicate their difference, the most striking and effective of which were the exotic-sounding names applied to the family members, their relatives, and their associates: the "Tribe of Ishmael," the "Ishmaelites"—both of which suggested Islam in the late-nineteenth-century imaginary—and the "American Gypsies" and "Grasshopper Gypsies." These titles enabled McCulloch and his successors to stigmatize the Ishmaels by subtly exploiting contemporary Orientalist stereotypes of the Islamic East as a culture in decline and of Gypsies (Roma) as a threat to settled urban communities.

When McCulloch first employed the name "Tribe of Ishmael," his original intent was not to argue that the Ishmaels of Indiana were actually Muslim, but that they resembled their biblical namesake in the threat they posed to civilized Christian society. Similarly, when he likened the Ishmaels to Native Americans, he generally intended the comparison to be symbolic rather than literal, although he sometimes attributed certain Ishmaelite traits to a "half breed" Indian ancestor. McCulloch's underlying ideological assumption was that poor whites like the Ishmaels and their associates, who did not live by middle-class norms, were functionally equivalent to outcast groups such as Muslims, Native Americans, and Roma. Indeed, they were even more dangerous to respectable society than those more easily identifiable outsiders, since the white physical appearance of most Ishmaelites disguised their true perfidy.

The symbolic racialization of the Ishmaelites places their story within a broader historical narrative that the scholar Theodore Allen has called "the invention of the white race."[5] Rather than viewing whiteness as a biological category, Allen and others have argued that it represents a social construction, historically grounded in factors such as class, culture, and country of origin. Nineteenth-century Irish immigrants constitute what is probably the most striking example of this phenomenon.[6] Despite their typically pale skin, Irish immigrants were frequently likened to blacks and labeled "white niggers" because of their disproportionate participation in unskilled labor and their cultural and religious differences from the Anglo-Saxon elite. Similarly, the Ishmaelites, depicted by McCulloch as eschewing wage labor entirely and engaging in a host of aberrant practices, did not fit neatly into the emerging social category of whiteness and were therefore characterized as belonging to a separate and unequal tribe of savages. The Ishmaelites had failed to become white.

Because of McCulloch's efforts, the Ishmaels became virtually synonymous with the undeserving poor in the United States from the 1880s
until the Great Depression. This category, which dated back to the
Elizabethan poor laws of early-seventeenth-century England, reflected a
moral distinction between poor people who supposedly deserved charity and those who did not, resulting in what Michael Katz has called the
"transmutation of pauperism into a moral category."[7] Traditionally,
members of the so-called deserving poor included widows, orphans, the
infirm, and the elderly—in other words, those who were unable to support themselves or their dependents because of circumstances beyond
their control. By contrast, unwed mothers and especially able-bodied
men who were seen as refusing to work constituted the undeserving
poor, or, as they were popularly known, paupers. For such individuals,
poverty did not result from bad luck; rather, like the proverbial scarlet
letter, it signified moral failing. Those who accepted this distinction
viewed giving charity to the undeserving poor as immoral, since it had
the effect of rewarding and even encouraging sloth, licentiousness, and
other sins. In the United States, being labeled a member of the undeserving poor carried a special stigma because in rhetoric, if not always
in reality, America was supposed to be "the best poor man's country," a
place where ambitious individuals were not bound by the rigid socioeconomic hierarchies of Europe and could radically transform themselves through hard work.[8]

So ubiquitous did the association between the Ishmaels and the
undeserving poor become that in *How the Other Half Lives,* his
groundbreaking work on urban poverty, Jacob Riis explicitly invoked
the family in order to signify the entire pauper population of New York:
"Frauds, professional beggars, training their children to follow in their
footsteps—a veritable 'tribe of Ishmael,' tightening its grip on society
as the years pass, until society shall summon up the pluck to say with
Paul, 'if any man will not work neither shall he eat,' and stick to it."[9]
Riis's reference to the Tribe of Ishmael indicates that by 1890, the name
had already entered the lexicon of social reformers as a catchphrase for
the undeserving poor in general, rather than just a specific group in the
city of Indianapolis.

It is no accident that the myth of the Tribe of Ishmael began to take
shape soon after Horatio Alger published *Ragged Dick,* his blockbuster
novel about a young urban "vagabond" or "street Arab"—as such children were then known in both Great Britain and the United States—
who goes from rags to riches by dint of good breeding and hard work.

Horatio Alger's fictional hero would become an important model for American notions of the deserving poor: an ambitious individual who was "frank and straight-forward, manly and self-reliant. His nature was a noble one, and had saved him from all mean faults."[10]

Oscar McCulloch's hereditarian portrait of the Tribe of Ishmael, in turn, represented the flip side of the Horatio Alger myth. Instead of the noble individual who pulls himself up by his bootstraps, the Ishmaelites were depicted as an atavistic clan that was both unable and unwilling to better itself, no matter how much aid was given to its members. They were, in short, born losers.[11] In the following decades, the myth of the undeserving poor symbolized by the Tribe of Ishmael—clannish, racialized, morally and physically degenerate—would prove to be as enduring and as influential as Horatio Alger's fictional hero.

The Ishmaels reached their height of infamy—and had their greatest impact on public policy in the United States—during the 1920s, when the increasingly powerful eugenics movement transformed the family into a potent symbol for the dangers of unrestricted immigration, the growing epidemic of "feeblemindedness," and a host of other social problems, both real and imagined. Derived from a Greek root meaning "well born," the term *eugenics* was originally coined in the 1880s by Francis Galton, a cousin of Charles Darwin. According to the principles developed by Galton, genetically worthwhile people possessed two responsibilities to society. First, they needed to reproduce "like to like," as the eugenicists were fond of saying, so that their positive traits would be passed on to future generations. Second, they needed to prevent so-called *cacogenic* individuals (i.e., those with inferior genes, from the Greek term *kakos* or "bad") from blindly passing on their traits by reproducing with one another.

In the early 1920s, the eugenicists and their political allies presented the Ishmaels as crucial evidence during the Congressional hearings that led to the passage of the draconian Immigration Restriction Act of 1924. The eugenicist Harry Laughlin played such a central role in this drama that Ashley Montague later wrote, "It is perhaps not as well known as it should be that the United States Immigration Act of 1924 was based on the ill-considered, prejudiced, and scientific judgments of the late Mr. Harry Laughlin."[12] At first glance, the Ishmaels were unlikely poster children for the threat supposedly posed by immigrants from Asia and eastern and southern Europe. After all, they were descended from old-stock Americans who had lived in the country since at least the beginning of the eighteenth century.

Yet the eugenicists subtly manipulated the Ishmaels' Islamic sounding surname to invoke the "Asiatic Menace" that contemporary racist ideologues such as Madison Grant and Lothrop Stoddard warned would soon swamp Anglo-Saxon civilization unless drastic measures were taken. As in Oscar McCulloch's day, therefore, Orientalist stereotypes concerning Islam and the East also helped to shape the popular image of the Ishmaels during what has been called the "tribal twenties."[13] Thus, the Ishmaels were transformed into white, Midwestern surrogates for the "hordes" of Jews, Arabs, Chinese, and other "Asiatics" who threatened to turn the United States into a colony of Asia if they were allowed to enter the country.

Throughout the 1920s, the Ishmaels served as archetypal representatives of the country's cacogenic underclass. The following quote from Albert Edward Wiggam, a nonscientist who served as the Johnny Appleseed of the eugenics movement in America, exemplifies the attitude toward the Ishmaels during this period:

> A few generations ago, down in Old Virginia, this family was composed of but two members, Old Man Ishmael and his wife, helpless, anti-social, thriftless incompetents. By the finest thing in civilization, kind-heartedness, the Ishmaelites were kept alive; not only that, they were given a better chance to reproduce their kind than the school teachers, preachers, business men, skilled mechanics, doctors and lawyers who tried to teach their empty brains to clothe and shelter their filthy bodies and, by expensive legal procedures, prevent them from being hanged. There were two of them then; there are nearly twelve thousand now![14]

Like his professional counterparts in the eugenics movement, Wiggam repeated canards and exaggerations about the Ishmaels. Wiggam, who once authored a eugenics version of the Ten Commandments and liked to brag that "had Jesus been among us he would have been president of the First Eugenics Congress," expressed his views in a populist idiom.[15] Others—including David Starr Jordan, the first president of Stanford University and a prominent eugenicist, who advocated involuntary sterilization of so-called degenerates, Charles Davenport, the head of the influential Eugenics Records Office, and Arthur Estabrook, the most prolific eugenics field-worker of the day—depicted the Ishmaels more scientifically, if no less grotesquely.

Estabrook, the young eugenicist who published a follow-up study on the Ishmaelites in the early 1920s, also helped to formulate and enforce the State of Virginia's notorious Racial Integrity Act of 1924, which legally prohibited "miscegenation." As Paul Lombardo has demonstrated, the role that eugenicists like Estabrook played in lobbying for this legislation was critical and, until recently, largely overlooked, even in studies of the eugenics movement.[16] Estabrook's own private papers contain letters from Virginia state officials asking him to perform background checks on racially "suspect" individuals requesting marriage licenses. As a result of Estabrook's genealogical research, people who had lived their entire lives as whites were officially designated as black because they possessed a single African American ancestor, a policy popularly known as the "one-drop rule." The ramifications of such a reclassification were enormous. In some cases, couples were prevented from marrying; in others, children were expelled from schools they had attended for years; in still others, previously "white" individuals were now forced to drink from colored water fountains.

What kept eugenicists like Arthur Estabrook up at night, however, was not the risk posed by blacks or by the recent waves of immigrants from eastern and southern Europe. Although such people were seen as genetically inferior by the eugenicists, they were also typically identifiable by a wide range of physical, linguistic, and/or cultural markers and, therefore, sexual unions between them and genetically superior individuals (i.e., middle- and upper-class whites of northern European background) could be regulated via the antimiscegenation laws and restrictive immigration policies that the eugenics movement helped to pass in the 1920s. No, what most bothered men like Estabrook and his boss, Charles Davenport, was another group that they considered to be even more dangerous to American society than blacks and immigrants: genetically inferior, native-born whites, like the Ishmaels. As Edward Larson has noted in his history of the eugenics movement in the Deep South: "Eugenicists' overriding concern [was] with purifying the Caucasian race. A typical example of this concern appeared throughout an article in the *Journal of the Medical Association of Georgia* during the 1937 campaign for eugenic sterilization in that state. According to the article, the 'South's "poor white trash," so aptly named by the Negro,' threatened to choke civilization 'in a wilderness of weeds.' Physicians must sterilize this 'human rubbish,' it warned, or the 'time may come when it will be necessary to resort to euthanasia.'"[17]

The danger posed by people like the Ishmaels lay in the very fact that they possessed the same names, physical appearance, and, frequently, some of the same ancestors as the genetically superior members of their communities, including, it should be noted, the eugenicists, themselves. Nevertheless, they also possessed defective "germ plasm"—the phrase eugenicists employed to refer to genetic material—which resulted in inferior intelligence. This feeblemindedness, in turn, contributed to a wide range of aberrant behaviors, including sexual licentiousness, laziness, and criminality, that together conspired to create the undeserving poor.

In some cases, eugenicists and their forerunners, such as the nineteenth-century Italian criminal anthropologist Cesare Lombroso, did try to argue that cacogenic individuals displayed physical signs of their genetic inferiority. Yet the absence of real evidence for such a connection led some eugenicists to doctor photographs to make supposedly cacogenic individuals look more like stereotypical criminals or deviants. These clumsy efforts betray the great difficulty in actually identifying cacogenic individuals by their physical appearance alone. Instead, preventing these individuals from interbreeding with genetically superior people required an elaborate system of background checks, intelligence testing, institutionalization, and, in some cases, compulsory sterilization.

Without these policies, the eugenicists argued, the entire white gene pool would be dragged down by "normal-looking" but genetically inferior individuals, a phenomenon that had already occurred within infamous cacogenic families such as the Jukes and Ishmaels. It is not coincidental, therefore, that the so-called family studies produced by eugenicists focused almost exclusively on poor white descendants of early American settlers, that is, people who shared the same physical appearance and ancestry as the Anglo-Saxon elite. Indeed, some of these families, including the Ishmaels themselves, could rightly claim membership in blue-blood organizations like the Daughters of the American Revolution.

As we have already seen, the process of demonizing the Ishmaels reached its apex in 1933, the same year that the newly elected Nazi government implemented a eugenically inspired campaign of forced sterilization in Germany. While the Nazis were drawing on a model sterilization plan authored by Harry Laughlin (who would later receive a medal from the German government and an honorary degree from the University of Heidelberg for his efforts), he and his colleagues were busy presenting the Ishmaels as one of America's worst family in the eugenics exhibit at the Chicago world's fair of 1933. Following this event, the rise of Nazism abroad forced the eugenics movement to retreat from the public sphere in the United States, although sympathizers continued to work behind the scenes to influence policy for many years to come. By the eve of World War II, the Ishmaels had disappeared from the nation's consciousness as dramatically as they had first entered it. For the next four decades, the once notorious Ishmael family was but a vague memory among residents of Indiana and a footnote for scholars of the eugenics movement.

Then, in the strangest twist in an already extraordinary story, the Ishmaelites were resurrected a century after Oscar McCulloch first identified them as a distinct community and two centuries after the original patriarch, Benjamin Ishmael, had taken up arms to fight the British. Like McCulloch, Hugo Prosper Leaming, the man who rediscovered the Ishmaels in the 1970s, was a liberal Protestant minister and social activist who possessed a keen interest in Islam. In 1977, Leaming published a book chapter entitled "The Ben Ishmael Tribe: A Fugitive 'Nation' of the Old Northwest," in which he turned the standard image of the Tribe of Ishmael on its head.

Rather than a cacogenic community of old-stock whites, Hugo Leaming argued, the Ishmaelites had really been a "tightly knit nomadic community of African, Native American, and 'poor white' descent," that "could only be categorized as 'colored,' therefore 'Negro' or African-American (but including others, by marriage or adoption)."[18] Instead of being feebleminded paupers and petty criminals, Leaming claimed that the Ishmaelites had founded the city of Indianapolis and developed their own distinct forms of architecture, music, and literature. And, finally, in the most stunning assertion of all, Leaming hypothesized that rather than being a "white trash" patriarch, Ben Ishmael had actually been a Muslim of African descent who had established the first Islamic community native to the United States.

After being driven underground in the first few decades of the twentieth century, members of this community had then supposedly helped to found the Moorish Science Temple and the Nation of Islam, the earliest African American Islamic groups. In short, according to Hugo Leaming, the Tribe of Ishmael was

> an older branch of this tree of African-American Islam. It is suggested that behind the millions of African-Americans who have been affected by Islam in recent years . . . behind the Nation of Islam founded by the Divine Imam Master Wallace Fard Muhammad and led so long by the Honorable Elijah Muhammad, behind the Moorish Science of the Divine Imam Noble Drew Ali . . . there stands one more earlier Islamic saint or Imam, Ben Ishmael, and one more earlier Islamic community, the Tribe of Ishmael, a bridge between African and American Islam, a lost-found nation in the wilderness of North America.[19]

On the surface, Leaming would seem to have made one of those rare discoveries that most historians only dream about. His assertion that the

Tribe of Ishmael was a "tri-racial" Islamic community was nothing less than astounding. It literally revolutionized the standard picture of organized Islam in the United States. Put into comparative perspective, the first community of Muslims native to the United States was now revealed to be contemporary with the American Revolution rather than with World War I. Leaming had apparently transformed the standard narrative of class, race, and religion in America.

In the years since Leaming's essay on the Tribe of Ishmael was first published—it has since been reprinted—his version has become the most widely repeated and influential among contemporary readers, far outstripping the impact of Oscar McCulloch's work or that of his successors in the eugenics movement. Books and Web sites dedicated to uncovering the previously hidden history of "tri-racial" and Islamic communities in the United States have taken Leaming's portrait of the Ishmaelites as gospel.[20] For example, one internet discussion group posted a message entitled "The first true Ummat [Muslim community] in America (1750–1920)," which informed its readers about "a nomadic group of Muslims called 'The Tribe of Ishmael.' This group was composed of Africans (African-Americans), white-Americans, and Native Americans. In short, it reflected what America claims to be—a melting pot. This group was persecuted severely by local governments and, eventually, the federal government."[21] In response, another member of the discussion group wrote, "it is a tragedy that we have no record of the descendants of this tribe. were they killed off? did they convert to other religions? or did they just lose the fire in the belly to maintain their faith once the tribe was forcibly disbanded?"[22]

Significantly, Leaming's portrait of the Ishmaels has also influenced some printed histories of the eugenics movement in the United States. One author of a recent work speculated that the Ishmaelites "may have been composed initially of Shawnee Indians, blacks of the nomadic Fulani Tradition, and a Celtic gypsy-like population called the Tinkers."[23] Another uncritically described the Ishmaelites as a "tribe of racially mixed white gypsies, Islamic blacks and American Indians."[24]

There is only one problem with Hugo Leaming's ingenious and inspiring portrait of the Tribe of Ishmael: it isn't true. Ben Ishmael was not an "Islamic saint or Imam," his name does not reflect a corruption of the Arabic "ibn Ishmael," as Leaming also suggested in his essay. Nor was Ben Ishmael of African descent. Moreover, the Tribe of Ishmael was never an Islamic community, and the vast majority of the people identified as Ishmaelites over the years were of Western European background, although a relatively small minority did possess some African or Native American ancestry. Indeed, as I will show, a careful examination of all the published and unpublished sources on the Tribe of Ishmael reveals that only one of Leaming's major claims remains a possibility, namely, that some of the individuals identified as Ishmaelites may have become early members of the Moorish Science Temple and the Nation of Islam. In light of the available evidence, however, even this assertion does not rise beyond the level of conjecture.

If the evidence is so weak, how and why did Hugo Leaming arrive at his startling conclusions? Leaming had complex personal reasons for reimagining the Tribe of Ishmael as a primarily African American Islamic community. Born into a white, middle-class Christian family from Virginia, Leaming decided later in life that he was actually triracial and, despite his upbringing, became a member of the Moorish Science Temple, the first African American Islamic group. In short, Hugo Leaming assumed the same racial and religious identity that he invented for the Tribe of Ishmael. While Leaming's own dramatic metamorphosis helped shape his interpretation of the Ishmaelites, broader cultural and ideological currents also influenced his portrait.

Unlike Oscar McCulloch, who "discovered" the Tribe of Ishmael when Islam was widely seen in the West as a religion in decline, Leaming produced his study of the Tribe of Ishmael in the immediate aftermath of the civil rights era in the United States, when prominent African American Muslims such as Malcolm X and Muhammad Ali had become cultural icons. At the same time, Islamicists in other countries were attacking Western imperialism and their own corrupt governments. By the 1970s, far from being a symbol of decay, as it had been for Orientalists during the nineteenth century, Islam had now come to signify in the eyes of many—including Hugo Leaming—robust and popular resistance to colonialism, racism, and economic oppression.

It is also important to appreciate that Leaming was able to reimagine the Tribe of Ishmael as Muslim because earlier authors had already exploited contemporary tropes of Islam in their own portraits, beginning, of course, with the Islamic sounding names coined for the group. In this respect, the Tribe of Ishmael's story sheds new light on what Vijay Prashad has evocatively referred to as "the undisciplined world of U.S. orientalism."[25] Contrary to popular belief, Americans did not encounter Islam for the first time in the second half of the twentieth century. Indeed, the roots of Islam in America date back centuries to the numerous Muslim slaves brought to these shores from Africa. Nor did it take Malcolm X or even the members of Al Qaeda for Islam to become part of America's collective consciousness. Instead, Islam has been present in the popular American imagination for centuries. As I will argue throughout this book, each stage of the Tribe of Ishmael's story corresponds to a different phase in this fascinating but largely unwritten history of American Orientalism.[26]

One way of understanding Hugo Leaming's radical reinterpretation of the Tribe of Ishmael, therefore, is that he literalized elements of their identity that had previously functioned on a symbolic level. Earlier writers like McCulloch and Estabrook had depicted the vast majority of the tribe's members as white Upland Southerners of Anglo-Saxon ancestry. At the same time, however, McCulloch and Estabrook symbolically likened all of the Ishmaelites—white and nonwhite alike—to marginalized groups such as Gypsies, Native Americans, and Muslims. In his revisionist study of the Ishmaelites, Leaming flipped the actual ethnic and racial proportions of the tribe's members so that African Americans now dominated numerically and culturally. Leaming also literalized the previously symbolic association of the Ishmaelites with Islam. Almost alchemically, he had transformed a collection of poor, overwhelmingly white, Upland Southern migrants into an African American Islamic community.

Despite its mythical quality, Leaming's version of the Ishmaelites' story illuminates a number of recurring themes in the history of African American Islam. The first is the powerful role that reinvention has played in the creation of new and distinctly American Islamic identities. In this respect, Leaming's transformation of the Tribe of Ishmael into an Islamic community and Ben Ishmael into an "Islamic saint or Imam," recalls the equally dramatic religious transformations of individuals such as Elijah Muhammad and Malcolm X. The second theme is best expressed by the Nation of Islam's phrase "lost-found nation," that is, the idea that the original Islamic identity of African Americans needs to be recovered and restored. Seen from this perspective, Leaming's revisionist interpretation of the Tribe of Ishmael fits into a broader pattern of reclaiming the supposedly obscured Islamic roots of all African Americans.

Finally, Leaming's identification of the Tribe of Ishmael as a "colored" community reflects a common American tendency to racialize Islam and, more specifically, to view it as a religion of nonwhites. To appreciate how deeply this racialization of Islam has penetrated the consciousness of many Americans, we need only recall Malcolm X's great surprise upon encountering blond-haired, blue-eyed Muslims on his pilgrimage to Mecca or, more recently, how governmental profiling of terrorist suspects has relied on narrow and misleading assumptions of what Muslims are *supposed* to look like.

Just as Hugo Leaming's portrait of the Tribe of Ishmael was influenced by contemporary shifts in the image of Islam, so too was it shaped by important changes in how the undeserving poor were represented in the United States. Following World War II, the popular image of the undeserving poor in America underwent two major revisions. The first was a shift from etiological explanations that emphasized biology to those that stressed culture. The second was the emergence of a primarily African American "underclass." Together, these phenomena had a major impact on Leaming's reconstruction of the Tribe of Ishmael as an African American community possessing its own distinctive culture.

During the first few decades of the twentieth century, eugenicists had argued that members of the undeserving poor such as the Ishmaels were doomed to engage in immoral behavior because of their inferior genes. By shifting the focus away from morality and toward biology, the eugenicists radically redefined the category of "undeserving." What had once been a moral category was now recast as a biological one. In this brave new world, the Ishmaelites, Jukes, Kallikaks, Wins, and other supposedly cacogenic clans did not *deserve to reproduce,* not primarily because they acted immorally—though they did, according to the eugenicists—but because they possessed bad genes.

The retreat of the eugenics movement in the 1930s coincided with the rise of the New Deal, whose policies were predicated on the assumption that the federal government had a responsibility to help the poor. Together, the leveling effects of the Great Depression, the decline of the eugenics movement, and the rise of the New Deal combined to drive the image of the undeserving poor from the popular imagination. For several decades, no major theory emerged in the United States to replace the biological model championed by the eugenicists. Then, as Michael Katz has written, "in the early 1960s intellectuals and politicians rediscovered poverty."[27]

Rather than bad genes, scholars like Oscar Lewis and Michael Harrington—despite their differences—argued that the most intractable cases of poverty were rooted in culture. According to Lewis, certain individuals, families, or even entire communities, were mired in a pathological "culture of poverty" that "tends to perpetuate itself from generation to generation because of its effects on the children."[28] Lewis identified sixty-two traits that characterized this condition, including many that basically reproduced the stereotypes previously associated with the undeserving poor. Indeed, Lewis even invoked the specter of degeneration that had earlier played a major role in McCulloch's portrait of the Tribe of Ishmael, writing that "the low level of organization . . . gives the culture of poverty its marginal and anachronistic quality in our highly complex, specialized, organized society. Most primitive people achieved a higher level of socio-cultural organization than our modern urban slum dwellers."[29]

In 1965, the culture of poverty took on a decidedly racial cast when Daniel Patrick Moynihan submitted a jointly authored report to President Lyndon Johnson entitled *The Negro Family: The Case for National Action*. Although Moynihan did not refer explicitly to Lewis's work, his description of poor African Americans as constituting a "subculture" dominated by families with a "matriarchal structure" that lay at the root of a "tangle of pathology," employed many of the same tropes as the "culture of poverty" theory, as well as the earlier family studies produced by the eugenicists.[30]

By the middle of the 1970s, the popular media had begun to label this latest version of the undeserving poor the "underclass." Gunnar Myrdal had originally employed the phrase in 1963 to describe "an unprivileged class of unemployed, unemployables and underemployed who are more and more hopelessly set apart from the nation at large and do not share in its life, its ambitions and its achievements."[31] Then, in 1977, a seminal article in *Time* magazine entitled "The American Underclass: Destitute and Desperate in the Land of Plenty," introduced the label to the broader American public. *Time* described the underclass in language that could have been taken directly from earlier studies of the Tribe of Ishmael: "More intractable, more socially alien and more hostile than almost anyone had imagined. They are the unreachables: the American underclass."[32] The underclass label soon became associated with a host of adjectives echoing earlier hereditarian stereotypes of the undeserving poor, including "intergenerational," "biological," "hereditary," and "trapped."[33]

Not coincidentally, Leaming's revisionist essay on the Ishmaelites appeared in the same year that *Time* magazine introduced millions of middle-class readers to the latest incarnation of the undeserving poor. From the vantage point of the 1970s, the Tribe of Ishmael would have looked to many contemporary observers like classic denizens of the underclass. Yet Leaming asserted that the Ishmaelites—and by implication, the contemporary American underclass, as well—actually possessed a rich and vibrant culture of their own. The key was being able to recognize it. Thus, for example, Leaming interpreted the multiple sexual partners of some Ishmaelites as a sign of polygamy, perhaps influenced by Islamic tradition, rather than a mark of licentiousness. Similarly, he argued that depictions of powerful Ishmaelite women—whom he called "queens" in his account—indicated a matriarchal social structure instead of a pathological breakdown of the family. Most fundamentally, rather than being "intractable" and "hostile" degenerates—per contemporary stereotypes of the urban underclass—Leaming reimagined the Ishmaelites as pioneering "race rebels," whose only real crime was being ahead of their time.[34]

By recovering what he claimed was their true identity, Leaming sought to redeem not only the Ishmaelites of Indiana but also their symbolic descendants in America's contemporary inner cities. Once put on display at the World's Fair as America's worst family, the Ishmaels had now been transformed into an allegory for why categories like the undeserving poor and the underclass should be abandoned forever. Against this backdrop, Leaming's work on the Tribe of Ishmael should be seen as an imaginative, if historically inaccurate, intervention in the postwar debate about the poor, as well as another link in the centuries-long chain of American fantasies about Islam.

Like the character Zelig in the Woody Allen film of the same name, the Ishmaels have appeared and reappeared under different guises throughout American history. Present at the American Revolution, the settling of the frontier, the economic Panic of 1873, the Roaring Twenties, and the Great Depression, the Ishmaels are a quintessentially American family. Rather than generals, presidents, and other "great men," the central characters in this book's narrative were poor people whose hardscrabble lives were written out of history except when they could be rendered into crude cautionary tales. Unlike Zelig, however, the Ishmaels and their neighbors in Indianapolis were flesh-and-blood people whose own story is as meaningful and illuminating as the fantasies projected upon them.

Instead of an atavistic tribe of urban savages, a cacogenic clan, or an African American Islamic community, the Ishmaelites of Indiana were poor people trying to survive during an era marked by rapid industrialization, urbanization, and other radical dislocations. Some were petty thieves and prostitutes, others were more hardened criminals, but most of the people identified as Ishmaelites by Oscar McCulloch and his successors struggled to navigate the "shady world" between legitimate and illegitimate economies, supporting themselves by working "off the books"—to borrow Sudhir Venkatesh's phrase—in occupations that ranged from fixing umbrellas and recycling trash to skimming grease and making throw rugs from dog pelts.[35]

Ultimately, the competing fantasies inspired by the Ishmael family over the last century and a half reveal a great deal about how successive generations of Americans have deployed and manipulated race, religion, and science in order to shape the popular image of the poor in the United States and to formulate public policy based on these shifting representations. Just as this book revises standard notions of American history, so, too, does it raise important questions about the nation's mythology and, in particular, the "pull yourself up by your bootstraps" narrative known as the American Dream. If everyone should be able to succeed in America through hard work, what does that imply about those individuals or, worse, entire families who are unable to escape grinding poverty after years or even generations of struggle? In the first half of the twentieth century, the eugenics movement answered this question by positing that such people, including members of the Ishmael family, were born not made. As the world's fair exhibition of 1933 glumly put it, "their hereditary equipment lacked the basic qualities of intelligence and character on which opportunity could work." By contrast, I argue that the desperately poor people once labeled the Tribe of Ishmael *were made, not born*. For, as Thomas Paine observed in 1795, the same year that Benjamin Ishmael, the patriarch of the Ishmael family, left Pennsylvania for Kentucky in search of a better life, "Poverty . . . is a thing created by that which is called civilized life. It exists not in the natural state."[36]

CHAPTER I

How Oscar McCulloch
Discovered the Ishmaelites

With his dapper good looks and easy charm, Oscar McCulloch, the Protestant minister who first discovered and named the Tribe of Ishmael, was sometimes mistaken for a traveling salesman. This confusion was understandable, since McCulloch had spent several years peddling wares for a wholesale drug company before entering the Chicago Theological Seminary in 1867.[1] Settling in Indianapolis a decade later, he parlayed the same skills he had honed while hawking hair tonic and pep pills into a national reputation in the newly emerging fields of organized charity and hereditarian theory.

Oscar McCulloch was born in 1843 in Fremont, Ohio, to a solidly middle-class family with roots in New York and Connecticut. Carleton McCulloch, Oscar's father, was a pharmacist and store owner who regularly moved his family around the upper Midwest to take advantage of new business opportunities. Both he and his wife, Harriet, were devout Presbyterians at a time when the denomination held fast to traditional Calvinistic doctrines such as predestination. Oscar, the eldest of five children, experienced a religious conversion when he was fourteen that inspired him to dedicate his life to God. After entering the business world as a young man, McCulloch maintained this vow by volunteering in church missions and delivering lay sermons.

Like many young men of his generation, McCulloch was caught up in the Protestant revival that swept the country in the middle of the nineteenth century. He eventually decided to give up his career as a

Figure 2. Oscar McCulloch, undated. (University
Library Special Collections and Archives, Indiana
University–Purdue University, Indianapolis)

salesman and enter the Chicago Theological Seminary, an institution
whose Congregationalist character better reflected McCulloch's
increasingly liberal theological views. After graduating in 1870,
McCulloch experienced the first of a series of physical breakdowns
that would plague him over the course of the next two decades. On this
occasion, with—or, more likely, despite—the help of dubious contemporary remedies such as burning the lower part of his nose and drinking strong coffee, McCulloch recovered sufficiently to assume his first
position as a minister in Sheboygan, Wisconsin. Photos from this
period reveal a sensitive-looking man with a high forehead, discerning
eyes, and a bushy mustache that lent him the air of a kinder, gentler-
looking Nietzsche.

McCulloch spent a few years in Sheboygan, where he caused a stir for attempting to harmonize Darwin's theory of evolution with the New Testament. In 1877, after a period of intense soul-searching, McCulloch accepted a new pulpit at the Plymouth Church in Indianapolis. The city that greeted him was in the throes of the economic crisis known as the Panic of 1873. In that year, the collapse of the New York banking house Jay Cooke and Company had triggered a nationwide financial depression that would last for almost a decade. In Indiana alone, nearly a thousand businesses, with a combined value of fourteen million dollars, went under between 1873 and 1876.[2]

In Indianapolis, the crisis reached a boiling point in June 1877, when the city teetered on the edge of a "blood or bread" uprising.[3] Violence was averted only at the last minute when John Caven, the longtime Republican mayor of Indianapolis, led a march of unemployed workers to the city's bakeries, where he purchased loaves of bread out of his own pocket and distributed them to the hungry masses. The next day, Caven arranged for hundreds of men to begin working at the Belt Line Railroad and union stockyards. The construction of new railroads and canals had only recently transformed Indianapolis into an important transportation hub. Unfortunately, it also made the city's economy especially vulnerable to the railroad strikes that crippled the nation in the summer of 1877. In response to the strike, factories in Indianapolis laid off hundreds of industrial employees. Those lucky enough to remain on the job saw their wages—which were often paid in scrip—decline precipitously.

By the time McCulloch arrived in Indianapolis, the situation had become so desperate that armies of the unemployed had taken to the streets searching for work. Most of these streets were unpaved, which lent Indianapolis the air of an overgrown town, despite the city's dramatic growth in population, from 18,611 in 1860 to 48,244 in 1870 to nearly 75,000 in 1877.[4] Most of the newcomers had come to build the railroad or to work in industries such as the pharmaceutical company Eli Lilly and the Kingan stockyards, which belatedly brought large-scale capitalism to Indianapolis. From 1860 to 1880, the number of manufacturing establishments grew from one hundred to almost seven hundred, while the number of industrial workers ballooned from seven hundred to ten thousand, including fourteen hundred women.

Many of these industrial workers had recently migrated to Indianapolis from rural farming areas that had suffered economic devastation since the end of the Civil War. These residents were crowded into an urban area not much larger than a square mile, which had only recently acquired some of the basic municipal services that other cities in the region took for granted, such as a waterworks, a sewerage system, and public garbage collection. Because of the fiscal crisis, however, garbage collection was unreliable, and people continued to dump their trash in privy vaults and on the streets, where professional scavengers (later identified by McCulloch as belonging to the Tribe of Ishmael) hauled it away to be sorted and recycled.

Besides the rural flavor, one other factor gave Indianapolis a distinctive profile compared to other northern cities: the decidedly southern character of much of its population. By 1880, 22.3 percent of the non–Indiana-born population of the city was from the Upland South (Kentucky, North Carolina, Tennessee, Virginia, and West Virginia), with Kentucky alone providing 14.2 percent of the city's population. In this respect, the city once again reflected the overall situation of Indiana, where by mid-century, 44 percent of the total population of nonnative residents came from the South, as compared to an average of only 28.3 percent from the upper Midwest. If one focused on the south-central portion of the state, the figure was even more dramatic, with a full 91.5 percent of the nonnative Hoosier population—as residents of Indiana are known—consisting of Southern migrants, particularly those from Upland South states.[5] The number of Hoosiers with roots in Kentucky was so large that a popular joke asserted, "Kentucky had taken Indiana without firing a shot." By contrast, the percentage of migrants from New England and the Mid-Atlantic was lower than in any neighboring state—comprising only 8.8 percent of the total population, compared to 19.8 percent for the upper Midwest.[6]

Like their white neighbors, most African American residents of Indianapolis hailed from Upland Southern states, especially North Carolina, Kentucky, and Tennessee. In 1860, there were 498 African Americans in the city, only 2.6 percent of the total population. These numbers jumped dramatically following the Civil War and the failure of Reconstruction in the South. By 1880, there were 6,504 African Americans in Indianapolis, and ten years later, the number had increased so dramatically that only six cities in the North had larger black populations.[7]

Poor black and white migrants from the Upland South had much in common, culturally. As Berry Sulgrove (1827–90), the author of one of the most important early histories of Indianapolis, cynically noted, "Among the early settlers were a good many from the slave states of the class since widely known as 'poor whites,' who brought here all the silly superstitions they had learned among the slaves at home."[8]

The colorful accounts of nineteenth-century travelers and residents alike make it abundantly clear that the culture of Indianapolis was heavily influenced by the many white and black migrants from Kentucky and other Upland Southern states. The impact of these mostly hardscrabble men and women could be felt in the city's religion, language, politics, and social norms. In 1870, nearly one-third of the churchgoing population of Indianapolis belonged to evangelical Methodist and Baptist congregations that were popular among Southerners.[9] Yet many migrants from places like Kentucky did not join these established churches, instead preferring the more emotional environment of revival meetings. Others were "indifferent" to organized religion, according to Berry Sulgrove. Indeed, he observed that "among a considerable section of the Southern immigration disparaging or even scandalous jokes on preachers and prominent church members were no unusual entertainment of social or accidental gatherings."[10]

In addition to their frequently iconoclastic attitudes toward institutionalized religion, some Southerners apparently brought a love of whiskey and fighting with them to Indianapolis. Oliver Johnson (1821–1907), whose family migrated from Kentucky around the time the city was founded, later recalled in the Southern-inflected dialect widely spoken in Indianapolis, "Throughout the day and the evenin the whisky bottle . . . set on the table for anyone to help himself whenever he wanted a drink."[11] Sulgrove confirmed that "the use of liquor was hardly less general or habitual than the use of coffee."[12] Fueled by locally distilled whiskey like Bayou Blue and a deeply ingrained sense of honor, some migrants from the South were quick to fight. As Johnson put it, "The gentleman class of the early days got satisfaction by using swords and pistols, but the common class that settled the land in these parts had more sense and used their fists."[13] A less sanguine position was taken by the *Indiana State Sentinel,* an Indianapolis newspaper, which complained that "the moral influence of a dozen churches is not enough to check the vicious propensities of our population."[14]

Whether drinking and fighting were seen as socially acceptable activities depended largely on the cultural background of the observer. As the historian Andrew Cayton has observed in his work on frontier Indiana, customs like drinking and fighting were "something more than the evidence of moral breakdown that reformers saw. From the perspective of rural and working people, they were critical components of a traditional masculine culture that valued competition and personal honor. Imbibing alcohol, betting on sporting events, and having a good time were long-standing customs for southern rural males."[15] On the other hand, many residents originally from the Northeast viewed these same activities as dangerously undermining the industrialized Victorian society that they were attempting to create in Indianapolis. Commenting on one such resident's "antipathy to the fiddle," for example, Sulgrove noted that "the Eastern immigrant brought his bigotry . . . and made the whole social structure redolent of it."[16] Southerners responded in kind, as Oliver Johnson recalled: "Some thought the Easterners was kind a stuck up on account of havin more book learnin than we did."[17]

By the 1870s, wealthy and middle-class residents of Indianapolis inhabited comfortable homes, while their poorer neighbors crowded into slums with colorful names like Dogtown, Poverty Flats, Holy Row, Happy Hollow, Greasy Row, and Brickville. Named for its many brick-yards, this last neighborhood was in particular home to numerous set-tlers from Kentucky. During the warmer months, the Kentuckians worked as brickmakers, but when winter arrived, according to one observer, "like the untameable red man, they would bury the hatchet and come in to the government agent—i.e., the township trustee, to be fed." The same author described the Kentuckians as "a law unto themselves and as defiant as they dared be of the powers that were." Many kept dogs—including one notorious resident who had thirty "savage sheep-killing brutes"—to keep the taxman and other unwanted visitors away.[18]

The denizens of these rough and tumble neighborhoods patronized brothels like Long Branch and Park House, strolled along Rag Alley (Columbia Street from Ohio to Michigan) and Cockroach Row (a stretch of Massachusetts Avenue near Pennsylvania Street), and gathered in juke joints like The Crib, The Nest, Lindenbower Station, Chism's Fence ("a resort for the lowest class of blacks and whites"), Hoplight Station ("so called because the beaux and belles of the neighborhood used to congregate there and dance of moonlight nights"), and Sleigho, which stood just across a canal nicknamed the St. Lawrence from another dive called Canada. Putting to shame the most extravagant fashions of the disco era, the "typical Brickville dandy" dressed for a night on the town in "a compound of brilliant colors with red, blue and yellow stripes in his trousers, a red undershirt crossed with bright hued suspenders, and a gaudy neckerchief, with cowhide boots upon his feet and a broad-brimmed brown hat surmounting all."[19]

Relations between working-class whites and blacks, who generally lived in a neighborhood called Bucktown, were both intimate and volatile. Despite or, perhaps, because of the cultural closeness between white and black migrants from the Upland South, Sulgrove observed that in the early days of the city, "The race prejudices of the South were imported with its dialect. . . . The colored man counted for little and claimed nothing."[20] By the 1870s, however, blacks in Indianapolis had started to make inroads into business and politics. In 1879, for example, the Bagby brothers, Robert, James, and Benjamin, had begun to publish the *Leader,* the first black newspaper in the city. (Eventually there would be at least ten such publications.)[21] Two years later, in 1881, James Hinton, a Republican from Indianapolis, became the first African American elected to Indiana's House of Representatives.

By that time, the growing number of black voters had become critically important to Republican political success in Indianapolis. In 1876 this alignment led to the worst riot in the city's history when a rumor spread that African American Republicans were being turned away from voting booths in the Democratically controlled Sixth Ward. When a group of blacks marched to the ward to demand their rights, a pitched battle ensued between them and the area's Democratically inclined Irish residents, who had earlier been denounced in Republican-owned newspapers as "Irish tramps," "Hibernian heifers," and "Romish herds."[22]

This brief tour through 1870s Indianapolis reveals the colorful and complex socioeconomic landscape that Oscar McCulloch encountered when he arrived in 1877. Deeply divided between haves and have-nots, Northerners and Southerners, blacks and whites, urban professionals and transplanted rural laborers, Indianapolis in the late 1870s was a city of contrasts. As a middle-class white clergyman with Northeastern roots, McCulloch joined a small but powerful minority that sought to transform Indianapolis from an overgrown frontier town into a modern, industrialized metropolis. Like the author who compared the rough-edged Kentuckians of Brickville to the "untameable red man," these bourgeois citizens saw themselves as forming a vanguard in the struggle to bring civilization to Indianapolis, hoping to enact a kind of Manifest Destiny in microcosm. The objects of this civilizing mission inhabited run down tenements like the Dirty Dozen, named for the twelve "dirty looking girls" who lived there, or they squatted on the banks of the White River in the "grotesque" shanties of Dumptown, which anticipated the Hoovervilles of the Great Depression by half a century.[23] Poor but proud, many of these individuals fiercely resented the efforts to make them adopt middle-class norms, even as they were forced to seek charity from the very people applying this pressure to conform.

By the time Oscar McCulloch set foot in the city, the ongoing economic depression had widened the gulf between middle- and upper-class residents on the one hand and poor and working-class folk on the other. As more and more laborers were thrown out of work, wealthier residents confronted the question of what, if anything, they should do to improve the living conditions of their down-and-out neighbors, while still furthering their agenda to make Indianapolis into a modern city. Oscar McCulloch's discovery of the Tribe of Ishmael must be seen within this environment. Indeed, it is impossible to understand the true significance of the Ishmaelites without appreciating the historical context in which they were first identified as a distinct community.

On January 18, 1878, about a year after arriving in the city, McCulloch recorded the following entry in his diary under the heading "A case of poverty": "A family composed of a man, half blind, a woman, two children, the woman's sister and child, the man's mother, blind all in one room ten foot square. One bed, a stove, no other furniture. When found they had no coal, no food. Dirty, filthy because of no fire, no soap, no towels. It was the most abject poverty I ever saw. We carried supplies to them."[24]

McCulloch had encountered this down-and-out family during one of the many charitable visits he paid to the city's poorest residents. Profoundly shocked by the sight of such intense poverty, McCulloch initially responded with what might be termed traditional Christian charity—a phrase whose meaning he would soon turn on its head, however. In order to learn more about the unnamed family, McCulloch decided to visit the office of the Center Township Trustee, an elected official in charge of distributing public charity funds to Indianapolis's needy citizens.[25] What he learned during this visit would not only disturb the good reverend, it would end up changing the course of his life. Unfortunately, the original files for the township trustee are no longer extant. Nevertheless, some files were copied into the case records of the Charity Organization Society, an Indianapolis institution later founded by Oscar McCulloch. Among those is a report dated August 20, 1877, which depicts the Ishmaels in starkly animalistic terms.[26]

Two days after apparently reading this dehumanizing township trustee report, which conflated the Ishmaels proper with other, supposedly interconnected families, Oscar McCulloch took time from his busy Sunday schedule to record his own impressions. In his diary entry for

January 20, 1878, we find the following description under the heading "The Ishmaelites":

> The case alluded to under date of Friday seems to be a case similar to that of the 'Jukes.' I went to the office of the township trustee this morning and found them under the above name [i.e., the Ishmaelites]. They are called 'The rest-house mob'. Real name is not known but called so from wandering habits. They are a wandering lot of beings, marrying, inter-marrying, cohabitating, etc. They live mostly out of doors, in the river bottoms, in old houses, etc. They are largely illegitimate, subject to fits. There have been in all one hundred and thirteen who have sought aid at different times from the county—of this family and its connections. Five years ago they lived out of doors all winter. Most of the children die. They are hardly human beings. But still they can be made something of, by changed surroundings. The children ought to be taken from them and brought up separately.

Oscar McCulloch had discovered the Tribe of Ishmael, though it would be another decade before he published his groundbreaking study of the community.[27] Two things in particular stand out from his brief observations of January 18: the family's terrible living conditions and the blindness of several of its members, a detail that would become a trope in later accounts of the Tribe of Ishmael. In those accounts, the blindness of various "Ishmaelites" would be attributed to syphilis (and, therefore, to sexual licentiousness) or to the lifelong abuse of blue vitriol (copper sulfate solution), also known as blue stone water, a substance that enabled individuals to feign blindness temporarily and, consequently, to beg more effectively. Blindness would thus become an important sign of the Tribe of Ishmael's moral, social, and physical decay.

By January 20, McCulloch had learned that the poor family's surname was Ishmael, though in his diary, he referred to them and their "connections" (i.e., the other families they had intermarried with) by the more tribal sounding name "The Ishmaelites." This decision reflected McCulloch's initial, though mistaken view that Ishmael was not the central family's real name but a derogatory nickname applied to them on account of their habits. By transforming Ishmael into Ishmaelite, McCulloch stressed the name's symbolic function and also began the rhetorical process of transforming the poor family he had encountered into the central unit of the Tribe of Ishmael.

In order to unpack the significance of the names Ishmaelite and Tribe of Ishmael during the nineteenth century, we must first begin with the Hebrew Bible, where Ishmael is portrayed as the eldest son of Abraham by his concubine Hagar, an Egyptian slave. In Genesis 16, Sarah, Abraham's barren wife, suggests to Abraham that he have a child with her servant, Hagar, yet she reacts jealously when the woman becomes pregnant. To avoid the wrath of her mistress, Hagar escapes into the wilderness, where an angel of the Lord appears to her and declares that her unborn son will be named Ishmael (Hebrew for "God hears") because God heeded her suffering. The angel adds that Ishmael's descendants will be "too many to count," and that "he shall be a wild ass of a man; his hand against everyone, and everyone's hand against him; he shall dwell alongside of all his kinsmen" (16:12). In the next chapter, God blesses Ishmael and makes him the father of twelve chieftains but also tells Abraham that His covenant will be established with Isaac, the patriarch's yet unborn son with Sarah. Later in Genesis, Ishmael is described as living in the "wilderness" and his descendants, a wandering "caravan of Ishmaelites," are depicted as selling Joseph to the Egyptians after acquiring him from his brothers. Other biblical references to the Ishmaelites portray them as enemies of Israel who plunder the land.

In the Hebrew Bible, therefore, Ishmael functions as the prototype of the older sibling displaced by a younger brother, a dynamic repeated in the story of Esau and Jacob, the father of the twelve tribes of Israel. Paul later employs the same trope in the New Testament's Letter to the Galatians, where he contrasts the descendants of Abraham's two sons. The older son's descendants, the Ishmaelites, are slaves, while the younger son's descendants, the Israelites, are free men. In an ironic twist, however, according to Paul's allegorical interpretation, the Jews have become like the Ishmaelites, while the Christians have superseded them as the New Israel.

Post-biblical Jewish authors like the historian Josephus identified the Ishmaelites as the ancestors of the Arabs (based on a genealogical list found in Genesis 25). Later, during the medieval period, this link led to the association of the Ishmaelites with Islam. Indeed, seventh-century non-Muslim authors frequently referred to adherents of the new religion as members of the "Tribe of Ishmael."[28] Muslim sources, in turn, depicted Ishmael, rather than Isaac, as the favored son whom Abraham almost sacrificed, and some even claimed that Muhammad himself was Ishmael's direct descendant. Perhaps responding to the Muslim attempt to replace Isaac with Ishmael, the eleventh-century French rabbi known as Rashi, described Ishmael in his Bible commentary as a "thief" whom "everyone hated and fought with."[29]

By the middle of the nineteenth century, the name *Ishmaelite* had acquired the meanings "outcast" and "thievish" in the English language.

American documents from this period reveal the use of Ishmaelite as a biblically inflected term connoting deception, savagery, and nomadism. For example, in 1861, a Union Army soldier serving in Missouri wrote a letter in which he condemned the local Confederate sympathizers for acting like Ishmaelites: "I can not describe the misery and confusion that everywhere prevail. Law and order are abolished, and a miserable horde of Ishmaelites are roving the country, burning bridges, stealing property, and slaughtering or driving away all those who are suspected of having the least particle of love for the Union. Too cowardly, or too sensible of their inability to meet the Federal troops in a fair engagement, they are content to lie in wait, like the cunning savage, and strike a blow at some unguarded point."[30]

As a Christian minister, avid reader, and amateur Orientalist, Oscar McCulloch was undoubtedly well aware of these symbolic associations when he decided to call the supposedly degenerate community he had discovered the Ishmaelites. In his diary McCulloch likened the Ishmaelites of Indianapolis to their biblical namesake, a wild ass of a man who wandered the wilderness bordering the civilization of the camp and always fighting with his settled neighbors: "a wandering lot of beings . . . largely illegitimate, subject to fits . . . hardly human beings." In the Bible, the Ishmaelites signified a kind of atavism, an earlier stage of development that had since been superseded but continued to survive on the margins of the chosen community of Israelites. Similarly, the modern-day Ishmaelites represented an itinerant way of life that was tolerated when Indianapolis was still a frontier town but, in the eyes of McCulloch, was now completely out of place in a city that was seeking to transform itself into a modern, bourgeois metropolis.

The biblical image of Ishmael as a wild man and wanderer prefigured the coon cap–wearing pioneer of the American frontier. Like Ishmael's relationship with Isaac, the American frontiersman served as a kind of displaced older brother to the urban settler. McCulloch made it clear in his published account of the Tribe of Ishmael that the Ishmaelites were descendants of early pioneers who had arrived in Indianapolis from Kentucky, Tennessee, and other Upland Southern states. Just as Isaac superseded Ishmael in the Bible, so too would middle-class residents from the Northeast supplant the so-called Ishmaelites of Indianapolis; at least, that is what McCulloch and other reformers hoped.

By employing the name Ishmaelite, therefore, McCulloch had tapped into a biblical narrative that resonated with many Protestant Americans who saw themselves as the New Israel. To be an Ishmaelite within this context signified kinship with, but ultimately exclusion from, the chosen community. Ironically, however, it also represented the stubborn survival of an earlier American ideal: the restless wanderer of the frontier. It was this heroic, if ambivalent, image that James Fenimore Cooper had earlier exploited in his popular novel *The Prairie,* when he decided to name his wandering protagonist Ishmael. Like Cooper, McCulloch appreciated the powerful significance of the name, and in his future writings on the Tribe of Ishmael, he would deliberately exploit its different symbolic registers.

One of the most important of these registers involved the traditional identification of Ishmael with Islam. Unlike Hugo Leaming a century later, McCulloch never claimed or even implied that the Ishmaelites of Indianapolis were actually Muslims. Yet he subtly invoked contemporary views of the Islamic East as a culture in decline, bypassed by the supposedly more civilized Christian West, when he coined the Muslim sounding names "Tribe of Ishmael" and "Ishmaelites."

Happily for the historian, Oscar McCulloch was a precise man who diligently recorded the books he read in his diary. Indeed, he even went so far as to write down the price of each book he purchased. From these detailed diary entries, we know that in the period immediately preceding his discovery of the Tribe of Ishmael, McCulloch had become intensely interested in Islam and the Near East. Throughout 1877, he acquired a veritable library of contemporary Orientalist works, including Frederick Burnaby's *Ride to Khiva,* Robert Arthur Arnold's *Through Persia by Caravan,* and E. A. Freeman's *The Turks in Europe*—the last a bargain at only 15 cents.[31]

On April 17, 1877, McCulloch noted in his diary that besides completing Burnaby's book and beginning Arnold's, he had come across an essay by Edwin Godkin entitled "The Eastern Question."[32] Concerning his newfound passion, McCulloch observed rather glumly: "It is a good time to study up this Eastern Question if life is long enough." Less than a week before he discovered the Ishmaelites, on Monday, January 14, 1878, McCulloch recorded a diary entry under the heading "Mohammed's sermon on charity." Nor did his interest in Islam wane in the months following his discovery. For example, on February 17, 1878, McCulloch completed writing a "Sketch of the Rise and Growth of Turkish Power in Europe," while a week later, on February 26, he read the "Resemblance of the Arabs to the Old Testament People," contained in what he cited as Baskin's *Abyssinia.*[33]

Late-nineteenth-century Orientalists like Edwin Godkin and Frederick Burnaby diagnosed Muslims—aka Ishmaelites—as suffering from a terminal case of cultural decay. As Robert Arnold put it succinctly at the end of his five-hundred-page tome: "The religion of Islam is incompatible with progress, and must decline with the advance of civilization."[34] Indeed, decades before McCulloch first employed the names "Ishmaelites" and "Tribe of Ishmael" to identify his community of urban "primitives," Americans had already begun to characterize Turks, Arabs, and Muslims—the three were frequently conflated in the popular imagination—as savages. This phenomenon reflected a complex combination of political, religious, and cultural factors dating back to the very founding of the United States. One of the earliest phases in the development of this distinctly American brand of Orientalism was the conflict known as the Barbary Pirate War. This struggle raged on and off from 1801, when Thomas Jefferson first refused to pay tribute to North African (Barbary Coast) pirates in the Mediterranean, to 1815, when James Madison finally eliminated this threat to American ships. In addition to tribute, the Barbary pirates also took Europeans and Americans captive, sometimes selling them into slavery, an ironic and, for many outraged white observers, bitter reversal of the transatlantic slave trade.[35]

In 1819, a few years after the Barbary Pirate War ended, the first Christian missionaries were dispatched to the Middle East from the United States. Although they met with little success in converting local Muslims, Jews, or even Eastern Christians, their theological attitudes and their experiences in the Levant helped to shape the views of their fellow Americans back home. Nineteenth-century American Protestants inherited older Christian views of Muslims as both potential converts and implacable enemies who would eventually play a decisive eschatological role.[36] Many interpreted the New Testament's Book of Revelation 9:3–7, "from the smoke came locusts on the earth . . . their faces were like human faces," as referring to Muslims. This was an easy connection to make since Muslims had long been portrayed as rapacious, animalistic hordes threatening cultivated Christian lands. Similarly, the Ishmaelites of Indiana were pejoratively labeled "Grasshopper Gypsies" because they supposedly stole farmers' crops during their travels through the countryside.[37] Both groups of Ishmaelites, therefore, were explicitly likened to a biblical plague of voracious insects laying waste to civilization.

Early American travelers to the Near East viewed the places and people they encountered through a distinctly biblical lens. Since the

Bible portrayed the Ishmaelites as a tribe of nomads prone to thievery and violence, it is not surprising that when Americans in the Holy Land and elsewhere came across flesh-and-blood Muslims—"the sons and daughters of Ishmael" as one contemporary observer put it—they imagined them to be thievish and shiftless.[38]

During the same period that Americans began to physically encounter the Near East, they were also rapidly expanding westward in self-proclaimed Manifest Destiny. Like the Near Eastern frontier, Americans understood the West in explicitly biblical terms, frequently likening their conquest of the Indians to the Israelite conquest of the Canaanites. Some even explicitly compared the Indians to Ishmaelites. Thus, an official of the Smithsonian Institution's Bureau of Ethnology wrote in 1880: "The Shawnees were the Bedouins, and I may almost say the Ishmaelites of the North American tribes. As wanderers they were without rivals among their race, and as fomentors of discord and war between themselves and their neighbors their genius was marked."[39]

In light of these parallel historical and discursive processes, it makes sense that many American travelers to the Near East perceived similarities between the Muslim "savages" they encountered abroad and the Native Americans they had left behind. As George William Curtis noted, "the last inhabitants of the oldest land [i.e., the Levant] have thus a mysterious sympathy of similarity with the aborigines of the youngest [i.e., America]. For what more are these orientals than sumptuous savages?"[40] Following his own visit to the Near East, Mark Twain put it more succinctly, albeit more crudely: "They [Syrian villagers] reminded me much of Indians, did these people. . . . They were infested with vermin and the dirt had caked on them until it amounted to bark. . . . The children were in a pitiable condition—they all had sore eyes and were otherwise afflicted in various ways."[41]

Twain and other American observers painted "Orientals" and Native Americans with the same brush that Oscar McCulloch employed in his 1878 diary entry on the Ishmaelites. By the time McCulloch arrived in the state, Indiana—despite its name—had long been essentially emptied of Native Americans after years of vicious warfare had culminated in the famous Battle of Tippecanoe in 1811. In the absence of actual Native Americans or Bedouins in Indianapolis, McCulloch imagined the impoverished Anglo-American family he had come upon as their equivalents: thievish wanderers who lacked middle-class Christian morals. Hence, he called them the Ishmaelites, a name that evoked comparisons with both Muslims and Native Americans in the nineteenth-century imagination.

The Tribe of Ishmael thus was not the first case of a marginal community in the United States being associated with Islam, as Native Americans were frequently likened to Ishmaelites, both the biblical and contemporary varieties. Nor was the Tribe of Ishmael the first European American community to be symbolically likened to Muslims. Although it may seem surprising today, the most striking example of this phenomenon was the Mormons.[42]

From its very beginnings, Mormonism was identified with Islam. In 1831, only a few years after Joseph Smith, the founder of Mormonism, received his revelations, he was referred to as "the Ontario Mahomet," in recognition of the New York county where he first achieved prominence. In the following decades, other observers identified Smith and his prophetic successor, Brigham Young, by a host of Islamic titles, including the "American Mahomet," the "Yankee Mahomet," the "New World Mohammad," the "Yankee Turk," and the "modern Mahomet." One critic even observed in 1877 that Brigham Young was the "second Mohammed of American Mohamedanism,—Joseph Smith being the first."[43]

In addition to these monikers, critics drew a host of parallels between Mormonism and Islam during the nineteenth century. Such observers likened Mormon polygamy to the Muslim harem, the Mormon trek west to Muhammad's flight from Medina (the hegira), Salt Lake City to Mecca, and the Book of Mormon to the Koran. They also wondered whether Joseph Smith and his followers would "like a second Mahometanism . . . extend itself sword in hand."[44] The author of a book entitled *The Mormon Prophet and His Harem* disparagingly referred to "Mohammaedan Utah."[45] Other late-nineteenth-century and early-twentieth-century authors explicitly described Mormonism as "the Islam of America" and "Mohammedanism Yankeeized," and Mormons, themselves, as "the Mohammedans of America."[46]

Like the Mormons of Utah, the Ishmaelites of Indiana were not real "Mohammedans." But they, too, were depicted as symbolic Muslims at a time when Islam, particularly in the form of the Ottoman Empire, was seen as an acute threat to Christian civilization. As fate would have it, in the days immediately leading up to his discovery of the Ishmaelites, Oscar McCulloch's attention was drawn to the Russo-Turkish War, a bloody conflict over the Balkans that many European and American observers interpreted as the latest phase in an ongoing struggle between

Islam and Christianity. Indeed, on January 19, 1878, the very day before McCulloch composed his first diary entry on the Ishmaelites, *The Indianapolis News* ran a front-page story entitled "The Eastern War," on the Balkan conflict between Muslims and Christians.

Ironically, one of the things that made the Muslim Turks so dangerous in the eyes of many nineteenth-century Europeans and Americans was that they had adopted certain Western practices over the years. Thus, the Orientalist author E. A. Freeman warned that Turks were more treacherous than other "barbarians," such as sub-Saharan Africans, because the former had learned to "dress and talk like Europeans," while the latter still looked like stereotypical savages.[47] Similarly, according to McCulloch, the Ishmaelites were particularly threatening to the social order of Indianapolis because, like the Turks, they were able to "ape"—to borrow an expression from Freeman—the physical appearance of their more civilized neighbors while still engaging in barbaric behavior.

Indeed, McCulloch did not point out anything remarkable about the Ishmael family's physical appearance in his first diary entries—with the exception of their dirtiness—for a very simple reason: they basically looked like him. Had they possessed any outstanding physical traits that differentiated them from white Anglo-Saxons such as himself, it is likely that McCulloch would have taken the opportunity to note them. In the absence of such obvious signs, the family's difference would have to be represented in other ways, beginning with the oriental-sounding titles that McCulloch applied to them. Fortunately for McCulloch, the supposedly degenerate family already possessed an exotic-sounding surname that lent itself easily to further transformations. Had the Ishmaels possessed a more mundane name, McCulloch would have been compelled to invent an evocative pseudonym, as was the case with other cacogenic groups that were called by tribal sounding names, like the Kallikaks, the Win, the Nam, the Zeros, and the granddaddy of them all, the Jukes, a name that meant "to roost" and referred "to the habit of fowls to have no home, no nest, no coop, preferring to fly into the trees and roost away from the places where they belong."[48]

As his diary entry from January 20 makes clear, McCulloch was already aware of Richard Dugdale's famous study of the Jukes when he made his own discovery of the Ishmaelites. Several months earlier, on November 6, 1877, McCulloch noted in his diary that he had "Finished 'The Jukes' and shall work up into sermons." McCulloch saw his own work on the Ishmaelites as a continuation of the groundbreaking research done by Dugdale or, as he put it in his diary, the Ishmaelite tribe "seems to be a case similar to that of the 'Jukes.'"

Richard Dugdale had discovered the group of paupers and criminals he immortalized as the Jukes while conducting research in rural county jails on behalf of the Prison Association of New York in 1874. Three years later, he published his findings in a landmark book entitled *"The Jukes": A Study in Crime, Pauperism, Disease and Heredity,* considered the first of the eugenics family studies.[49] Many of the elements that would later come to define the genre were already present in Dugdale's work. These included an obsessive interest in genealogy, the predominantly white, Anglo-Saxon background of the individuals involved, an emphasis on the dangers of uncontrolled sexuality, the conflation of a number of families into a single, synthetic community identified by a tribal-sounding name, and a call for public policy reforms to address the social problems (crime, pauperism, etc.) caused by the group. Yet, in contrast to later eugenics family studies, Dugdale's book offered environmental as well as hereditarian explanations for why certain families seemed to engage in deviant behavior. Dugdale's approach helps to explain why McCulloch initially wrote in his diary that the Ishmaelites could "be made something of, by changed surroundings," an environmentalist view that he eventually abandoned in favor of a more strictly hereditarian perspective.

Over the next decade, McCulloch sought to gather more information about the Ishmaelites while simultaneously addressing the practical problems they posed to the city of Indianapolis. An opportunity to accomplish both goals soon presented itself on January 5, 1879, when McCulloch was elected president of the Indianapolis Benevolent Society.[50] Established on Thanksgiving Day, 1835, the Indianapolis Benevolent Society was the oldest and most venerable private charity organization in the city. Since its inception, the society had maintained the same rather quaint method for gathering and distributing charity. On a set day, each district in the city would be visited by a pair of volunteers—always a respectable gentleman carrying a basket and a lady carrying a purse—who would collect clothes, firewood, and money from residents. Once gathered, donated money would be handed over to the society's treasurer and the wood and clothing placed in a depository. The same couple that collected the donations would then be responsible for distributing it to needy residents of their district.

By the time McCulloch was elected president, the society had become moribund. This decline may be attributed to several factors, including the economic depression of the 1870s, which increased the number of charity applications while decreasing the number of donations; the ninefold increase in the city's population from 1850 to 1880, which put a strain on the society's antiquated mode of collecting charity; and the growing role of the township trustee in providing public assistance. Several months earlier, in November 1878, a special committee had even recommended that the society disband. Instead, with McCulloch at its helm, the organization decided to reinvigorate itself.

Looking back on those early days, McCulloch wrote in 1886, "The society had before it as its object: to distinguish between poverty and pauperism, to relieve the one and to refuse the other . . . to keep careful records of the cases; to do what it could to substitute work for alms."[51] The society's new mission was grounded in an ideology—rooted in Elizabethan poor laws—that sharply distinguished between real poverty and pauperism or, as it was also commonly phrased, between the deserving and undeserving poor. As noted in the introduction, during the late nineteenth century, such moral definitions of poverty became an increasingly important part of American public policy, Protestant theology, and early hereditarian theory.

Like many of his contemporaries, Oscar McCulloch believed that paupers—unlike the deserving poor—were morally to blame for their poverty and therefore undeserving of charity. By contrast, he complained, the township trustee's office in Indianapolis had long failed to make this distinction, with dire consequences. Noting that the number of families given aid by the township trustee had increased from 314 in 1870 to 3,000 in 1877, McCulloch condemned the office for its "practical pauperization of the city" in this period and compared the situation in Indianapolis to "the latter days of Rome." Indeed, McCulloch grumbled that the city had come to be seen as so "benevolent" that "thrifty township trustees" from other towns would actually ship their poor to Indianapolis in order to avoid supporting them. Indeed, the practice of directing the poor to other municipalities became so widespread throughout the country that it eventually resulted in the modification of what were known as settlement laws.[52] In McCulloch's opinion, morally deficient paupers and irresponsible township trustees alike were to blame for the dramatic increase in tax-supported charity in Indianapolis during the mid-1870s. Glaringly absent was any acknowledgement that the growth in poverty could be attributed to the terrible economic depression that had devastated Indianapolis's working-class residents during the same period.

After attending a meeting of the society on January 9, 1879, McCulloch lamented that it "had no system . . . no organization—No records kept, no reports. It is no easy work to organize it but it can be done. . . . I am to perfect a plan this week."[53] Never one to dawdle, McCulloch returned a week later with a proposal entitled "Methods of Charitable Relief in Large Cities," in which he called for the complete overhaul of the society along principles of "scientific charity," as opposed to the traditional almsgiving that had previously characterized the organization. As a result of his recommendations, the Indianapolis Benevolent Society was radically transformed into a centralized bureaucracy whose structure and methods anticipated modern social work agencies. Most significantly, the organization now required every application for charity to be thoroughly investigated in order to distinguish the deserving poor from paupers. The names of all applicants, as well as decisions concerning aid, were to be recorded for future reference and to prevent duplication of assistance.

By implementing these new methods, which he had carefully modeled on an earlier German initiative known as the Elberfeld Plan, McCulloch hoped to put an end to outdoor relief (such as alms and soup kitchens) to all "vagrants, beggars, and paupers" in the city of Indianapolis. Instead, these and other "defectives" who hailed "from miserable stock" were to be placed in the growing number of institutions being built in the state. In a diary entry from January 18, 1879, McCulloch described seeing "women going from house to house. I propose to make it an impossibility for them to get anything. The begging children tell their tale in the alleys, and I listen to them. I hope to see this done away [with]." The chief goal of the newly organized society, as he expressed it a month and a half later on March 3, was to "relieve the worthy poor without breaking down that sturdy self-dependence which is characteristic of the Teutonic races." On November 30, 1879, McCulloch would repeat this view at the Annual Public Meeting of the Indianapolis Benevolent Society: "While the poor we will always have with us, it is our fault and our disgrace if we have the pauper. The pauper is one whose Saxon or Teutonic self-help has given place to a parasitic life."[54]

McCulloch's glowing references to Anglo-Saxon self-dependence reflect the increasingly popular racial ideology in postbellum America known as *Teutonism*. Based on the writings of men like E. A. Freeman and his disciple John Fiske, these taxonomies placed members of the Anglo-Saxon branch of the Teutonic "race" atop the racial pyramid.[55] As Matthew Frye Jacobson has shown, one of the most articulate spokesmen for this position was Daniel Ullman, a Know-Nothing politician from New York, who delivered a speech in 1868 in which he emphasized the "inherent love of freedom of the Anglo-Saxons in England and America, which has been the hereditary characteristic of the Teutonic or Germanic race from the earliest period."[56]

Like Ullman, Fiske, and Freeman—whose writings he had read—Oscar McCulloch viewed the Teutonic race as the backbone of American democracy and economic self-sufficiency. Against this backdrop, Anglo-Saxon paupers such as the Ishmaelites represented a glaring exception that proved the rule. In the following decade, McCulloch would argue that the Tribe of Ishmael's debased condition testified to the deleterious effects of unscientific charity, on the one hand, and to an inherited propensity for begging, prostitution, nomadism, and criminality, on the other. McCulloch viewed the degeneracy of the Ishmaelites as evidence that even the Teutonic race could produce atavistic survivals of more primitive and, particularly in the modern context, socially undesirable behaviors.

McCulloch's reorganization of the Indianapolis Benevolence Society attracted the support of the city's wealthiest businessmen and professionals, including Benjamin Harrison, the future president of the United States, who agreed to serve on one of its committees. It didn't take long for dissenting voices to appear, as well. The most pointed critiques were leveled by the prolabor Indianapolis newspaper, *The People*. On March 8, 1879, the paper published the following stinging editorial:

> The great hobby of this Benevolent Society is "investigation". They believe in spending dollar upon dollar for investigation—but not one red cent to relieve "cases" until they have been investigated. . . . They harp upon the "chronic poor" of the city. In God's name how can one help from being a "chronic poor" person when he can get no work to put bread into his mouth or into the mouths of his suffering family? Does the Benevolent Society believe, for a moment that these "chronic poor" people remain the "chronic poor" of the city from choice? No doubt they would greatly prefer to be among the "chronic" rich. . . . Ask the poor people who apply to this Benevolent Society how they are treated, and you will have but a very poor opinion of the efficiency of the "Christian activity" which they so prate about. . . . God help the poor if they have no other dependence save this Indianapolis Benevolent Society and our township trustee's office.[57]

Over the next few months, *The People* continued to attack the society and its new president, asking, for example, "Who made Oscar C. McCulloch a judge of his fellows?" and exhorting him to model his behavior "more after his Savior and less after our little township trustee."[58] These charges of religious hypocrisy were intended to under-mine McCulloch's growing reputation as the foremost liberal clergyman in Indianapolis. From his pulpit in the Plymouth Church, McCulloch had quickly become one of the city's most vocal proponents of the Social Gospel, a newly emerging theological doctrine that rejected predestina-tion and, instead, argued that "applied Christianity"—that is, religiously inspired social work—could transform society.[59] Unlike their more con-servative evangelical counterparts, advocates of the Social Gospel did not interpret the Bible literally, and many even embraced Darwin's theory of evolution. Inspired by the writings of well-known contemporaries like Washington Gladden and Edward Everett Hale, Oscar McCulloch deliv-ered sermons with titles like "Problems of the City Poor" and "The Development of Benevolence in the Race and Individual."[60]

In these sermons and in published bulletins for the Indianapolis Benevolent Society, McCulloch exhorted the residents of the city to vol-unteer "a very little act of personal kindness or attention" on behalf of their impoverished neighbors.[61] But he also chided them for actually increasing misery through indiscriminate almsgiving. Christian charity, in his view, meant first and foremost distinguishing between the worthy and unworthy poor. Once this was accomplished through scientific methods of investigation, then deserving individuals could be reinte-grated into society and undeserving ones could be safely segregated in institutions. By contrast, as we have seen, prolabor voices like *The People* believed that McCulloch and his allies spent too much time and money on surveillance of the poor and too little on actual aid. While a small number of hustlers and malcontents might end up receiving char-ity, these opponents argued that a more generous approach would ensure that none of the truly needy went away empty-handed—some-thing that they claimed was already occurring under the newly organ-ized Indianapolis Benevolent Society.

In its editorials, *The People* also accused McCulloch of being "in league with the township trustee" and of supporting "his disgraceful system of espionage upon the poor." McCulloch was highly critical of what he viewed as the township trustee's policy of indiscriminate giving during the first half of the 1870s. From 1874 to 1876 alone, the amount of relief given by the office had nearly doubled from $33,601 to $55,542—hardly surprising, given the increase in population and the effects of the depression during the same period. This changed dramat-ically, however, after B.F. King was elected trustee in November 1876. During his first few months in office, King assembled a team of twenty paid and volunteer workers to investigate every application for aid. As a result of these practices, the amount of relief given by the township trustee actually decreased to $31,733 in 1877, plummeted to an astonishing $8,780 in 1878, and then fell even further, to $6, 743 in 1879. It would not break the $10,000 mark again until 1884.[62]

These numbers reveal that Oscar McCulloch's policy initiatives with the Indianapolis Benevolent Society did not occur in a vacuum. On the contrary, the city had already introduced surveillance of the poor in the year preceding his arrival. McCulloch expressed his support for the township trustee's new approach in a letter to the editor of the *Indianapolis News* on March 3, 1879: "Of over eighteen hundred applicants for aid in 1876 only forty are now receiving help. . . . I believe the management of that office to be thorough, efficient and in the best interests of the people."[63]

The joint efforts of McCulloch and the township trustee to restrict aid could not have occurred at a worse time for the growing ranks of the city's poor. Instead of attributing the increase in need to socioeconomic factors, such as the influx of desperately poor white and black rural laborers and the lingering effects of the economic collapse of the 1870s, McCulloch and his allies blamed the so-called undeserving poor and their unwitting benefactors.

In December 1879, encouraged by the positive response of the city's upper classes to his work with the Indianapolis Benevolence Society, McCulloch established the Charity Organization Society.[64] Under his leadership, the COS, as it was also known, assumed responsibility for investigating families requesting aid, while the Benevolence Society remained in charge of actually distributing the aid approved by the investigators. McCulloch modeled the COS after a similar society in Buffalo established by Benjamin Gurteen, who was in turn inspired by the London Charity Organization Society. All these groups belonged to a new movement known as "associated" or "organized" charity.[65] As the *Yearbook of Charities, 1888–1889* made clear, the chief goal of the movement was to adopt "the principles of scientific charity as distinguished from mere relief or almsgiving societies." The constitution for the Buffalo society spelled out exactly what this meant:

1. To see that all deserving cases of destitution are properly relieved.
2. To prevent indiscriminate and duplicate giving.
3. To make employment the basis for relief.
4. To secure the community from imposture.
5. To reduce vagrancy and pauperism, and ascertain their true causes.[66]

Over the next few years, Oscar McCulloch succeeded in transforming the Indianapolis Charity Organization Society into the city's central hub for the distribution of aid to the poor. During this period, the COS worked closely with the township trustee, the police, clergymen, and prominent businessmen, although McCulloch's relationship with the city's capitalists later soured after his views took a decided turn to the left. The COS minutes from 1880 mention an impressive list of financial contributors, including the Indiana National Bank, George Kingan (a local meat-packing mogul), Merchants Bank, Eli Lilly and Company, and the *Indianapolis Journal* and the *Indiana State Sentinel,* the city's two most prominent newspapers.[67] Emboldened by this support, McCulloch eventually sought to eliminate the office of the township trustee—the other main distributor of charity in Indianapolis—on the grounds that it was no longer necessary. By the end of the 1880s, McCulloch had once again become so critical of the township trustee, despite its adoption of many of the principles of "scientific" charity that he himself championed, that he even accused holders of the office of trading charity for votes.

Criticism of McCulloch's efforts with the Charity Organization Society was not confined to *The People.* One letter to the editor of the *Indianapolis Journal* sarcastically referred to the agency as the "society for the suppression of benevolence" and complained that "the poor—the deserving poor, the superlatively, double-distilled, deserving poor—get only fifty cents out of each dollar collected. It is a beautiful work."[68]

Undaunted, McCulloch continued to expand the reach of the COS throughout the 1880s. Under its auspices, he helped to establish a range of important social services in the city, including free public baths, the Indianapolis Free Kindergarten Society, and the Dime Savings and Loan Association for poor investors. He tirelessly argued for reforms in the area's decrepit jails, hospitals, and insane asylums and unsuccessfully campaigned for the construction of low- and moderate-income public housing. On another front, McCulloch established the Plymouth Institute—inspired, in part, by the Working Men's College in London—which offered courses to working people for a nominal fee, as well as a literary club and a lecture series that included talks by John Dewey, Mark Twain, Felix Adler (founder of the Society for Ethical Culture), Matthew Arnold, Henry Ward Beecher, Charles Dickens, and the explorer Henry Stanley, who supposedly received the telegram that sent him on his quest for Dr. Livingstone while staying in McCulloch's Indianapolis home. During the same period, McCulloch himself gave numerous public lectures, on topics like "Contributions of Darwinism to Religion," "March of the Teuton," and "The Higher Socialism."[69]

During his days as a traveling salesman, McCulloch had learned to appreciate the power of advertising. Taking advantage of his good relations with the city's main newspapers in the early 1880s, McCulloch began to publicize his social programs in a regular column in the *Indianapolis Journal*. Here, for the first time, he discussed in print the pauper community that he had previously referred to in his diary as the Ishmaelites. In a column published on April 16, 1880, McCulloch thanked the township trustee for granting him access to "histories of over 7,000 cases," containing "family connections and lines of descent through three and four generations . . . [offering] an opportunity to the student of crime and pauperism unequaled, it is believed in the country." A few weeks later, on May 1, McCulloch published a column in which he referred to 459 "knots or groups of families" who reflected the "law of retrogression" and were "connected by blood or marriage and form a mass of parasitic growth."[70] Although he chose not to identify this cluster of pauper families by name, McCulloch was clearly referring to the so-called Ishmaelites he had discovered nearly two years earlier. In these columns, McCulloch began to formulate the rhetoric of regression and parasitism that he would later employ so chillingly in his 1888 published account of the Tribe of Ishmael.

In the same year that these columns appeared, McCulloch was invited to give a speech before the National Social Science Association in Saratoga, New York. The text of this lecture was published under the title "Associated Charities" in *The Indiana State Sentinel* and in a national publication called *Good Company*.[71] At the conference, McCulloch illustrated his remarks with a diagram (no longer extant) consisting of more than four hundred supposedly deviant individuals related by blood or marriage who were "underrunning our society like devil grass," as he put it. In the following decades, such charts would become a staple of the eugenics family studies genre. Apparently wishing to preserve the anonymity of the Ishmaels, McCulloch referred to them in his lecture as an "Indianapolis family" whose members were caught in a spiral of public aid, infant mortality, and incest. As in his diary, McCulloch described going to "the office of the township trustee, where the historical records of all applicants for public aid are registered," adding, "Here I found that I had touched one knot of a large family known as 'American Gypsies.'"

Significantly, instead of calling them the Ishmaelites in this lecture, McCulloch identified the community as Gypsies, another equally exotic sounding title. McCulloch never suggested in either his published or unpublished writings that the Ishmaels were genuine Gypsies, or, as they call themselves, Roma. Instead, he hoped to symbolically associate the community with another outcast group then in vogue. Indeed, Roma were the subject of innumerable articles in the 1880s.[72] Contemporary works such as George Smith's *Gipsy Life: Being an Account of our Gipsies and their Children, with Suggestions for their Improvement* (1880) and Charles Leland's *The English Gipsies and Their Language* (1874) provided a literary backdrop for McCulloch's discursive choice, just as Orientalist writings on the Islamic Near East had earlier influenced his identification of the community as the Ishmaelites.

It is also possible that McCulloch was influenced by direct contact with actual Roma who were part of the great waves of immigration from Eastern and Southern Europe that began reaching America's shores in the 1880s.[73] Late-nineteenth-century birth records for Marion County, Indiana—where Indianapolis is located—list "gypsies living in a tent" as the "occupation" of at least one couple.[74] Whether these itinerant folk were Roma, Ishmaelites, or the British Isles people known as Travellers is now impossible to say.

Like the Ishmaelites, Roma were consistently portrayed during the nineteenth century as wanderers and thieves. One self-appointed English expert on the Roma declared that "all their peculiar vices . . . are obviously traceable to their wandering life. This engenders idleness, ignorance, poverty, a fierce lawless temper. . . . They have so many opportunities, when unobserved, of indulging their thievish propensities, that they are bold and unblushing in the practice."[75] Like McCulloch, the author of this passage was a social reformer who believed in surveillance—note his reference to the trouble the Roma get into when "unobserved"—as well as the removal of children from their parents, a recommendation that McCulloch had also made in his diary entry of January 20, 1878.

McCulloch probably knew that the English word "Gypsy" reflected a bastardization of the word "Egyptian," based on a common—though mistaken—belief that the Roma originated in Egypt before arriving in Europe. Indeed, early English sources even referred to them as "Egipcyans" or "counterfayte Egipcians." This provided a symbolic link to the name "Ishmaelites" since Ishmael himself was depicted as the son of an Egyptian slave in the Bible and his descendants were later identified as Arabs. Like the name "Ishmaelites," therefore, the title "American Gypsies" conjured up threatening Orientalist stereotypes of a degenerate tribe of wanderers and thieves living on the margins of civilization.

Today, Oscar McCulloch's untiring activism on behalf of Indianapolis's working poor on the one hand and his strident condemnation of the Ishmaelites on the other appear contradictory and even paradoxical. In his day, however, as we have seen, it was not uncommon for social reformers and other progressives to differentiate sharply between the ranks of the deserving and the undeserving poor. Poor individuals whose labor was defined as socially productive (typically those who worked in trades, factories, and farms) were deemed worthy of help; those whose labor was stigmatized (e.g., collecting junk, begging, prostitution) or who did not work at all were stereotyped as social parasites. The eugenics movement would later attract a large number of progressive activists to its ranks, including, most notably, Margaret Sanger, the founder of the organization now known as Planned Parenthood.[76] Given this broader trend, it is not surprising that during the middle of the 1880s, McCulloch began to turn away from his close ties with Indianapolis's business community and started to champion a more progressive prolabor ideology that he and others called Christian Socialism. In McCulloch's words, "Every public spirited man is in this sense a Socialist."[77]

In the summer of 1885, after more than half a decade of laboring in vain to eliminate the scourge of poverty in Indianapolis, a frustrated McCulloch began to deliver sermons with titles like "A Defense of Labor and Endorsement of Trades Unions" and "An Honest Definition of Socialism." He praised labor unions as expressions of Christian self-sacrifice since "the good of the individual must be submitted to the good of his class. Each must think of all, must lay aside some of his wages for some suffering brother, for a union locked out or on a strike."[78] Whereas McCulloch's earlier efforts had been heavily publicized by the city's main newspapers and criticized by its prolabor press, this time the situation was reversed. For instance, Thomas Gruelle, the president of the Central Labor Union and publisher of the Indianapolis *Labor Signal,* wrote an editorial on February 18, 1886, in which he declared, "The working people of Indianapolis should rally as one man to the support of Rev. Oscar C. McCulloch, who stands alone among the ministers of this city as the champion of labor—the defender of our faith."[79]

McCulloch cemented his newfound reputation as a man of the people following the infamous Haymarket Riots of 1886, in which the Chicago police fired into a crowd of union supporters after a bomb went off at a labor gathering in the city's Haymarket Square. Altogether, seven police officers were killed in the explosion. In response, the police killed several workers and injured hundreds more. Eventually, eight union leaders were put on trial, and four were hanged for inciting the deadly disturbance, although an investigation later indicated that the bomb may have been planted by an agent of the police as a pretext for a crackdown on organized labor.

McCulloch's diary entry from May 7, 1886, reveals how deeply disturbed he was by the incident. Although he opposed violent revolution, McCulloch sympathized with the workers: "The one thought in my mind is the Labor trouble [in Chicago]. I wish that I could speak on that and nothing else. . . . When there is revolution there is reason for it in the oppression of the people. . . . They are brought in here by railroads who wish cheap labor, by coal syndicates, by rolling mills, etc. They are the *Frankensteins* of modern society. . . . But the Christ is behind them."[80]

Half a year later, McCulloch decided to make his views public in a sermon at the Plymouth Church. Warning his congregation beforehand that they would probably disapprove of his position, McCulloch went on to criticize the trial of the Chicago anarchists as unfair. The reaction was swift. Labor sympathizers sent him letters of thanks, but opponents boycotted his church and rescinded at least one invitation to lecture. Refusing to be cowed, on November 30, 1886, McCulloch sent a letter to the editor of the *Indianapolis Journal* in which he defended his position: "They [the anarchists] see hundreds of men out of work. . . . They see machinery displace men who then go about vainly for work. . . . There are thousands today who feel that they were not legally tried; that they were too severely sentenced. It is not by repression, by 'blood and iron,' that such things are stamped out, but by remedying the causes."[81]

Those in power were not amused, as the pro-establishment editor of the *Indianapolis Journal* made clear in his response: "Of course Mr. McCulloch has a perfect right to think the bloody wretches in Chicago should have a new trial, or that their sentences should be mitigated; and he probably has the right to stand in his pulpit and say so, even at a time when their cases are still in process of judicial consideration; but we think that neither Mr. McCulloch nor any other man has the right to use a pulpit of a leading and intelligent church in which to utter unmitigated 'hogwash.'"[82]

The controversy over the labor troubles in Chicago appears to have taken a toll on McCulloch's already precarious health, and in April 1887 he fell into a coma for several days following an operation. After recovering, McCulloch took a leave of absence from his duties at the Plymouth Church and spent the next six months in Europe, much of it in London.[83] Given his interests, McCulloch could not have arrived at a more opportune time, for the city was in the midst of a social crisis brought about by rapid industrialization, immigration, and urbanization.[84]

A few years earlier, Andrew Mearns—like McCulloch, a Congregationalist minister and social reformer—had issued a clarion call with the publication of *The Bitter Cry of Outcast London* (1883). In its pages, Mearns took his readers on a virtual tour of London's worst slums. His vivid descriptions of urban families mired in poverty recall McCulloch's own diary account of his first encounter with the Ishmaels. For example, Mearns wrote that "every room in these rotten and reeking tenements houses a family, often two. . . . Here are seven people living in one underground kitchen, and a little child lying dead in the same room."[85] Mearns's incendiary pamphlet kindled a firestorm of public debate in England that eventually led to the implementation of important legal reforms such as the Housing of the Working Classes Act of 1890. It also inspired other investigations of London's poor districts, including Charles Booth's studies of the notorious East End, which he first presented before the Royal Statistical Society in May 1887, around the time that McCulloch was visiting London.

Booth argued that London's one million poor residents should be divided into four classes, identified by the letters, A, B, C, and D. Booth condemned those in class A as leading a "savage life, with vicissitudes of extreme hardship and occasional excess," and those in class B as being "shiftless, hand-to-mouth, pleasure loving, and always poor," respectively, and called them a threat to the well-being of the city. By contrast, he sympathetically described the other two classes, those who made up the deserving poor, as "victims of competition" (C) and as living "hard lives very patiently" (D).[86]

When McCulloch reviewed Jacob Riis's *How the Other Half Lives* (1890), a trailblazing book that exposed the problem of urban poverty in America, he praised Booth's work on London's poor as similarly important. In his review, McCulloch also provided a list of related books, including Helen Campbell's *Prisoners of Poverty,* General William Booth's *In Darkest England,* and Henry Morton Stanley's *In Darkest Africa,* that might interest his readers.[87] At first glance, Stanley's account of his adventures in Africa seems out of place in what is otherwise a collection of pioneering works in urban ethnography. Stylistically and ideologically, however, the colorful accounts of intrepid Victorian explorers like Stanley provided a model for the guided tours of dark slums and their supposedly savage residents published by social reformers during this era.

It should come as no surprise, therefore, that William Booth, the founder of the Salvation Army, would name his own urban exposé after Stanley's enormously popular travelogue. After all, Booth asked, "As there is a darkest Africa is there not a darkest England? Civilization, which can breed its own barbarians, does it not also breed its own pygmies? May we not find a parallel at our own doors, and discover within a stone's throw of our cathedrals and palaces similar horrors to those which Stanley has found existing in the great Equatorial forest?"[88] By warning that civilization breeds its own "pygmies," Booth was implicitly invoking the frightening specter of degeneration, which emerged during the last half of the nineteenth century as a powerful counterweight to the era's essentially optimistic theories of progress and evolution.[89]

Echoing the words of Booth and Stanley, McCulloch concluded his newspaper review of *How the Other Half Lives* with a question of his own: "Shall there be a 'Darkest Indianapolis'?" McCulloch and his counterparts saw many parallels between supposedly primitive people in colonized places like Africa and their own impoverished neighbors in the slums of London, New York, and Indianapolis.[90] Influential thinkers like Ray Lankaster, a scientist whose work would later influence McCulloch's published account of the Tribe of Ishmael, Max Nordau, one of the founders of political Zionism, and Cesare Lombroso, the Italian criminal anthropologist, rejected the idea that human society "moves incessantly from less good to better, from ignorance to science, from barbarism to civilisation," as the Larouse dictionary entry on *progress* phrased it in 1875.[91]

Instead, they asserted that certain individuals or, in some cases, entire groups or communities, could survive as atavistic throwbacks to earlier stages of human development, what Lombroso, in his inimitable and offensive style, referred to as "lubricious and ferocious orangutans with human faces."[92] Even more frighteningly, they argued, civilized society itself could actually encourage the degeneration of some of its members by not properly addressing the environmental and biological factors that could lead to their social and physical devolution.

Like his European colleagues, McCulloch believed that the newly industrialized cities of Europe and America were fertile breeding grounds for tribes of degenerates. As early as 1880, he had publicly declared: "Pauperism is steadily on the increase in almost every city in the land. . . . Into our cities pour, in addition to the discharged convicts, the families of convicts left without support; the tramp; the alms-house children, all these sink to the bottom forming a morass. The law of degeneration is as active as that of gravitation."[93] Ten years later, in 1889, McCulloch exhorted an audience of organized charity professionals in San Francisco to see themselves as the latest links in a long chain of urban reformers stretching back to the first Christians: "All great movements have been developed in cities. Christianity took possession of the great centres of civilization—Rome, Antioch, Ephesus."[94]

The nineteenth-century fantasy of urban jungles rivaling the equatorial forests of darkest Africa would (mis)inform social reformers, politicians, and artists on both sides of the Atlantic for generations. We need only look at 1970s films like *Fort Apache: The Bronx* and *The Warriors* to see how deeply and tenaciously the idea of the city as a tribal space inhabited by urban primitives like the Ishmaelites would take hold of the popular imagination in the following century.[95] Within this genealogy, Oscar McCulloch's published account of the Tribe of Ishmael, which he produced soon after returning from Europe in 1888, represents an early and important stage of development.

CHAPTER 2

In Darkest Indianapolis

In July 1888, Oscar McCulloch traveled to Buffalo, New York, to attend the National Conference of Charities and Correction (which later became the National Conference of Social Work), an organization whose presidency he would assume in 1891. At the gathering, McCulloch finally went public with the results of his ten years of research into Indianapolis's pauper community. To illustrate his speech, McCulloch brought along a twelve-foot-long diagram containing the names of 1,720 supposedly interrelated individuals compiled by Kate Parker, who was the registrar of the Charity Organization Society, and James Frank Wright, who had been enlisted by the county commissioners to help McCulloch in his investigation. The speech, entitled "The Tribe of Ishmael: A Study in Social Degradation," was published a year later, and the diagram, now reduced to a nearly illegible 29 × 66 inches, was made available to the public by the Charity Organization Society for the reasonable price of fifty cents.[1] Anyone could now purchase a genealogical chart of the Tribe of Ishmael that one observer later likened to "a cross between a seismographic reading of the San Francisco earthquake and an electrocardiogram of a man who has just sat through a triple feature of X rated movies."[2]

McCulloch began his report on the Tribe of Ishmael by invoking the earlier work of Ray Lankester on the physical degeneration of certain species. He argued that Lankester's conclusions about crustaceans and other animals were as relevant for the "student of social science" as they were for the "student of physical science." In fact, Lankester himself had earlier established this link, when he noted in one of his works that "with regard to ourselves, the white races of Europe, the possibility of degeneration seems to be worth consideration."[3] Although he did not quote Lankester's statement for support, McCulloch made it clear in the remainder of his study on the Tribe of Ishmael that such a process of degeneration had already occurred among the paupers of Indianapolis.

In order to illustrate the immanent danger posed by the Ishmaelites, McCulloch borrowed an example from Lankester's research into the animal world: the *Sacculina*. This tiny crustacean, McCulloch wrote, "has left the free, independent life common to its family, and is living as a parasite, or pauper," attached to the body of its host, the hermit crab. At birth, the *Sacculina* resembled its independent cousin and was "a free swimmer." As it aged, however, the *Sacculina* attached itself to the crab and henceforth "became degraded in form and function."[4]

McCulloch attributed the source of this degeneration to heredity and suggested that the same process occurred in human beings:

> An irresistible hereditary tendency seizes upon it, and it succumbs. A hereditary tendency I say, because some remote ancestor left its independent, self-helpful life, and began a parasitic, or pauper life. Not using its organs for self-help, they one by one have disappeared . . . until there is left a shapeless mass, with only the stomach and organs of reproduction left. This tendency to parasitism was transmitted to its descendants, until there is set up an irresistible hereditary tendency; and the Sacculina stands in nature as a type of degradation through parasitism, or pauperism. I propose to trace the history of similar degradation in man.[5]

McCulloch's remarks about the devolution of the *Sacculina* into parasitism reflected the influence of Lamarckism, a since discredited theory that physical changes experienced by an individual during its lifetime could be passed down to its descendants—a view also known as the inheritance of acquired characteristics. In the case of the *Sacculina,* a lazy crustacean ancestor whose limbs had atrophied from lack of use had supposedly passed down this physical disability to future generations of crustacean paupers.

As his diary reveals, McCulloch was well versed in the writings of Charles Darwin, Herbert Spencer, and a host of lesser lights in the burgeoning field of evolution, including Oskar Peschel and John Fiske. Although McCulloch believed that evolution operated in human societies, a doctrine that became known as Social Darwinism, he disagreed with Herbert Spencer's view, in *The Principles of Sociology* (1883), that an unregulated society would inevitably result in the survival of only its fittest members. Instead, on the basis of his research on the Tribe of Ishmael, McCulloch argued that natural selection alone could not guarantee the elimination of a society's weakest and, from a genetic point of view, most dangerous members. Reforms and other interventions were necessary in order to prevent degenerate individuals and communities, such as the Ishmaelites, from reproducing.

The parable of the parasitic crustaceans would be almost comical if its social implications were not so disturbing. For McCulloch firmly believed that he had discovered a "history of similar degradation" in the Tribe of Ishmael. After acknowledging the influence of Dugdale's study of the Jukes, McCulloch explained that "the name, 'the tribe of Ishmael,' is given because that is the name of the central, the oldest, and the most widely ramified family" of 250—supposedly—interconnected families that together comprised the degenerate community of Indianapolis. Dipping into his diary, McCulloch then recounted the events of January 18, 1878, when he first encountered a branch of the Ishmael family in their rundown lodgings. For some reason, however, McCulloch stated that he had come across the Ishmaels in the late fall of 1877, rather than the winter of 1878. This would be the first of several glaring contradictions between McCulloch's published work and his unpublished writings on the tribe.

McCulloch's reasons for calling the group the Tribe of Ishmael were more complicated than he admitted in print. First and foremost, McCulloch must have appreciated the symbolic value of the name Ishmael. After all, he could have called the community the "Tribe of Owens" or the "Tribe of Smith," two of the other pauper families he mentioned in his study. But neither *Owens* nor *Smith* possessed the multiple associations of the name Ishmael, particularly when combined with the word *tribe*. The Tribe of Ishmael—unlike, say, the Tribe of Smith—could effectively conjure up images of modern-day savages inhabiting the urban jungle that McCulloch believed he had discovered in his own backyard. To a former traveling salesman like McCulloch, the name must have sounded like a winner.

The name "Tribe of Ishmael" also resonated for another reason. During the second half of the nineteenth century, middle-class America experienced a love affair with the signs and symbols of the Middle East, a phenomenon that was the flip side of the explicitly negative Orientalist stereotypes that were popular in the same period. Small towns in

Indiana and Illinois were named after Muslim cities like Cairo, Mecca, and Medina; traditional Islamic architecture influenced the design of grandiose buildings like South Dakota's famous Corn Palace (built in 1892); and members of secret societies like the Ancient Arabic Order of the Nobles of the Mystic Shrine (the Shriners, or Nobles, as they also called themselves) wore fezzes, employed Arabic terminology, and built lodges that looked like mosques in places like Springfield, Missouri, and Des Moines, Iowa.

The case of the Shriners is particularly illuminating. The first Temple of the Nobles of the Mystic Shrine, known as the Mecca Temple, was established by the "Illustrious Noble" (aka "The Shayk" or "The Ancient") Walter Fleming in New York City on September 26, 1872. Fleming and other early members of the group claimed close connections to Islam. So close, in fact, that a document issued by the organization's Imperial Council (est. 1876) actually traced the group's origins to Mecca, Arabia. Even a brief excerpt from this remarkable work reveals the degree to which Muslim history, liturgy, and theology influenced the early Shriners:

> In the Name of God, the Merciful, the Compassionate!
> The Order of the Nobles of the Mystic Shrine was instituted by the Mohammedan Kalif Alee (whose name be praised!), the cousin-german and son-in-law of the Prophet Mohammed, in the year of the Hegira 25 (A.D. 656), at Mekkah, in Arabia. . . . The only connection the Order ever had with any sect of Dervishes was with that called the Bektash (White Hats) [a Sufi group]. This warlike sect undertook to favor and protect the "Nobles" in a time of great peril, and have ever since been counted among its most honored patrons. . . . The salutation of distinction among the Faithful is "Es Selamu Aleikum!"—"Peace be with you!" to which is returned the gracious wish, "Aleikum es Selaam!"—"With you be Peace!"[6]

In many ways, this text resembles the histories produced by Muslim Sufi orders, which also typically trace their lineage back to the Imam Ali (or Alee). Yet the men who became Nobles of the Mystic Shrine were not Persian or Arab Muslims but a group of middle-class American men with names like William Florence, Walter Fleming, Charles McClenachan, and John Moore (all founders of the Mecca Temple in New York). It still remains a mystery how such men acquired their knowledge of Islam, in general, and of Sufi traditions, in particular. According to Walter Fleming, the order was established in the United States by William Florence who was "initiated . . . by original Oriental source and authority." In a letter written in 1882, Florence mentioned that in 1870, while visiting Marseilles, he had come into contact with a man named Yusef Churi Bey, who was apparently a Sufi teacher. After this encounter, Florence made his way to Algiers where, his letter implies, he met weekly with members of a Sufi order.[7]

The Shriners found fertile soil throughout Middle America for their Sufi-inspired organization. Within decades, numerous temples with names like Ismailia, Mohammed, Medinah, and Al Koran were established in towns and cities such as Cincinnati, Cedar Rapids, Mobile, Atlanta, and Fargo. The Murat Temple of the Ancient Order of Nobles of the Mystic Shrine was established in Indianapolis in 1884, making it one of the first temples in the United States.[8] Ten years later, another fraternal organization incorporated itself in Indiana as the Tribe of Ben Hur, in honor of the famous novel by the Hoosier author Lew Wallace. In 1886, Oscar McCulloch invited Wallace, who had served as the United States representative to Turkey from 1881 to 1885, to deliver a lecture entitled "Turkey and the Turks," indicating McCulloch's continuing interest in the "Eastern Question" in the period when he began publicizing the Tribe of Ishmael. Other societies in Indianapolis that adopted Oriental-sounding names included the Sahara Grotto and the Order of the Eastern Star.

These borrowings represent a kind of homage—however fetishistic—to Islam and Middle Eastern culture. They are intriguing artifacts from a time when thousands of middle-class Americans adopted the symbols, language, and even the rituals of Islam in order to reimagine—if only temporarily and in a limited context—their own senses of self. While escapist, the attraction to this imaginary Islam stemmed from a deep yearning in big cities like New York, as well as in smaller towns like Sioux Falls, South Dakota, and Lincoln, Nebraska (which both established temples in the 1880s), for a more cosmopolitan identity. The construction of an imaginary Islam in the heart of the American Midwest reached its pinnacle in the Chicago World's Fair of 1893, where, for the price of a ticket, a farm boy visiting the big city could stroll through the Streets of Cairo exhibit on the Midway and marvel at belly dancers, camel drivers, and other seemingly fantastic denizens of the Near East.

At the same time, the 30 million visitors to the World's Fair could also come into contact with flesh-and-blood Muslims seeking to instruct American audiences in the beliefs and practices of Islam for the first time. At the Parliament of World Religions, for example, a Muslim named Jamal Effendi led prayers in Arabic and was joined by several thousand Shriners in a display that blurred the boundaries between real and imaginary Islam.[9] A visitor to the fair might also encounter

Mohammed Alexander Russell Webb, widely considered to be the first European American convert to Islam. With the help of wealthy Indian and Arab supporters, Webb founded the American Moslem Brotherhood and the Moslem World Publishing Company in New York. At the Parliament of World Religions, the turban-wearing, heavily bearded Webb served as the chief spokesman for Islam.[10]

In the same period that these Islamically inspired fraternal organizations, architecture, and world's fair exhibitions appeared in America's heartland, Islam emerged as a significant theme in the nation's literature. Washington Irving, Nathaniel Hawthorne, Ralph Waldo Emerson, Henry David Thoreau, Herman Melville, and a host of lesser literary lights all explored Islam in their writings. While these authors typically sympathized with Islam—or, at least, with what they imagined it to be—their romantic portrayals also betrayed many of the same stereotypes found in more explicitly negative Orientalist works.

Among the most enduring tropes adopted by these authors was that desert-dwelling Arabs—also called Bedouins or Ishmaelites—were predatory, thievish, and, in a more positive light, freedom loving. Better known today for his *Knickerbocker Tales,* Washington Irving also wrote a massive biography of Muhammad in which he described the typical denizen of Arabia as "apt to lay contributions on the caravan or plunder it outright in its toilful progress through the desert. All this he regarded as a legitimate exercise of arms; looking down upon the gainful sons of traffic as an inferior race. . . . Such was the Arab of the desert, the dweller in tents, in whom was fulfilled the prophetic destiny of his ancestor Ishmael. 'He will be a wild man; his hand will be against every man, and every man's hand against him.'"[11] In his journal, Ralph Waldo Emerson presented a similar portrait of "the Bedoween, who from the first year of recorded time up to this moment has preserved his savage Ishmaelitish independence, who is lavishly hospitable and a ferocious robber."[12] Most famously, of course, Herman Melville exploited the image of Ishmael as an archetypal wanderer in his novel *Moby Dick*. A devoted Orientalist, Melville traveled to the Near East and incorporated Islamic references throughout his work, including his long poem *Clarel,* in which an Arab bandit named Ishmael leads a group of marauding nomads. Against this complex backdrop, Oscar McCulloch's savvy choice of the name "Tribe of Ishmael" appealed to the contemporary craze for things Oriental while still exploiting overtly negative stereotypes of Islam.

At the same time that romantic Orientalists like the Shriners and Herman Melville—who once came to a masquerade party dressed as a

Turk—were performing their own versions of an Islamic identity, actual Arabs and Turks (the two were often equated) continued to be vilified in a variety of ways within the popular American imagination.[13] By the second half of the nineteenth century, the stereotypical image of the Arab as a thievish nomad had been transformed into a model for a range of urban characters—all of them negative. For example, in *How the Other Half Lives* Jacob Riis famously referred to the "outcast waifs" of New York as "Street Arabs." According to Riis, "the Street Arab has all the faults and all the virtues of the lawless life he leads. Vagabond that he is, acknowledging no authority and owing no allegiance to anybody or anything . . . he is as bright and sharp as the weasel, which, among all the predatory beasts, he most resembles."[14]

Riis did not invent the name "Street Arab," nor was its use limited to the mean streets of New York or even the United States. Rather, the phrase had entered the American lexicon from England, where it functioned as Victorian slang for an urban homeless child who wandered the city getting into trouble. As early as 1848, Lord Shaftesbury, a member of the English parliament, had lamented that "City arabs . . . are like tribes of lawless freebooters . . . and utterly ignorant or utterly regardless of social duties."[15] In 1851, the satirical journal *Punch* published an article entitled "The Monkey Tribe of the Metropolis" that referred to the street Arabs of London as "Bedouins" who behaved like the "Arabs at BATTY's Hippodrome" (a theater)[16] By 1868, *Harper's Weekly* in New York had followed suit and was titillating its readers with descriptions of

> street folk [who] . . . all belong to the nomadic race. Every where they are found they can be recognized as true Arabs. . . . Those who have once adopted the semi-savage and wandering mode of life in early youth seldom abandon it, but continue to the end of their existence Arabs by second nature. Among the "Street Arabs" of New York . . . are to be included pickpockets, beggars, and prostitutes that *prey* upon the populace, as well as the itinerant sellers, buyers, etc., who profess to make some return for what they receive.[17]

During the same period, in Baltimore the phrase "Street Arab" inspired the slang terms *Arabber* (pronounced "A-rabber") and *Arab* (pronounced "A-rab"), to describe individuals who sold fruits and vegetables from horse-drawn carts and, in the early years of the tradition at least, also carted away unwanted objects for recycling. The names initially referred to poor whites, who dominated the Arabber trade in the late nineteenth century. By the 1940s, however, almost all of the Arabbers were African Americans. Like the Ishmaelites of Indianapolis, whom they resembled in important respects, Arabbers in Baltimore were frequently marked by what the folklorist Charles Camp has called "the stigma of huckstering and borderline vagrancy." Even today, when only a few still carry on the tradition, Camp has noted that "Arabbers continue to contend with persistent stereotypes that cast them as people who live at the margins of working America—people who favor a way of life in which they may choose to work or not to work, as they prefer."[18]

Like the Orientalist monikers "Street Arabs" and "Arabbers," the names "Ishmaelites" and "Tribe of Ishmael," symbolically racialized poor urban whites who eked out a marginal existence outside the newly emerging wage-labor economy by casting their difference from middle-class white society in exotic, ethnic terms. In all of these cases, the people being depicted possessed stereotypically white physical features—as Riis made clear in the posed photographs of Street Arabs accompanying his text and McCulloch did by describing the Ishmaelite children as "tow-headed" (i.e., white blond)—but their aberrant behavior placed them beyond the pale. These examples confirm Edward Said's observation that during the nineteenth century "the Oriental was linked thus to elements in Western society (delinquents, the insane, women, the poor) having in common an identity best described as lamentably alien."[19]

Despite their shared Orientalist vocabulary, Oscar McCulloch was far more critical of his impoverished subjects than was Jacob Riis. Indeed, McCulloch actually believed that members of the Tribe of Ishmael had devolved to a more primitive state. On March 16, 1877, after reading Godwin Smith's *Ascent of Man,* McCulloch had written in his diary, "Vice is not a diabolical inspiration but the remnant of a previous animal connection slowly being sloughed off." According to this logic, the vice-ridden Ishmaelites represented the atavistic survival of a "previous animal connection" right in the heart of Indianapolis. Later, in his published account, McCulloch explicitly attributed the licentiousness, prostitution, and incest that supposedly characterized the Tribe of Ishmael as "an animal reversion, which can be paralleled in lower animals."[20]

McCulloch's study of the Tribe of Ishmael may be read as a parable about the social threat posed by poor whites who have essentially become like blacks, Gypsies, Muslims, Native Americans, and other subaltern groups. As the sensationalistic *Harper's Weekly* article on Street Arabs emphasized, by becoming homeless, engaging in petty crime, or even—like Baltimore's Arabbers—by working as itinerant sellers, poor, urban whites could essentially devolve to the state of "true Arabs" or "Arabs by second nature."

Remarkably, McCulloch devoted less than two full paragraphs of his published study to describing the Ishmaels themselves, despite his claim that they were the "most widely ramified family" in the tribe. He stated that in 1840 the Ishmaels arrived in Indianapolis from Kentucky, where they had wound up after first settling in Maryland and Pennsylvania. The founder of the family was one Ben Ishmael, who fathered eight children, according to McCulloch. Some of Ben's descendants remained in Kentucky, where they became "prosperous, well-regarded citizens." Another son, named John, married a "half-breed" woman and left the Blue Grass State for Marion County, Indiana, where he ended his travels around 1840 because he was "diseased."

John Ishmael and his wife had seven children, according to McCulloch. Two remained in Kentucky, one disappeared, one never married, and the remaining three sons married three sisters from a "pauper family" named Smith. These unions produced the supposedly cacogenic branch of the Ishmael family in Indianapolis. McCulloch claimed that this branch had a "pauper record" dating back to 1840 and had since then "received continuous aid from the township." He asserted that members of the family had spent time in the almshouse, the Women's Reformatory, penitentiaries, and other institutions and that the Ishmaels had intermarried with over two hundred other families in the city to form a "pauper ganglion."

Although he neglected to flag the shift, at this point in his study, McCulloch began to use the word "family" to refer to the entire tribe of paupers, rather than to the Ishmael family alone. This would emerge as a common strategy in future eugenics studies. By shifting back and forth seamlessly between individual families and a larger group while making broad assertions concerning character or behavior, the authors of these studies sought to make the point that all degenerate families— and individuals—were essentially alike and that the part could substitute for the whole. As McCulloch confidently put it, after claiming that he had traced the history of over five thousand members of the tribe: "Pick up one, and the whole five thousand would be drawn up."[21] The underlying ideological assumption was that so-called degenerates, unlike respectable people, lacked individuality. And in a highly individualistic society like America, that meant they lacked humanity.

Having made this important, if unspoken, transition, McCulloch then went on to describe the "family history" of the entire tribe. "In this family history," he wrote, "are murders, a large number of illegitimacies and of prostitutes. They are generally diseased. The children die young. They live by petty stealing, begging, ash-gathering. In summer they 'gypsy,' or travel in wagons east or west. We hear of them in Illinois about Decatur, and in Ohio about Columbus. In the fall they return. They have been known to live in hollow trees on the river-bottoms or in empty houses. Strangely enough, they are not intemperate to excess." Later in the account, while discussing the Owens family, McCulloch once again stressed that "There is much prostitution, but little intemperance."[22]

McCulloch made no moral distinction between any of the phenomena he attributed to the Ishmaelites. On the contrary, he argued that all were part of a matrix of degeneracy, or as he put it: "physical depravity is followed by physical weakness. Out of this come the frequent deaths, the still-born children, and the general incapacity to endure hard work or bad climate. They cannot work hard, and break down early. They then appear in the county asylum, the city hospital, and the township trustee's office."[23] According to McCulloch's jaundiced view, the disease and infant mortality that afflicted the tribe did not result from the miserable conditions and lack of health care that affected all poor people but, instead, from the licentiousness of its members. Likewise, the inability of some Ishmaelites to "work hard" or withstand cold weather signified their moral decay, rather than the debilitating effects of long-term poverty. In other words, members of the Tribe of Ishmael did not suffer from disease, unemployment, or, even the cold—unlike the deserving poor—but were actually guilty of these things, just as they were guilty of murder and theft.

As evidence of the tribe's supposed criminality, McCulloch claimed that its "criminal record is very large" and that "nearly every crime of any note belongs here." When it came down to specifics, however, McCulloch was remarkably vague, noting that there "have been a number of murders" without providing any statistics and asserting that the "first murder committed in the city was in this family" without offering further details. Since, according to McCulloch, the Ishmaels were the oldest family in the tribe and had arrived in Indianapolis in 1840, for his second claim to be correct, no homicide could have occurred between 1821, when the city was founded, and 1840. Yet as accounts of this period reveal, this simply wasn't true.[24] Even McCulloch was forced to admit that the majority of the Ishmaelites' crimes consisted of prostitution and "petty thieving, larcenies, chiefly," rather than violent offenses such as murder. And, according to McCulloch's own sources of information, most of these petty thefts were motivated by hunger.

The only bright spot in McCulloch's otherwise gloomy portrait of the tribe was his assertion that the Ishmaelites did not suffer from alcohol abuse. Like many reformers of his day, McCulloch saw alcohol as the source of a wide range of social ills. In 1857, a pioneering criminal anthropologist from France named B. A. Morel had argued that alcoholism led to hereditary degeneration and was organically linked to other problems such as insanity, criminality, and epilepsy. By the middle of the 1880s, the role of alcoholism in hereditarian ideology was so well established that the Women's Christian Temperance Union even published a *Journal of Heredity,* in which they reprinted Francis Galton's writings on eugenics. Other early eugenicists such as Caleb Williams Saleeby and Montague Crackanthorpe passionately condemned alcohol as a "race poison" that damaged germ tissue and produced generations of genetically inferior individuals.[25]

McCulloch took the issue of alcohol abuse so seriously that he even convinced an ice cream parlor in Indianapolis to sell glasses of buttermilk as an alternative to the harder fare offered in the city's many taverns. Ironically, however, the one positive thing that McCulloch had to say about the Tribe of Ishmael was repeatedly contradicted by his own sources—James Frank Wright's notes and the Charity Organization Society case records. Rightly or wrongly, these unpublished documents depicted many of the tribe's members as heavy drinkers, a far cry from McCulloch's assertion that "they are not intemperate to excess." Indeed, the same Owens family that suffered from "little intemperance," according to McCulloch, was described by Wright as being notorious for its love of liquor. Given his overwhelmingly negative attitude towards the Ishmaelites, McCulloch's decision to ignore the ample evidence for their intemperance is inexplicable.

In his prolabor writings and sermons, McCulloch argued that environmental factors such as worker exploitation had helped to create the problems of the deserving poor in Indianapolis. By contrast, he implied that such factors had little or no impact on hereditary paupers like the Tribe of Ishmael—with one notable exception. This was the "almost unlimited public and private aid" given to the Ishmaelites by "the benevolent public . . . thus encouraging them in this idle, wandering life, and in the propagation of similarly disposed children." According to McCulloch, "fully three-fourths" of the relief distributed by the township trustee had gone to the Tribe of Ishmael over the years. He acknowledged that this aid had plummeted from its high point in 1876, but still accused the township trustee of political corruption, essentially claiming that holders of the office bribed voters with aid in order to assure their own reelection. This harsh view represented a dramatic reversal of the more sympathetic statements McCulloch made concerning the township trustee during the early 1880s.

Nor was McCulloch any more favorably disposed to the "private benevolence" of the city's well-meaning citizens, whom he righteously— some might say, self-righteously—condemned in religious terms:

> The so-called charitable people who give to begging children and women with baskets have a vast sin to answer for. It is from them that this pauper element gets its consent to exist. Charity—falsely so called—covers a multitude of sins, and sends the pauper out with the benediction, 'Be fruitful and multiply.' Such charity has made this element, has brought children to the birth, and insured them a life of misery, cold, hunger, sickness. So-called charity joins public relief in producing still-born children, raising prostitutes, and educating criminals. . . . Some persons think it hard that we say to the public, Give no relief to men or boys asking for food, to women begging, to children with baskets, ill-clad, wasted, and wan. "I can't resist the appeal of a child," they say. Do you know what this means? It means the perpetuation of this misery. . . . Two little boys sell flowers at the doors of church and theatre. They ring bells at night, asking to get warm. . . . Your kindness keeps them out in the cold.[26]

In McCulloch's eyes, the Bible's first commandment in Genesis 1:28 only applied to people who could afford to "be fruitful and multiply" and not to the poor parents who sent their children out to beg or sell flowers on the street. Whereas many residents of Indianapolis viewed their handouts to these children as traditional Christian charity, McCulloch saw their actions as fueling the fire of pauperism. The pitiful cases with which McCulloch illustrated the "vast sin" of private charity indicate that he saw begging in public as one of the chief criteria distinguishing the deserving poor from paupers like the Tribe of Ishmael. The poor were supposed to keep their poverty to themselves, only sharing their stories with experts at the Charity Organization Society who could scientifically determine how much and what kind of aid they needed. People like the Ishmaelites, who sought charity on the streets, by contrast, were paupers who threatened the civic order that McCulloch and his supporters were working to establish in Indianapolis.

Was being a pauper enough then to make someone a member of the Tribe of Ishmael? There is no simple answer to this question. At times,

McCulloch implied that every pauper—not to mention every petty thief and prostitute—in the city of Indianapolis belonged to the Tribe of Ishmael. For example, he claimed that "over seven thousand pages of history are now on file in the Charity Organization Society," documenting more than five thousand members of the Tribe of Ishmael—out of a total city population of 105,000 in 1890. These figures suggest that McCulloch had basically equated the entire pauper and criminal population of Indianapolis with the Tribe of Ishmael. At other times, however, McCulloch was quite specific about whom he considered to be an Ishmaelite. He identified the core of the tribe as consisting of thirty families who originally hailed from the Upland South of Kentucky, Tennessee, and North Carolina. Without providing any evidence, he further speculated that their "parasitism, or social degradation" could be attributed to ancestors "from the old convict stock which England threw into this country in the seventeenth century."

These statements indicate that McCulloch viewed the Tribe of Ishmael as a distinct community of Upland Southern background. With the exception of two "half-breed" (i.e., part Native American) women— John Ishmael's aforementioned wife and an "illegitimate, half-breed Canadian" who married into the Owens family—McCulloch depicted the tribe as ethnically Anglo-Saxon. This, as we shall see, contrasts sharply with Hugo Leaming's later portrait of a triracial community dominated by escaped African American slaves and their poor white and Native American allies. Unlike Leaming, McCulloch did not discuss the tribe's religious practices, perhaps because they did not strike him as out of the ordinary for poor whites of Upland Southern origin. Significantly, the only observation he did make regarding religion was that one member of the Owens family was a Presbyterian minister. This directly contradicts Leaming's later assertion that "not a single Ishmaelite was ever known to belong to any of the churches of the majority society."

If we accept McCulloch's characterization of their background as accurate, the Ishmaelites were part of a much broader Indianapolis community hailing from states like Kentucky and Tennessee. Many of these residents and, in particular, those who occupied the bottom rungs of the economic ladder, continued to preserve cultural traditions from the Upland South long after moving north to Indiana. Throughout the nineteenth century, this led to tension with other residents of Indianapolis over a wide range of social issues including child rearing, compulsory education, law enforcement, and the use of public space. Despite the importance of this dynamic in shaping the city's character, McCulloch was blind to the possibility that much of the Tribe of Ishmael's distinguishing behavior could be linked to the distinctive cultural background of its members.

For example, one of the things that most bothered McCulloch about the Ishmaelites was their extensive "wandering" or, as he also put it, their "annual gypsying." McCulloch offered two explanations for this behavior, both hereditary. On the one hand, he suggested that the tribe's "wandering blood" along with the "poison and passion" that characterized the group, had come via a "half-breed mother." On the other hand, he attributed it to the tribe's hypothetical English convict ancestry. As he explained, employing two derogatory slang terms for poor whites, "We find the wandering tendency so marked in the case of the 'Cracker' and the 'Pike.'"[27]

Although it seems ridiculous today, early-twentieth-century eugenicists such as Arthur Estabrook and Charles Davenport would follow McCulloch's lead in describing wandering or, as they typically called it, nomadism, as an inherited trait. Davenport, perhaps the most powerful man in the American eugenics movement during its heyday, even devoted an entire study to the subject of nomadism, which he clinically defined as a "sex-linked, recessive, mono-hybrid trait." In a 1915 work, *The Feebly Inhibited: Nomadism, or the Wandering Impulse with Special Reference to Heredity,* published by the Carnegie Institution, Davenport argued, "I am inclined to use the word 'nomadism' just because it has a racial connotation." He claimed that children and "primitive" tribes were both prone to wandering, while so-called civilized peoples and most adults either no longer possessed the impulse or were "capable of inhibiting it." Nevertheless, some "feebly inhibited" individuals, families, and even entire cultures still retained the "nomadic trait." According to Davenport, the atavistic survival of this primitive behavior was typically linked to other socially undesirable activities, such as a "thieving propensity, or at least a lack of appreciation of property rights."[28]

For Oscar McCulloch and his successors in the eugenics movement, therefore, nomadism was hardly a neutral activity. On the contrary, it was a clear-cut sign of degeneracy. Yet McCulloch's own descriptions of the tribe's journeys suggest that they were not the aimless or instinctual wanderings he claimed them to be. He stated that the tribe had a regular route, ranging from Columbus, Ohio, in the east to Decatur, Illinois, in the west. Because he believed that the Ishmaelites possessed a hereditary impulse to wander, McCulloch offered no explanation for why they would follow a fixed itinerary on their annual trips. However, there is good reason to believe that individuals identified as belonging to the tribe regularly journeyed to places like Columbus and Decatur in order to visit relatives who lived there. Far from reflecting the influence of heredity, therefore, the travels of the "Tribe of Ishmael" appear to have developed out of the close kinship ties that constituted—and still constitute—an important part of trans-Appalachian and Upland Southern culture.

While ignoring this cultural explanation, McCulloch unwittingly alluded to an economic motivation for the tribe's travels when he described them making the rounds searching for work: "There is scarcely a day that the wagons are not to be seen on our streets; cur dogs; tow-headed children. They camp outside the city, and then beg. Two families, as I write, have come by, moving from north to south, and from east to west. 'Hunting work'; and yet we can give work to a thousand men on our gas-trenches."[29] Elsewhere, McCulloch indicated what kind of work they were looking for: "The people have no occupation. They gather swill or ashes; the women beg, and send the children around to beg; they make their eyes sore with [blue] vitriol [to feign blindness]."

Because he possessed a narrow though widely shared definition of legitimate work, McCulloch refused to believe that the Ishmaelites engaged in real labor. However, his own comments reveal that they eschewed wage labor in favor of other economic activities that enabled them to retain their independence. Thus, the Ishmaelite men used their carts to collect ashes, swill, and other trash that the city was unable or unwilling to recycle, while the women and children contributed to the family income by begging.

Like their annual travels to visit kin and search for seasonal work, the apparent refusal of people identified as Ishmaelites to take jobs in the city's factories may have grown out of their Upland Southern rural background. While the majority of residents from the Upland South eventually became integrated into Indianapolis's newly industrialized economy, others who rejected the draconian conditions of nineteenth-century factory work may have attempted to carve out an alternative niche for themselves on the margins of the city's economy. In some cases, these individuals may have seen their activities as continuing in spirit, if not in content, the independent lifestyle of their pioneering ancestors on the frontier.

It is also likely that the people identified with the Tribe of Ishmael were forced to take on stigmatized activities like trash collecting and begging because they could find no other way to eke out a living. McCulloch vehemently dismissed the possibility that a lack of jobs could have forced the Ishmaelites into their marginalized economic status. As evidence he referred, as quoted above, to the numerous jobs created in the city when natural gas fields were discovered in northern Indiana in 1886. Although the discovery of natural gas did dramatically transform Indianapolis's economy, it did not eliminate the problem of unemployment in the city.[30] In any case, Oscar McCulloch had first identified the Ishmaelites as a pauper community back in 1878, that is, at the height of the worst depression in the city's history and well before the gas fields were discovered. This suggests that, despite his claims to the contrary, the actual economic situation in Indianapolis had little to do with his attitudes towards the city's "undeserving poor."

Although McCulloch insisted that it was the Tribe of Ishmael's dependence on charity that bothered him, this was belied by his own admission that the township trustee's aid to the city's poor—including the Ishmaelites—had actually decreased to a trickle, beginning in 1878. Nor did McCulloch's Charity Organization Society pick up the slack when it came to families identified as belonging to the tribe. By the 1880s, at least, the people identified as Ishmaelites appear to have supported themselves through a combination of odd jobs, trash collecting, and begging from private citizens. Ironically, therefore, what really appears to have disturbed McCulloch about the group was not their rather minimal dependence on public charity but their independent lifestyle and refusal to join the masses of urban wage laborers.

In a period when America was rapidly becoming an industrialized society, this refusal was tantamount to rejecting whiteness, for as David Roediger has written, "The phrase *working men* speaks at once . . . of a class identity and of a gender identity. But its actual usage also suggests a *racial* identity, an identification of whiteness and work so strong that it need not even be spoken."[31] To refuse to participate in wage labor during the second half of the nineteenth century, therefore, was to refuse to be white. Now that the frontier had been settled, whites were no longer supposed to travel the countryside in horse-drawn carts, live off the land, or sleep in "hollow trees on the river-bottoms." Whether they liked it or not, the grandchildren of pioneers and frontiersmen were expected to assimilate into the modern industrial economy and to conform to middle-class notions of morality. Because the Ishmaelites apparently did neither,

McCulloch attributed their aberrant behavior to the influence of a "half-breed" ancestor, thereby linking the tribe's members to Native Americans, who were popularly seen as "overly independent . . . improvident, sexually abandoned 'lazy Indians.'"[32] This, of course, is precisely how McCulloch portrayed the Tribe of Ishmael. Just as the U.S. government sought to confine the Sioux and other vanquished Native Americans in reservations at the end of the nineteenth century, so Oscar McCulloch and his allies hoped to "reform" the Tribe of Ishmael, if necessary via confinement in a range of institutions.

Not coincidentally, during the same period of intense urbanization and industrialization in which McCulloch was attempting to tame the Ishmaelites of Indianapolis, across the Atlantic similar efforts were underway to domesticate the itinerant Celtic community known as the Travellers or Tinkers. A comparison of the two campaigns reveals a common set of cultural assumptions, as well as a shared sense of how best to deal with people whose lifestyles conflicted with the socioeconomic expectations of a modern industrialized state.

Although Traveller caravans had long plied the roads of Great Britain, it was not until the second half of the nineteenth century that "efforts at settlement and the promotion of wage labour" began to target them intensively.[33] Like the Ishmaelites, the Travellers were seen as a distinct community of paupers; as one observer put it in 1835, "Ordinary beggars do not become a separate class of the community; but wandering tinkers, families who always beg, do. Three generations of them have been seen begging together."[34] Similarly, in his study of the Ishmaelites, McCulloch noted with horror that "In my own experience, I have seen three generations of beggars among them."[35] Both groups were also characterized as having the same division of labor. Thus, according to another observer in Great Britain, "The wives and families accompany the tinker while he strolls about in search of work, and always beg. They intermarry with one another, and form a distinct class."[36]

Like the Ishmaelites, many Travellers earned a living by collecting and recycling trash and also planned their travels around visits to "geographically distant kin."[37] Just as the predominantly Anglo-Saxon Ishmaelites were racialized as a distinct tribe and called American Gypsies, so the Travellers were frequently described as a "wandering tribe" and, despite their Celtic origins, were often conflated with ethnic Gypsies. Given these parallels, it is not surprising that the Travellers were also regarded as morally suspect and prone to licentiousness—wife-swapping being a particularly common accusation leveled against the group.

In response to the perceived threat posed by the Travellers, British social reformers and government officials alike sought to end the group's migratory practices and eliminate their traditional sources of income. Much of their policy was framed in terms of protecting Traveller children or, as it was more colloquially known, "child-saving." In the words of one government deputy, "the children of these people do not attend school and grow up illiterate, learning nothing but the elements of crime to which their conditions make them easy addicts."[38] McCulloch also made child-saving a central feature of his own proposal to eradicate the Tribe of Ishmael, since, as he put it, "The children reappear with the old basket. The girl begins the life of prostitution, and is soon seen with her own illegitimate child."

For a host of similar reasons, therefore, both Travellers and Ishmaelites were perceived as dangerously out of step with the modern societies being constructed around them. As the nineteenth century drew to a close, interconnected phenomena such as increasing urbanization and the centralization of state authority combined to undermine the independence and, ultimately, the very existence of these and other people who had traditionally inhabited the margins of settled society.

In addition to these structural affinities, the Travellers and Ishmaelites may have also possessed a historical connection—a possibility first suggested by Hugo Leaming.[39] Around the year 1847, small groups of Travellers began to immigrate to the United States as a result of the Irish Potato Famine. After first settling in the Northeast, these Travellers made their way to states like Kentucky and Tennessee, where, according to Jared Harper, one of the few scholars to investigate this secretive community, they "camped by the roadside in a friendly farmer's field, living in wagons and tents, and in later years in house trailers."[40]

Over the years, some Traveller families made the short journey from Upland Southern states to Indiana, where they may have become part of the so-called Tribe of Ishmael, thereby helping to explain the itinerant lifestyle of some of the families identified as Ishmaelites. Supporting this possibility is a case file from the Charity Organization Society that mentions a family named Maiden that supposedly belonged to the Tribe of Ishmael. An investigator who visited the Maiden family at home submitted a report that described them as providing lodging to several families of Travellers who lived in wagons most of the time, except when the weather was too cold."[41] Whether these were actual Travellers or whether this was just another name for Ishmaelites is impossible to determine from the case file, but it does raise the possibility of a historical connection between the two groups.

Such speculation also raises an important question about the Tribe of Ishmael, one that Oscar McCulloch completely ignored. The Travellers saw—and continue to see—themselves as a culturally distinct community, one set apart from outsiders, whom they call "country people." But was this also the case with members of the Tribe of Ishmael? If we focus on McCulloch's expansive definition of the tribe as basically comprising all of the paupers, prostitutes, and petty thieves in Indianapolis, such a self-identification makes no sense. Things become less clear, however, if we limit ourselves to the more narrow definition McCulloch sometimes offered, namely, that of a core of Upland Southern families organized around the Ishmael family, who collectively engaged in annual migrations, trash recycling, and door-to-door begging by women and children. We know that these families did not see themselves as members of a "Tribe of Ishmael," per se, since McCulloch invented this title in 1888. Nevertheless, the question remains whether the families identified as Ishmaelites by McCulloch considered themselves to be culturally distinct from the larger poor and working-class Upland Southern community of Indianapolis or whether such a separate identity only existed in McCulloch's fertile imagination.

In chapter 3 we will get a sense of how the people identified as Ishmaelites may have seen themselves. For the present, however, it is important to stress that Oscar McCulloch's portrait of the Tribe of Ishmael closely resembles the negative stereotypes that were frequently applied to *all* Upland Southern and Appalachian migrants to northern industrial cities like Indianapolis, Detroit, and Chicago. Within this broader historical context, McCulloch's study of the Tribe of Ishmael represents an early example of what would eventually become a century-long pattern of casting migrants from the Upland South in a decidedly unsympathetic light. When we examine other examples of this phenomenon, the Ishmaelites begin to look less and less like a distinctive subculture of their own and more like transplanted Upland Southerners and Appalachians in general—at least as seen through the disapproving eyes of northern whites like McCulloch.

The Great Migration of southern blacks to northern cities has become part of America's official historical narrative, revisited in scholarly studies, documentaries, popular music, and works of fiction. Far less acknowledged, however, is the significant migration north of rural whites during the same period. Even Detroit, a city synonymous with

the transformative effects of the Great Migration, actually attracted
twice as many white migrants (64,735) from the South as nonwhites
(29,975) in the crucial years 1940–45.[42] Like their black counterparts,
these intrepid men and women were often greeted with suspicion,
insults, and worse.

In their new urban homes, these white migrants were popularly
known by a variety of nicknames, including "briers," "ridge-runners,"
and the ubiquitous "hillbillies," and "white-trash."[43] As their presence
became more pronounced in the period after World War II, a series of
magazine articles with provocative titles like "The Hillbillies Invade
Chicago" and "Down from the Hills and into the Slums" began to
employ many of the same images that had earlier appeared in
McCulloch's study of the Tribe of Ishmael. Unlike McCulloch, however,
the authors of these articles described their subjects in socioeconomic
rather than hereditarian terms. As one of them put it in 1964, "they
arrive in places like Chicago with no training to compete in the job
market and no preparation to make the difficult transition from rural
living. In the city, the Southern whites become the victims of old slum
problems while creating some new ones. They are undernourished, uneducated, unwanted, and unable to cope with a society that does not
understand them or their ways. Lacking leadership, organization, or
political power, these descendants of the pioneers are a lost people."[44]

Like the so-called Ishmaelites before them, twentieth-century
migrants from the Upland South "prided themselves on the very traits of
mobility and independence which employers found most objection-
able."[45] The author of one article referred to their "reckless and unre-
flective pioneer spirit," while a resident of a Detroit neighborhood with
a sizable Appalachian population explained, "to me, a hillbilly is the
people who are dirty and they shuffle back and forth and all."[46] The
"Anglo-Saxon ghettos" where these migrants settled were marked by a
"constant turnover" as families traveled in search of work or to visit
kin. According to a social worker for the Chicago Commission on Youth
Welfare, the mobility of these families made it difficult for their children
to succeed in school: "You know, when a kid finally gets adjusted, his
family moves on again."[47]

In dramatic contrast to the genial buffoons of *Lil' Abner, Ma and Pa
Kettle,* or *The Beverly Hillbillies,* real migrants from the Upland South
were frequently stereotyped by their new neighbors as dirty, violent, diseased, and prone to incest. The comments of an Indianapolis woman
quoted in an article from 1956 reveal how little attitudes among some in

the city had changed since McCulloch first discovered the Ishmaelites nearly a century before: "Those people are creating a terrible problem in our city. They can't or won't hold a job, they flout the law constantly and neglect their children, they drink too much and their moral standards would shame an alley cat. For some reason or other, they absolutely refuse to accommodate themselves to any kind of decent, civilized life." Concerning this woman, the article's author noted ironically that she was "not a New Yorker denouncing Puerto Ricans or a San Franciscan belaboring Mexicans. . . . The subject of her diatribe was an ethnic group usually considered to be the most favored in American society—white Anglo-Saxon Protestants. Her term for them was 'hillbillies.' "[48]

In an echo of McCulloch's earlier comments about the Ishmaelites' "physically weakened condition . . . general incapacity, and unfitness for hard work," a personnel director from Cincinnati complained that his Appalachian workers "seem to do everything wrong because of lack of training and poor physical stamina."[49] Other residents of Cincinnati suspected that many migrants from the Upland South were attracted to their city because of its relatively generous welfare policy, another claim made by McCulloch concerning the Ishmaelites. Yet a sociological study revealed that "migrants' names appear on relief rolls no more frequently than do their Cincinnati neighbors.' "[50]

Even this brief survey reveals how much twentieth-century stereotypes of Upland Southern and Appalachian migrants to the North had in common with McCulloch's late-nineteenth-century portrait of the Tribe of Ishmael. While some of these stereotypes reflected real socioeconomic and cultural differences, all were leavened with unhealthy doses of prejudice and fear. Unfortunately, McCulloch's own commitment to hereditarian theory blinded him to the fact that his image of the Ishmaelites was shaped by the same set of cultural anxieties that would later affect his successors in cities like Detroit, Chicago, Cincinnati, and Indianapolis.

Instead, McCulloch was convinced that the Ishmaelites "are a decaying stock; they cannot live self dependent," and, after describing the tribe as a "festering mass," claimed that "of this whole number, I know of but one who has escaped, and is to-day an honorable man. I have tried again and again to lift them, but they sink back."[51] Like the young *Sacculina* that inevitably developed into a parasite, McCulloch argued "we have the same in the pauper. All the organs and powers that belong to the free life disappear, and there are left only the tendency to parasitism and the debasement of the reproductive tendency." What to do in such a case? McCulloch concluded his study on the Tribe of Ishmael with his own modest proposal: "First, we must close up official outdoor relief [i.e., aid from the township trustee]. Second, we must check private and indiscriminate benevolence, or charity, falsely called. Third, we must get hold of the children."

McCulloch's final recommendation sounds ominous today. It would have sounded less so, however, during the late nineteenth century, when many Indiana residents had already accepted the idea of poor children being removed from their parents and placed elsewhere. As early as the 1850s, the Children's Aid Society, founded by the Reverend Charles Loring Brace in New York City, had begun to ship orphaned, poor, and so-called idle children—the street Arabs—by the trainload to Midwestern states to serve as cheap labor on depopulated farms. Once they arrived, these children were taken from the stock cars and, as one account put it, "herded like cattle on an auction block." Farmers would then select the children whom they wanted to work on their farms. Over the course of the 1850s and 1860s, Indiana accepted more of these "bound children" than any other state. By the time McCulloch arrived in 1877, the number had reached into the thousands.[52]

Reflecting this zeitgeist, McCulloch had already recommended back in 1882 that local boards be created throughout Indiana to "have power over the young vagrants and beggars, the cruelly treated [children], and those who grow up in the midst of bad associations."[53] Although his efforts did not immediately meet with success, he continued to search for what he called "the best means for caring for and reforming . . . 'street waifs.'" In 1889, only a year after publicly recommending that Ishmaelite children be taken from their parents, McCulloch drafted a bill calling for the creation of children's welfare boards in Indiana townships with over seventy-five thousand people. At the time, this applied only to Center Township in Indianapolis, but McCulloch viewed it as an important accomplishment since it granted such boards the authority to remove children from their homes. When later that year the Indiana state legislature voted the bill into law, a pleasantly surprised McCulloch wrote in his diary on March 8, 1889, that he considered it to be "the most radical bill ever passed."

McCulloch's ongoing efforts to place children in more nurturing environments appeared to contradict his own hereditarian assertion that "each [Ishmaelite] child tends to the same life, reverts when taken out."[54] If changing the environment had no impact on the deviant behavior of Ishmaelite children, what was the point of removing them from their homes? Unless, of course, the goal was to permanently isolate them from the rest of society in institutions where their behavior could be constantly monitored and regulated. McCulloch himself does not appear to have endorsed such a view, although it would later become a staple of the eugenics movement. Instead, he remained torn between his optimistic belief that social reform could solve the problems of the less fortunate and his pessimistic conviction that certain people were doomed to failure because of their ancestry.

Only a few months before his death from Hodgkin's disease in 1891, Oscar McCulloch delivered the presidential address to the National Conference of Charities and Correction in Indianapolis. He ambitiously called for the registration of all dependents, defectives, and delinquents, as well as the restriction of immigration to "strong, honest, healthy men, from whom to make good Americans."[55] The organization's chief goal, he told the audience, should be to "make the strongest, most intelligent, and most sympathetic men and women, physically, mentally, and spiritually, the world has ever seen." Although he did not live long enough to witness it, McCulloch's rousing words would help to inspire the rise of the American eugenics movement. In the years to come, McCulloch would be fondly remembered by his successors as one of the pioneers of their discipline and his groundbreaking study of the Tribe of Ishmael would help to transform the state of Indiana into a veritable eugenics laboratory.

CHAPTER 3

How the Other Half Lives

Oscar McCulloch would eventually achieve fame within the eugenics movement for his discovery of the Tribe of Ishmael. But the man who actually conducted most of the research was McCulloch's chief investigator, James Frank Wright.[1] Unlike his mentor, Wright was a native of Indiana. Born in 1851 to an upper-middle-class family, Wright first clerked in his father's law office before deciding to become a journalist. During the closing decades of the nineteenth century, Wright served as the city editor for the *Indiana State Sentinel* and as a court reporter for the *Indianapolis Journal*. Inspired by his contact with the city's most downtrodden citizens, he also became a member of the Board of Children's Guardians of Indianapolis, a position that he held for twelve years. With his combination of local knowledge, investigative skills, and civic concern, Wright was the ideal person to help McCulloch in his research. From 1880 to 1895, Wright compiled close to three hundred pages of unpublished notes on families identified as belonging to the Tribe of Ishmael.[2]

In addition to a detailed history of the Ishmael family itself, Wright composed vivid thumbnail sketches of several hundred individuals from other families who supposedly belonged to the tribe. He personally visited and interviewed many of his subjects. Perhaps because he did not intend to publish his observations, he composed them in an earthy, even gossipy style, full of peculiar spellings. He quoted his informants extensively, although it is impossible to know how faithfully he reproduced these comments. Unlike McCulloch, Wright readily admitted that not all of the Ishmaelites were happy to share their stories with him. For example, one man, named Fletcher McCherry, "was surprised to find one who knew a great deal of his past life, and as soon as he learned this he refused to talk further about it," while another, Berry Rogers, "had a remarkable way of closing his eyes before beginning an answer to any question which he did not particularly fancy, and before the answer was complete he would startle the interrogator with the wildness of his stare which would be directed at him."[3]

Despite these and other challenges, Wright appears to have developed personal relationships with many of his informants over the years. These ties encouraged him to portray at least some of the Ishmaelites as individuals and not simply as members of a criminal subculture. Unfortunately, many of Wright's portraits also reveal the same crude prejudices that tainted Oscar McCulloch's work, and therefore we must read them with a healthy dose of skepticism.

That Wright continued to investigate the Ishmaelites for nearly half a decade after McCulloch's death in 1891 indicates that he had developed his own independent interest in the subject. Wright's notes also reveal that he did not always see eye to eye with McCulloch. Although Wright believed that "misapplied charity is a millstone about the necks of those to whom it is given," he preferred, unlike McCulloch, to attribute the supposed moral decay of the Ishmaelites to environmental rather than to hereditarian causes. As he put it in his characteristically folksy style:

> Morals are no more a matter of inheritance than shoes. Had the home influence in these families been of proper character; had the children been educated in the schools, and been taught to believe in a tenet higher than that which is generally taught among the social outcast . . . then there is reason to believe that they might have been as useful, as honored in society as any in the land. "Blood will tell" is the common answer which condemns this class. It is the answer of selfishness or of ignorance of conditions. If it were true that (in morals) "blood will tell" we must then discover some valid reason for the saying "Preachers boys are always the worst boys in the community."[4]

Another important difference between Wright and McCulloch concerned their views of the tribe's religious beliefs and practices. In his study of the Ishmaelites, McCulloch had expressed little interest in the subject of religion, despite his own background as a man of the cloth. By contrast, Wright made pointed observations concerning the dubious religiosity of various families and individuals belonging to the tribe. Even Ishmaelites who claimed to be good Christians and attended church regularly were hypocrites, according to Wright, including John Owens, a man whom McCulloch had described as a Presbyterian minister. According to Wright, however, Owens only "pretended to be a preacher," and he cynically added, "One of the children thus gave me the old man's creed. 'Well, Pap called himself a Presbyterian, but he wasn't a bit straight-laced. He was a very broad man. He believed any man had a right to get drunk if he wanted to, but he didn't allow that any man had any right to make another man drunk ag'in his will.'"[5]

As for the Ishmael family itself, Wright claimed that all of its members avoided church like the plague and instead believed in a host of "ghosts, demons, witches, [and] 'sperrets.'"[6] Wright's observations concerning the Ishmael family jibe with Berry Sulgrove's characterization of Upland Southern migrants to Indianapolis, in general. In his 1884 history of the city, Sulgrove complained that many poor whites from states like Kentucky and Tennessee remained "indifferent" to church and held tightly to "a belief in witchcraft . . . [and] a score of omens and portents and prophetic dreams" long after settling in Indianapolis.[7] Indeed, as late as 1964, a Chicago policeman informed a journalist that transplanted Upland Southerners "had religion down there, but they don't have their churches up here, so they stop going to any church at all."[8] These sources suggest that generations of Upland Southern migrants became alienated from institutional religion after settling in northern cities like Indianapolis and Chicago. At the same time, many of these migrants continued to embrace a wide range of folk beliefs from back home. These interrelated factors illuminate the Ishmael family's non-normative religious practices—at least by the standards of northern Protestants—far more than Hugo Leaming's later suggestion that Ben Ishmael and his descendants were crypto-Muslims.

Wright also painted a different portrait of the Tribe of Ishmael's ethnic and racial make-up. With the exception of two "half-breed" Indian ancestors, Oscar McCulloch depicted the Ishmaelites, en masse, as white Anglo Saxons with "tow-headed" children. In Wright's account, whites from Upland Southern states like Kentucky, Tennessee, and North Carolina still constituted a large majority of the tribe's members, but he also mentioned several immigrants from Ireland and Germany, as well as a number of individuals with varying degrees of African American ancestry. In discussing these individuals, Wright employed the complex racial taxonomy of nineteenth-century America. Thus, he described several of the tribe's members as "octoroons," two as possessing a "trace of negro blood," one man as a "mulatto" and his wife as a "very black woman," and the child of one mixed race couple as "yellow."

The use of racial designations such as octoroon and mulatto—which derives from a Spanish word for a young mule—reflects the reality of sexual unions between blacks and whites in the nineteenth century. As early as 1842, such mixed-race unions had inspired so much fear in Indiana that the state had passed legislation prohibiting marriages between a white person and any person possessing one-eighth or more "negro blood." Those found guilty were subject to fines of $1,000–$5,000 and to prison terms ranging from one to ten years. A year later, a second statute declared such marriages "absolutely void, without any decree of divorce or other legal proceedings."[9] These antimiscegenation laws were still on the books when James Frank Wright investigated the Ishmaelites during the 1880s and 1890s. Indeed, legislation against mixed-race marriage remained in effect in Indiana until the 1960s, when that state, along with Delaware, Florida, Maryland, Mississippi, and North Carolina, finally repealed its long-standing statutes.

It is important to understand that these draconian legal prohibitions existed, in part, because people from different racial backgrounds *did* seek to get married, despite the enormous pressures against such unions. In some cases, light-skinned blacks passed as whites in order to avoid persecution—and prosecution—for marrying whites. Perhaps more surprisingly, we also find cases from nineteenth-century Indiana of individuals who appeared to be white yet claimed to be black in order to marry African Americans. For example, an Indiana publication called the *Locomotive* reported on August 5, 1848, that a "buck nigger, as black as the ace of spades, named Peter Tilman," had married "Miss Pamelia Powell, a white girl." The couple secured a license by telling the clerk that "the girl had negro blood in her, but she is in every appearance as white as a lily." The journalist sarcastically congratulated the groom for being a "man of taste," and wished the bride "much joy of her conquest."[10] We are left to wonder whether Pamelia Powell was actually "black" or whether she was merely trying to pass in order to marry her beloved.

In the city of Indianapolis, poor and working-class blacks and whites from the Upland South frequently lived in close proximity to one another, often shared suspicious or even antagonistic attitudes to the law, and were less inclined to the strict Victorian moral codes of the day than middle-class residents. For these reasons, they were more likely to engage in mixed-race unions than their bourgeois counterparts.

Moreover, racial categories themselves were less strictly regulated and more fluid among members of the lower classes. Wright's notes on the Ishmaelites provide evidence for both of these phenomena.

For all of its problems—and there are many—Wright's unpublished manuscript still offers the reader a more nuanced perspective on the Tribe of Ishmael than McCulloch's tendentious study. In 1917, several decades after he completed his research, James Frank Wright lent his handwritten notes on the Ishmaelites to Arthur Estabrook, a young eugenicist who was then working on a follow-up study on the tribe. Estabrook not only employed Wright's notes as the foundation for his own work, he also had the notes typed up and a copy sent to the Board of State Charities of Indiana in 1922. Half a century later, Hugo Leaming discovered this typed manuscript in the collection of the Indiana State Library, where it had been gathering dust, and a light bulb went off.

Leaming drew liberally and, to a great extent, uncritically on Wright's manuscript for most of his information on the Tribe of Ishmael's history up until the year 1895. He sprinkled his work with numerous anecdotes borrowed directly from Wright and manipulated Wright's observations concerning religion and race in order to construct his own image of an "Islamic community . . . a bridge between African and American Islam, a lost-found nation in the wilderness of North America."[11] To understand how Leaming radically—and misleadingly— reworked Wright's portrait of the Ishmaelites, it is necessary to explore Wright's notes in detail.

Before examining Wright's manuscript, however, one other source on the Tribe of Ishmael needs to be introduced: the extant records of the Charity Organization Society (COS), established by Oscar McCulloch. In 1880, the COS began to send out caseworkers to investigate all applicants for charity in Indianapolis. Combining functions that would later be divided between social workers and welfare fraud investigators, these intrepid pioneers visited homes, conducted interviews, and did background checks on clients in order to differentiate between worthy and unworthy applicants for aid. Doctors, clergymen, schoolmasters, employers, the police, landlords, and inquiry officers were asked to provide testimony concerning the character of applicants. After completing their evaluations, the investigators presented recommendations to the Indianapolis Benevolent Society, which actually distributed the charity. This arrangement continued in Indianapolis until 1922, when the two societies joined with the Children's Aid Association and the Mother's

Aid Association to form the Family Welfare Society, which was renamed the Family Service Association in 1945.[12]

Since members of the Tribe and, in particular, the Ishmael family itself were supposedly notorious for their dependence on charity, one would expect to find them in great numbers in the files of the COS. Yet these records present a very different picture. Although some individuals identified by Oscar McCulloch and James Frank Wright as members of the Tribe of Ishmael do appear as applicants for charity, they constitute a small minority of the total, and even more strikingly, only a handful of actual Ishmaels are listed among the applicants.

How can we account for this phenomenon? One possibility is that families like the Ishmaels felt stigmatized by their encounters with the township trustee and Oscar McCulloch in the late 1870s and therefore avoided seeking aid from the COS during the 1880s and 1890s, except when absolutely necessary. Along these lines, there is evidence that anyone belonging to certain "Ishmaelite" families (including the Ishmaels and the Eads) was actively discouraged from applying for aid from the COS, since they had already been identified as members of the undeserving poor. Another possibility is that some of the poor people first identified as Ishmaelites in the late 1870s benefited from the economic recovery of the 1880s, and therefore fewer sought charity during this period. It is also possible that the Ishmaels and their "associates" were never as overrepresented on the charity rolls as McCulloch had first claimed in his published account of the Tribe of Ishmael.

Indeed, there is other evidence that McCulloch sometimes dramatically inflated numbers when it came to his charity work. In 1880, he wrote a newspaper article in which he claimed that the Charity Organization Society had registered 8,000 individuals in 1,779 families, whom he described as "a mass of parasitic growth . . . connected by blood and marriage," that is, in precisely the same terms that he employed elsewhere to refer to the Ishmaelites.[13] Since the entire population of Indianapolis was only 75,056 at the time, this represents over 10 percent of the total. In contrast to this impressive claim, however, the COS records from 1880 actually reveal that only several hundred people had been registered. This and other discrepancies have led one scholar to conclude that "McCulloch's study [on the Tribe of Ishmael] seems fraught with . . . fabrications."[14]

Perhaps, as I have already suggested, what really bothered McCulloch all along was not the number of Ishmaels or their "associations" who depended on charity but the fact that they refused to alter their distinct way of life even when they did accept aid. In other words, McCulloch and his fellow charity workers expected a kind of quid pro quo from the poor people who requested aid: in return for help, they were expected to conform to middle-class norms. Ironically, therefore, it may have been the Ishmaels' social independence rather than their economic dependence that made them seem dangerous and undeserving in the eyes of Oscar McCulloch and his colleagues.

The Ishmael case files indicate that many members of the family did not actively seek out aid from the COS. Instead, they attempted to scrape out a living by hauling, recycling trash, sweeping, doing other odd jobs, and, when necessary, by begging. As a result of McCulloch's prodigious efforts, however, these activities were put under increasing surveillance beginning in the late 1870s and early 1880s. After this period, the local authorities and many middle-class citizens alike appear to have tolerated hauling—although they didn't consider it legitimate work—but they viewed begging as immoral if not illegal. Thus, in the case files we find several mentions of private individuals who "reported" Ishmaels to the COS for the offense of begging. And, according to the "scientific" definition of charity embraced by the COS, begging was a sign that someone belonged to the undeserving rather than the deserving poor.

James Frank Wright's sketches and the COS case files enable us to reconstruct how the Tribe of Ishmael was imagined in the city of Indianapolis during the last two decades of the nineteenth century. These documents also provide us with fleeting glimpses into how some of the people identified as Ishmaelites may have seen themselves or, perhaps more accurately, how they chose to portray themselves to the various observers and investigators who visited them in this period. The resulting portrait, while colorful and compelling, sometimes conflicts with basic biographical details (dates of birth, number of children, etc.) contained in federal census lists, military records, and other official documents. Thus, there is an obvious gulf between the image of the people considered Ishmaelites during this period and the reality of their lives. What follows is a depiction of the Ishmaels and other connected families based on Wright's notes, with only occasional reference to independently verifying sources. In chapter 7, I will construct an alternate portrait based on a variety of sources and documents.

According to Wright, the Ishmaels first arrived in Nicholas County, Kentucky, sometime between 1785 and 1790. He traced the family's roots to either New York, Maryland, or Pennsylvania. The early Ishmaels were a "large, raw-boned class, coarse, rough in their manners and way of life, and primitive in their eating." Wright took great delight in describing the omnivorous eating habits of the family. Along with cornbread, "all was fish which came to their net," including bear, raccoon, deer, hedgehog, possum, and polecat.[15] What Wright didn't point out was that this diet was typical of the frontier families that had settled Kentucky. Nor was there anything "primitive" about living off the land and taking advantage of whatever animal protein was available. Indeed, a great many Kentucky families continued to hunt for their dinner long after moving to Indianapolis. So much so, in fact, that Oliver Johnson recalled in his memoir of life in early Indianapolis that the transplanted hill folk from Kentucky even gave names to their beloved flintlock rifles.[16]

Wright dismissed the early Ishmaels as an ignorant and uneducated lot, who preferred to associate with Indians and outlaws rather than with respectable folk. Almost none of the family ever accumulated any property, save for a simple horse- or donkey-drawn wagon used for their favorite activity: traveling the roads. Children typically had blond hair that became darker with age, while adults were notable for their "hang-dog, sneak thief" facial expressions, narrow, retreating foreheads, and eyes that one uncharitable observer described as looking "like the eyes of a pig." Wright claimed that "the family was of a low and thievish bent," and therefore their neighbors had nicknamed them the Ishmaels while they were still living in Kentucky. Yet he also acknowledged that this "disposition to steal was only from a desire to get some corn for the horses or bacon for the family use. There never [was] known a case of this family committing theft except in a small way."[17]

It was Ben Ishmael, the large-framed, "very ignorant, very rough" and "not particularly honest" founder of the clan, who arrived in Kentucky between 1785 and 1790 and there established a farm on refuse (worthless) land that later became part of Bourbon County. Citing a tradition that was supposedly passed down through three generations of Ishmaels, Wright wrote that old Ben left Kentucky for the west sometime between 1802 and 1810 and was never heard from again. For "some further romantic points" concerning Ben Ishmael's fate once he left Kentucky, Wright referred to James Fenimore Cooper's portrait of Ishmael Bush in *The Prairie*—an element that Hugo Leaming later borrowed and embroidered.

What neither Wright nor Leaming apparently realized was that Cooper could not have based his fictional character on Ben Ishmael. Even if the novelist and armchair frontiersman had somehow heard of an obscure pioneer named Ben Ishmael while he was writing *The Prairie* in New York and Paris, he could not have reimagined the latter's exodus from Kentucky for a very simple reason: Ben Ishmael did not leave Kentucky and disappear in the west during the first decade of the nineteenth century. Instead, the Ishmael patriarch remained in Kentucky until 1822, when he died in the bosom of his large family in Nicholas County. Rather than Cooper drawing on the figure of Ben Ishmael for inspiration, therefore, Wright and, following him, Leaming, both employed the rough-hewn character of Ishmael Bush as a model for their own portraits of Ben Ishmael.

The matriarch of the Ishmael clan was Ben's wife, Jennie, whom Wright described as being remarkably similar to her husband, that is, large in build, dirty, ignorant, lazy, and ready to fight. Before supposedly disappearing to the west with Ben, Jennie gave birth to nearly a dozen children. Of these, Wright was particularly interested in two, Samuel and John Ishmael. Samuel was significant because after coming to Kentucky with his parents, he married a Methodist woman who "reformed him." Alone among the Ishmaels, according to Wright, Samuel and his descendants became "good citizens," even building a church on the family farm that became known as "Ishmael's Chapel." Wright learned about this respectable branch of the Ishmaels from an Indianapolis physician named Wishard—probably Wiliam Wishard (1851–1941)—who became acquainted with Samuel's grandson, Dr. William Ishmael, when both were medical students in New York City in the 1870s. Dr. Wishard remembered William Ishmael as a "quiet, orderly man," who seemed likely to succeed as a small town physician.[18]

In marked contrast to his stable older brother, John Ishmael was given to wandering from a young age. Born in Nicholas County, John left Kentucky for southern Ohio, where he hung his hat for a few years before settling in Indianapolis around 1822–23, according to Wright.[19] The handful of Indians remaining in the city welcomed John Ishmael and his family with open arms since, as Wright put it, "John and his mongrel breed were so like the Indians in their habits of life, so lazy, so filthy, so primitive in their habits," that they were welcome where "genuine sportsmen and professional huntsmen and trappers," were not. It also helped that John's wife, Betsy Harbet, another native Kentuckian, was alleged to be a "half-breed Indian" herself. According to Wright, she was as bad tempered and "stolid, as devoid of mirth, as a Fenimore Cooper Indian." Betsy's grandson, George Ishmael, later described her as a "curious critter—must have been Dutch. She talked such lingo as I never heard any one talk, and nobody understood her." Leaming later quoted this line but omitted the phrase "must have been Dutch," in order to strengthen the impression that the "lingo" spoken by Betsy Harbet was a Native American language.[20]

Soon after arriving in Indianapolis, John and Betsy began to make regular treks to their former haunts in Ohio, as well as to a number of locales in Illinois, including Decatur, Bloomington, and Peoria, where other members of the Ishmael family lived. Whereas Oscar McCulloch had attributed the tribe's so-called wandering to heredity, Wright's account suggests a rather simple etiology for their travels. Like many families of Upland Southern origin, the Ishmaels retained close ties to their kin, and those who lived in Indianapolis would regularly travel outside of the city in order to visit other branches of their extended family and to search for work.

When they returned to Indianapolis from these journeys, John Ishmael and his family hunkered down in a strip of forest that later became the site of the city's Institute for the Deaf and Dumb. There, the Ishmaels would sleep in hollow logs, on railroad embankments, or, during the summer months, out in the open. John Ishmael, according to Wright, was considered "lazy, would not work, would steal, and was dependent upon charity. He was regarded with the same contempt as the few remaining Indians," whose love of hunting, fishing, and drinking he supposedly shared until the day he died, sometime between 1845 and 1848. (In fact, federal census lists indicate that John Ishmael actually lived until at least 1860.) John Ishmael was supposedly buried in Covington, Indiana, although Wright could not locate the grave when he visited the town's burial ground in 1893. Upon his death, John—Wright does not mention when Betsy died—left behind numerous children in Indianapolis and the surrounding towns.

One son named Tom Ishmael lived three miles northeast of Tipton, Indiana, in a "three cornered log cabin, perhaps the queerest structure in the state."[21] This unusual house was the only evidence that Hugo Leaming later needed in order to describe Tom as the third "patriarch" of the Tribe of Ishmael. By contrast, Wright admitted that "little is known of this man or his family," save for the fact that Tom's second wife was an octoroon woman. Significantly, this represents one of several marriages between members of the Ishmael family—including Tom's son, Joel—and people of African American descent. Wright gave no indication that these marriages were frowned upon by any of the Ishmaels. Indeed, Wright suggested that the Ishmaels welcomed the

mixed race members of their family with a refreshing openness, especially given the tense racial climate of nineteenth-century Indiana.

Fred Ishmael, another son of John and Betsy, was born in Nicholas
County, Kentucky.[22] He first married Mary Smith and, after she died, a
remarkable woman named Kate Thornton.[23] Wright didn't have much
to say about Fred, who supported himself by floating blocks of ice down
river to ice house chutes, but he took a shining to Kate, whom he
regarded as "truthful unless she was begging" and "not without a great
deal of intelligence."[24] According to Wright, Kate provided him with
most of his initial information about other Ishmaelites, and her stories
invariably turned out to be true when he checked them out.

Kate Thornton Ishmael was born in Ireland or as she used to say
proudly, "from the North of Ireland, and that kind of Irish won't lie."
After her father whipped her one too many times when she was a girl,
Kate snuck some gold coins from his purse and hit the road. By the following day, Kate was on a ship bound to New York, where, upon arrival,
she married a ne'er-do-well. It wasn't long before she abandoned him
and made her way to Indianapolis, where she met and married the one
true love of her life, Fred Ishmael. By the time Wright got to know Kate,
her beloved "Freddie" had already passed away. Between bouts of drinking "all she could get," Kate spent her time reminiscing and laughing
about their life together: "while she would relate some of his weak-
nesses, as his getting drunk or stealing corn, it would always wind up
with an apology for him, 'but he never meant any harm, he was the best
man in the world.'"

After Fred Ishmael died, Kate refused to remarry; she supported herself by selling bottles of liquid indigo on the street or by begging. When
Wright encouraged her to enter the poorhouse, she refused, explaining
"with a softened voice, and eyes suffused with tears, that she expected
to remain so she could die in the same bed 'where Freddie died.' This
was one last desire with her." Nor was Kate the only Ishmael to feel a
strong sense of loyalty to her spouse, for as Wright noted, "One of the
strange things in the history of the Ishmaels is that separations and
divorces were not so common as would be expected among such
people." Significantly, this statement directly contradicted Wright's own
public declaration before the National Conference of Charities and
Correction in 1890 that "it is a fixed fact that this class of people [the
Tribe of Ishmael] monopolize the divorce courts."[25]

Despite Fred Ishmael's faults, Kate Thornton Ishmael was fiercely
proud of her husband and deeply resented "the scorn with which she

was greeted (as 'the old Ishmael woman') and never failed to make a defense of the family." Wright's reference to Kate's being maligned for belonging to the Ishmael family suggests that by the 1880s, at least, the Ishmaels had earned a negative reputation among the other residents of Indianapolis. Whether this was due to their own behavior and/or to the persistent efforts of Oscar McCulloch and others to demonize them is uncertain. It should be noted, however, that in the early 1880s, Indianapolis newspapers explicitly referred to the Ishmaels as forming a criminal clan. On January 19, 1884, for example, an article in the *Indianapolis News* claimed, "The great progenitors of thieves and prostitutes in this city have been the Eads and Ishmael families." It is hard to imagine what it must have felt like to be an Ishmael in Indianapolis during this period of intense and very public stigmatization.

Loyal to the end, Kate Thornton Ishmael finally got her wish in June 1890, when she died in the bed she had shared with Freddie Ishmael. Unfortunately, it was a particularly hot summer day and by the time Kate's rotting body was discovered under a swarm of green flies, her face had turned black, and her hungry cats had devoured one of her arms.

Another notable member of the family's second generation in Indianapolis was Kate Thornton Ishmael's sister-in-law, Susan Ishmael (née Smith), a tall, thin woman who married Jim Ishmael (another son of John and Betsy) in Muncie, Indiana, sometime around 1840.[26] Susan's father, Jehu Smith, was an old friend of John Ishmael, and her sister, Mary, had been the first wife of Fred Ishmael. After going blind around 1870, Susan earned her keep by serving as a lucrative "begging card" for the rest of the family, according to Wright. Despite her infirmity, she also continued to join her fellow Ishmaels on their annual migrations until the spring of 1882, when poor health and cold weather forced her to seek temporary refuge on a farm in Hendricks County. Within a day or so, news of Susan's situation reached her son George Ishmael, who was still in Indianapolis. George hitched the rickety wagon he used to haul trash, ashes, and other refuse, and set out for the countryside. That evening he brought his ailing mother back to an old log house on Tennessee Street, just south of the Home for Friendless Women. A cold rain was falling the night that Susan Ishmael died, just plain worn out from years of hard living.

By the time Mrs. Bullitt, the matron of the Home for Friendless Women arrived to prepare Susan's body for burial, her hovel was filled to capacity with mourning relatives. After Mrs. Bullitt insisted that all the men leave the room before she undress the body, they stepped outside and stood stoically in the downpour. In the morning, the undertaker laid Susan Ishmael's corpse to rest in a roughly made cheap pine box. After placing this simple coffin in the back of his cart, the undertaker took off in the cold rain for the cemetery, followed by a long train of "queer little ash wagons of the mourners with from five to ten in each wagon, the wagons drawn by the worst apologies for horses and donkeys the city ever knew." The Ishmael wagons traveled on "wheels that did not match, sometimes with tires tied on with ropes, and spokes held in place by means of cross pieces nailed on," and were "filled to overflowing with men, women, children, who, with pieces of old umbrellas raised over them to keep off some of the rain, chased down the street."[27]

Wright was so impressed by Susan Ishmael's funeral procession that he concluded his thumbnail account of her life with the following testament: "Never before or since was anyone honored by the Ishmaels in the final act as was Susan. It seems as if they paid her such homage in life, and regarded her as a superior being, a mother or queen."[28] Later, Hugo Leaming cited Susan Ishmael's extraordinary funeral as evidence that the Ishmaelites had developed a tradition of matriarchal leadership or "queens." By contrast, Oscar McCulloch greatly downplayed the poignant events surrounding the woman's death, which he appears to have witnessed firsthand: "I was with a great-grandmother on her death-bed," he wrote in his published study of the Tribe of Ishmael. "She had been taken sick on the annual gypsying; deserted at a little town because sick; shipped into the city; sent to the county asylum; at last brought to the miserable home to die."[29]

Yet another version of Susan Ishmael's death appeared in the "City News" section of the *Indianapolis News* on October 14, 1881. The newspaper noted that "Mrs. Susan Ishmael, mother of the notorious Ishmael tribe, died in this city yesterday. She was one of the most accomplished beggars the city ever had to deal with."[30] Although brief, this anonymously authored obituary is significant for several reasons. First, the date given for Susan Ishmael's death is six months earlier than the one provided by Wright. This demonstrates how even the most basic biographical details can change depending on who is reporting them. In fact, Wright's biographical sketches are rife with factual errors. Second, the author—who may have been Oscar McCulloch, himself, since he sometimes wrote for the paper—employed the phrase "Ishmael tribe" nearly a decade before McCulloch delivered his "Tribe of Ishmael" lecture to the Conference on Charities. Finally, the article starkly confirms that by the early 1880s, at least, the Ishmael family had become the subject of public censure in the major media outlets of Indianapolis. Whether some members of the family deserved this notoriety or not, all Ishmaels in the city were painted with the same negative brush during this period.

The third generation of Ishmaels in Indianapolis produced more than its share of memorable characters. One of the more unusual figures was France Ishmael, son of Fred, who carved out a rather unusual economic niche for himself. According to Wright, France earned his living by killing St. Bernards, Newfoundlands, and other large dogs, typically by the undetectable means of poison. Posing as a good Samaritan, he would then notify the owners that their beloved pets had died, generously offering to remove the cumbersome carcasses for a mere quarter. France would then haul his canine victims to a secluded spot outside the city limits, where he skinned the dogs and sold their pelts for a dollar to eager rug makers. Henry Ishmael, though less colorful, also earned a brief mention in Wright's manuscript.[31] Another member of the family, Andy Ishmael, born in 1855, was a great fan of gypsying. Andy married a woman named Sarah or, as she was known to everyone, Sallie Williams.[32] Wright described Sallie, born around 1866, as a "coarse dirty woman" and "a passive observer of the wrongdoing of others."[33] Sallie's greatest vice was rum, which she drank so heavily during her last pregnancy in 1889, that it led to her death during labor, according to Wright.

Andy Ishmael's younger sister, Maggie, married Sallie's brother, George Williams.[34] Although Wright apparently met this couple only once, while he was visiting Kate Thornton, they made a powerful and lasting impression on him. In fact, the Williams family in general inspired Wright's curiosity and even his grudging sympathy. George and Sallie's father, Thomas Williams, was a North Carolinian by birth, whose wife, Elizabeth Lynch, had been dead for many years by the time Wright came unto the scene.[35] Williams was a longtime resident of Indianapolis who lived off public charity when he wasn't in prison—which wasn't that often. He was a "hard looking man, being short, rather of a heavy build, with hard lines in his face, well set, but cruel lips, and sharp-piercing eyes." According to Wright, Williams was so fond of liquor—and so destitute—that he frequently stooped to being a "gauger," underworld lingo for someone who made the rounds of the city's taverns, using a tin can to collect the dregs of stale beer from kegs left on the sidewalks by saloon keepers. In order to chase his beer with a smoke, Williams also became a "snipe shooter," gathering extinguished cigar butts on the street and smoking them.[36]

Thomas Williams's devotion to drinking was the rule rather than the exception among the Ishmaelites, according to Wright. This view contrasts sharply with McCulloch's published assertion that the tribe's members were "not intemperate to excess," and gives lie to Hugo Leaming's later claim that "Wright mentions one light drinker and no others." In reality, Wright depicted many of the Ishmaelites—rightly or wrongly—as raging alcoholics and drug addicts. Since Leaming referred to the supposed "Ishmaelite abstinence for alcohol" as a possible sign of Islamic influence, the complete lack of evidence for their intemperance further undermines his hypothesis that the Ishmaelites were crypto-Muslims.

By 1892, Thomas Williams had spent so much time incarcerated for petty theft that he actually stole a set of tools and turned himself in to the police, later pleading guilty, because he "felt more at home" in prison than he did in the outside world. Despite his hard life and long criminal record, Williams was not a violent man, and he inspired sympathy and affection in the police who got to know him over the years. When locked up in jail, Williams would smuggle in some beer or whisky, and soon he and the other prisoners would take over the cell block with "the jolliest, noisiest songs, laughing and drinking." Even Wright was won over by Williams, writing, "Tom had a heart in him, and was better than many men who have never served the state as he has."

James Frank Wright encountered Maggie Ishmael and George Williams in Kate Thornton's hovel in the summer of 1889, shortly after both had gotten out of prison. The couple had stolen eight horses and were on their way to Terre Haute, Indiana, when the law finally caught up with them. Although George got out early on good behavior, he had to wait for Maggie, who was given extra time for bad conduct. This was not surprising, Wright knowingly observed, since "a vicious woman is worse behind the bars than a vicious man." Maggie Ishmael was yet another tall, large-boned woman, and Wright considered her "not unhandsome." He did not know whether she was unchaste but admitted that "it was a general rule that all Ishmaels were, and Maggie was included in this general although unfair conclusion."[37]

Of all the women he wrote about, Wright found Maggie Ishmael to be the most compelling. Maggie Ishmael shattered Victorian notions of passive female propriety with her aggressive manner. She was a hardened ex-con who had spent most of her life gypsying and, according to Wright, did not regard "society except as her enemy." Wright praised Maggie for being a good judge of character and lauded "her evident contempt for her husband"—whom Wright viewed with a combination of disdain and barely suppressed jealousy—adding, however, that "she would have proven a tigress in his defense."[38] Although Wright tried to pass off his interest in Maggie as entirely professional—at one point he clinically referred to his desire "to study that woman"—he was both intimidated and titillated by her behavior, which "made the others in the room seem insignificant in comparison."

Wright consistently displayed sympathy for women, like Maggie Ishmael, whom he considered physically attractive. He even implied that a woman's potential for improvement lay in direct proportion to her looks and frequently lamented the contrast between a woman's physical beauty and her moral turpitude and poverty. For instance, Wright noted that Liddy Ann Uphold, a down-and-out prostitute and morphine eater known in police records as "Sugar Foot," was "a rather handsome woman," even though her fair white skin was always dirty. This inspired Wright to observe that it was a "strange thing to find a woman who had so much of fair appearance in such abject poverty." Likewise, one Lizzie Owens "was rather a handsome girl and might have been a good woman if she had been given an opportunity." Instead, she became a prostitute and "afterwards married a Hebrew" in Chicago. Finally, Wright noted that George Williams's sister Anna was "not a bad looking girl; indeed she might have been a good woman if she had been permitted by our social system."[39]

Unlike McCulloch, Wright did not assert that these women were doomed to become criminals, prostitutes, and paupers merely because they came from generations of so-called degenerates. Yet he did not totally reject a link between physical and moral traits, either. Instead, Wright viewed a woman's physical beauty as a sign that her moral character could be positively shaped by a healthy environment. By contrast, he interpreted an unattractive physical appearance as a mark of Cain, signifying that a woman deserved her low station in life.

Like many other men of the Victorian era, Wright was obsessed with maintaining the sexual purity of the so-called weaker sex, and he condemned the "human wolves" who took advantage of defenseless Ishmaelite women such as Luella Higgins, whom he described as "uneducated, rather attractive . . . the kind of prey the shrewd and unconscienceless villains would seek." The flip side of this obsession with sexual purity was an almost pornographic interest in women who had already fallen from grace. Nearly every woman in the Tribe of Ishmael was a prostitute, according to Wright, though some were worse than others. Bridget Otis, who "belonged to a class known as 'Fighting Irish'" was "a hard drinker, a morphine eater, and a prostitute" who "could swear like a drunken printer." Malinda Lynn was a "prostitute of the lowest kind. . . . Even the negroes could boast of being her lovers if only they would supply her with liquors." Despite his liberal use of the term, however, Wright never bothered to define what made a woman a prostitute, although he did imply that having sexual relations outside of marriage was enough to earn someone the moniker. Thus, Wright off handedly observed that Delilah Thacker, who "smoked a pipe and even chewed tobacco . . . must have been a prostitute since one of her sons was born two years after the death of her husband."[40]

Other Ishmaelite women who fascinated Wright were those who dominated—and, in some cases, terrified—their husbands. One such woman was Mary Hatfield, who had "a temper which would wreck a file." Wright claimed that "the evidence before the coroner, when her husband died, satisfied everyone that she had driven him to suicide by her tongue lashings." Another Ishmaelite woman named Lizzie Schwartz was "ignorant of those branches [of knowledge] usually taught in the public schools," but she was so skilled in the "art of unheard of oaths and flourishes" that an "Ohio river steamboat mate would appear small and insignificant beside her." Lizzie was a "woman of considerable energy, and had she married a man of any force of character would probably have been a very fair woman." Instead she married a "large, heavy, slow-moving, ignorant, lazy man, good natured as a rule, but clearly loving a fight." Wright observed pragmatically that if Lizzie had been "a woman with less of acid in her temper she might have starved. As it was John [her husband] feared her more than he hated work."[41] Wright's vivid descriptions of strong-willed "Ishmaelite" women such as Mary Hatfield and Lizzie Schwartz would later inspire Hugo Leaming to claim that "more female than male nobles or notables of the clans appear in the case studies. The queens of the tribe were not merely the consorts of the patriarchs but important personages in their own right."[42]

Unlike the passive men in the couples above, Wright portrayed George Williams, Maggie Ishmael's husband, as a cross between Billy the Kid and a Russian revolutionary: "thin, tall, hollow-eyed, with a sneer on his face that suggests the hyena; a stoop in his shoulders and a straggling beard of a sandy color, adds to his outlaw look. He is ignorant, vicious, immoral; drinks when he can get it; will steal if there is an opportunity, is not averse to any form of robbery, and is essentially cowardly. He is an anarchist of course, and he has the instinctive, envious dislike, so characteristic of his people, of anyone in a better condition than himself."[43]

Wright recalled that Williams had arrived at Kate Thornton's house after spending hours combing the city in search of broken umbrellas to repair. Upon seeing Wright, Williams launched into a passionate speech in which he "abused the law, the courts, the rich, factories—everything. He wanted every laundry burned and people compelled by law to give their laundry out to the poor." Wright dismissed Williams's angry remarks as a result of envy or even "instinct"—one of the few times that he used the word—rather than a reasonable frustration with the political and economic situation in Indianapolis. Yet the words that Wright quoted George Williams as delivering that day in Kate Thornton's room reveal a well-developed sense of class-consciousness. After condemning the rich and powerful, Williams passionately declared in a "loud harsh voice, with many oaths,—'I am better than any man that wears store clothes.'" These poignant remarks reveal the stigma that desperately poor people like George Williams and his Ishmael in-laws literally wore on their backs.[44]

At one point, Williams launched into a slang-filled soliloquy in which he angrily recounted the events leading up to his false—in his mind, at least—conviction for robbery. The story (including Wright's parenthetical translations of slang terms) is worth repeating in full for the window it opens unto the "thug life" of late-nineteenth-century Indianapolis:

> I was in a saloon and two men were there. They drank and I was offered some whiskey. Of course I drank it. It went to my head, and I ain't fitten (responsible) when whiskey shoots (affects the brain). Then one says to me he'll give another drink if I get him a woman. See. There's a fly (meaning that these two men had from the first planned the entire adventure in order to send him to prison). Well I couldn't dodge (think and act discretely) so I fell in (accepted the proposition). So I took him to my sister (Anna Graves) and she gathered him (accepted). Then I lays down in a corner and goes off (slept), and he and her went to bed. See! That shows that I did'nit follow (deliberately plot a robbery). So I got up swimming (drunk) and took out his pocketbook, and I took ten cases out (ten dollars). And then they never saw me take it. How could they make it play that way! (sentence me without an eye-witness). It wasn't held out in hock (shown clearly in court). But I had to wade (go over the road—to prison). The law is against us (meant to crush the poor).[45]

While George Williams raged, Wright's eyes were drawn to his silent but watchful wife. Later he recalled the scene with barely suppressed excitement: "How splendedly did Maggie appear that morning, as she paced two and fro across the room, like some fiend, who only awaited a signal from her master to begin the attack, for it was evident from their motions that I was going to be robbed." Apparently sensing Wright's discomfort, George Williams suddenly interrupted his soliloquy and reassured the visitor that he had nothing to fear and that "people were always afraid of him when he got earnest-like and made speeches." With more than a hint of competitive bravado, Wright responded that he "was not afraid of the biggest man in town." Following this exchange, Williams ended his speech, Maggie stopped pacing the room "liked a caged wild-cat," and the encounter came to a close. This lurid description reveals how much Wright relished his adventures with urban "savages" like Maggie Ishmael and her husband. Wright's purple prose echoed the florid literary style of nineteenth-century explorers. And why not? In the slums of Indianapolis, James Frank Wright had discovered his own Heart of Darkness.

Sarah Ishmael, Maggie's cousin, was another member of the family's third generation in Indianapolis who made a powerful impression on Wright. Sarah was described by the policemen who knew her well as the "Ishmael woman who walks like a man and talks bass."[46] According to Wright, Sarah played a prominent role in the history of the Ishmaels and many stories were later told about her. Unfortunately, Wright did not record any of these tales, but he did draw sketches of her four memorable, if brief, marriages.

Another tall, "raw-boned" woman, Sarah Ishmael first married a famous fiddler named "blind Henry Smith," who played at popular hangouts like the Hop-Light Station, the Crib, and the Nest. One night, Sarah took a shining to Henry and after plying him with whiskey, convinced him to marry her. The following morning, when Henry sobered up and realized what had happened, he abandoned Sarah. Apparently not one to let things get her down, Sarah moved on to Isaiah Eads, who, according to Wright, hailed from a rotten branch of a good Kentucky family.[47] Isaiah's father, James, was a "bad man in a small way . . . filthy, indescent, disgusting." As evidence of his perfidy, Wright cited one of James's activities: rafting deer carcasses down the river to New Orleans, where he waited for the meat to go bad before selling it to the Big Easy's wealthy citizens. As for Isaiah, it was rumored that he and his half-sister Rebecca Courter—who had supposedly seduced her own son and become his mistress—were discovered cutting rings off the fingers of men blown to bits in an engine explosion at the Indiana State Fair Grounds.[48]

After Sarah Ishmael and Isaiah Eads parted ways, she married Richard "Dick" Smith, the mixed-race son of Polly Hatton and Robert Chism, both of whom were notable in their own right. Indeed, Leaming would later describe Chism as the fourth patriarch of the Tribe of Ishmael. Polly Hatton ran the notorious night spot known as the Nest and held "quite a high rank among the Ishmaels." According to Wright, she "would have been a white woman had she used soap. A viler prostitute, thief, and all round criminal, it would be hard to find."[49] Wright implied that Polly Hatton had effectively assumed a black identity by living in dirty conditions, leading a life of crime, and cohabitating with Robert Chism, whom he described as a mulatto. Yet Wright also suggested that if Polly Hatton cleaned herself up, both literally and figuratively, she could lay claim to whiteness in a way that individuals who were born black never could.

It is easy to see why Hugo Leaming later considered Polly's charismatic paramour, Robert Chism, to be the tribe's final "patriarch." Wright probably devoted more space to Chism than to any other individual in his notes.[50] Significantly, the 1860 federal census lists Robert Chism as one of the wealthiest "Blacks and Mulattoes" in Marion County, where Indianapolis is located. With real estate valued at $2,000 and a personal estate of $75, only six other African American men in the county had more assets than Chism, who is listed as forty-five years old, a "cook" and, along with his wife, Milly, a native of Virginia.[51] James Frank Wright despised Robert Chism intensely, despite or, more likely, because of his financial success.

Wright claimed that Chism was born a slave in Virginia but somehow managed to gain his freedom while still a young man. Thereafter, he embarked on a life of adventure worthy of a Mark Twain novel. Living by his considerable wits, Chism worked as a gambler, thief, roustabout, and outlaw on boats plying the Ohio and Mississippi Rivers between Cincinnati and New Orleans. He was also a great ladies' man, who kept as many as fifteen mistresses in his house at one time, according to Wright. These mistresses, who included "many women belonging to the Tribe of Ishmael," as well as the wife of an evangelist who abandoned her husband to live with Chism for a year, called him by pet names like "Papa" and "Grandpa." Through all of his affairs, Chism remained married to his third wife, a "very black woman" named Milly Brown, who worked as a domestic for a wealthy lawyer named Lucian Barbour. Hugo Leaming would later interpret Chism's many dalliances as evidence that some members of the Tribe of Ishmael had engaged in

Figure 3. Robert Chism's house in Indianapolis, undated. This photo is part of the Tribe of Ishmael display in figure 1. (The American Philosophical Society)

polygamy or, as he put it, "There are indications that it [polygamy] was the prerogative of leaders, or nobility."[52]

Robert Chism built a three-story house on the corner of North and Blackford Streets that served as a refuge for worn-out veterans, desperate women, and criminals on the lam, including an infamous counterfeiter named Pete McCarney and a notorious criminal known to everyone by his underworld moniker, "Modoc." According to Wright, Chism was "the sworn enemy of the law and order and the chief defender of thieves and outlaws" in Indianapolis. As payment for the shelter and protection he provided, Wright claimed, Chism would take military pensions from retired soldiers, force his female guests to become his mistresses, and, like Fagan in *Oliver Twist,* turn their children into thieves and beggars. If a pauper had nothing to offer in return for a place to stay, Chism would head over to the township trustee and demand reimbursement for the lodging he was providing. On the many occasions when the police came looking for a suspect, six to ten officers were necessary to block the numerous escape routes built into Chism's oddly designed house.

In 1885, Chism published the first of two inflammatory pamphlets— Hugo Leaming incorrectly called them "books"—in which he accused the wealthy and powerful citizens of Indianapolis of robbing him. Chism was particularly enraged at a prominent attorney named William W. Leathers (known as Old Bill Leathers) and Lucian Barbour, his wife's employer. Barbour (1811–80) was a somewhat ironic target for Chism's ire, since he had been an early opponent of slavery and had abandoned the Democratic party following the Missouri Compromise. Indeed, Barbour had even played a central role in the most famous fugitive slave case in Indiana history. In 1853, Pleasant Ellington, a Methodist minister from St. Louis, had accused an African American resident of Indianapolis named John Freeman of being his escaped slave. Lucian Barbour, along with two other attorneys, successfully defended Freeman and prevented him from being handed over to Ellington.[53]

In his second pamphlet, Chism accused a number of well-respected public officials, including Dr. John Oliver, the superintendent of the Indianapolis City Hospital, of being frauds and charlatans. Unfortunately, neither of Chism's publications has survived, although Leaming later claimed—apparently without any evidence—that "both books created wide if whispered interest in the Midwest."[54] Wright's description of their contents suggests that Robert Chism saw himself as a champion of the downtrodden and, despite his racial background, as the social equal of the city's most powerful residents.

Robert Chism was still going strong in 1895, the year Wright completed his research on the Tribe of Ishmael. When a visitor commented on how good he looked for his advanced age, Chism responded: "Yes, I am 82 years old and in perfect health. I attribute it to the fact that I have always been a prohibitionist." Wright sardonically observed that in the same conversation Chism had admitted drinking large quantities of rum, but since he never got drunk, Chism reasoned, he remained a prohibitionist. Despite his Robin Hood–like qualities—or more likely, because of them—Wright could only see Chism's bad side. As he put it, "There are but few in this history who have such remarkable traits of character who are so utterly abandoned, and who have the source of so much that is bad and so little good."[55]

To return to Sarah Ishmael, she and Robert Chism's son, Dick Smith, had three children together before they separated. After they parted ways, Sarah Ishmael married her fourth and final husband, Henry Sharpe. The couple was married for only two years before Sharpe went insane while journeying home to Indianapolis from a "Gypsy tour" in Illinois. Soon after, Sharpe returned to his home state of Ohio and "was never heard of again," bringing to a rather ignominious end the long marital career of Sarah Ishmael.[56]

Sarah's brother, George Ishmael, was born in Indianapolis to Susan (of the famous funeral) and Jim Ishmael, one of John's sons. Wright sympathetically described George as willing to work—once even refusing charity when he was sick—and praised him as "the most intelligent of the Ishmaels . . . [who] really does think at times." Like his aunt Kate Thornton, George expressed pride in being an Ishmael. He even believed that the Ishmaels were physical descendants of their biblical namesake. Thus, Wright quoted George as declaring: "I reckon ours is the oldest family in the world. I have heard tell of one of our family being named in the Bible."[57]

George's first wife was Sarah Purcell, a light-skinned descendant of freed slaves from Kentucky. Despite mentioning this and other examples of white "Ishmaelite" men marrying African American women, Wright publicly asserted in a speech to the National Conference of Charities and Correction in 1890, "There are many instances [in the Tribe of Ishmael] of the marriage of white women to negro men, but our research has failed to show where a white man has married a colored woman."[58] The only way to explain this contradiction is that Wright, like so many whites of his day, was unable to acknowledge publicly what everyone knew to be true in private: white men could be sexually attracted to black women. Instead, Wright preferred to perpetuate the racist myth that white men— even "degenerate" ones like the Ishmaelites—did not sexually desire black women, while white women, unless they were carefully monitored, would easily fall victim to supposedly rapacious black men.

After Sarah Purcell died, George Ishmael married Caroline Bartlett, a white woman previously married to Matthew Tillberry, a mulatto who had owned some property.[59] Caroline brought her three children to live with George Ishmael, and together they had six more children of their own. Every year the entire family traveled to Illinois on the "Gypsy tours." On one of these trips, the story was told, George encountered a bad omen in the form of a stick in the road pointing straight at him. He turned the caravan around and brought the family back to Indianapolis, where they spent the summer. This was probably the same summer that George gathered up his blind mother, Susan, at the farm where she lay dying and brought her back to Indianapolis to pass away among her kin.

Joel Tillberry, George Ishmael's oldest adopted son, was a great lover of music who "must have been a marked character among those who knew him," according to Wright, "on account of the trace of negro blood in his veins, his long coarse strit and very black hair, and his cadaverous looks." Yet Wright's own description of Joel's warm relationship with his adoptive Ishmael family suggests that his features only made him a "marked character" among those with racist views. Indeed,

Wright seemed surprised at the close bond between Joel and George Ishmael, noting that Joel was "never impressed with the ludicrousness of the situation when he addressed George Ishmael as 'paw,' he being over head and shoulders the taller of the two."[60]

After Joel married a mixed-race woman named Mary Josie Dobbs in 1889, Wright expressed amazement at the closeness between him and his Ishmael relatives. Wright's description, perhaps unwittingly, captures the gritty ingenuity and warm spirit of cooperation among the Ishmaels:

> While a visitor from the trustee's office was visiting Andy and Sallie Ishmael, in the month of February of that year, a crowd of Ishmaels came into the house, swearing and discussing some project very earnestly. It proved to be Andy, Henry, George and France Ishmael who were planning Joel's future with him. The immediate subject at that moment was how a bed was to be prepared for the couple [Joel and Mary]. Henry agreed to furnish certain side pieces, France would furnish the nails which he said he had in his wagon, and Henry said Joel could steal enough of the weather boarding from a deserted frame house across the street to complete the structure. Probably it was carried out according to the plans. The last known of this couple they had a funny little yellow boy whom they named Sam, in honor of Mary's father.[61]

It is easy to see how an episode like this could have inspired Hugo Leaming to describe the Tribe of Ishmael as a harmonious triracial community. The problem with Leaming's characterization, however, is that not all of the families identified by James Frank Wright as belonging to the tribe shared the Ishmaels' apparent racial tolerance.

The most notable counterexample to Leaming's idealized portrait was the Owens family. Elijah Owens, the family patriarch, hailed from Laurel County, Kentucky, where he "probably owned some slaves," according to Wright. His son, William, moved to Indiana, where he became known as an "ignorant loafer, drunkard, and good-for-nothing." William eventually abandoned his family and tramped his way to California, where he was last heard from "in the best of health—much to the regret of his wife." In marked contrast to Oscar McCulloch's blanket assertion that there was "little intemperance" in the Owens family, Wright concluded a sketch of one of the family's female members with the remark: "Like all the rest of the Owens breed she is a great lover of peach brandy." He also noted that one of William Owens's sons, William Walker Owens, co-owned the notorious Indianapolis tavern known as Brighton Beach, where "he became the best customer

of his own bar." Another son, Elijah, died in prison after being incarcerated for stealing a box of cigars.[62]

Brook Owens, another son of the original Elijah, was born and raised
in Kentucky, where he operated a peach brandy distillery. According to
Wright, "Brook Owens was also noted for one thing more. This was his
love of slavery. He was a large man and those of his family which came
to this state [Indiana] were of large frame. For this reason, perhaps,
Brook and his sons were often called upon by some of the neighboring
farmers and slave owners to aid them in the whipping of a refractory
slave. Thus, to the Owens family such an occasion was in some degree a
holiday."[63]

It would be hard to invent a family more at odds with Hugo
Leaming's description of the "tribe's origin in escape from slavery."[64]
Yet this disjunction did not prevent Leaming from including the Owens
family in his version of the Tribe of Ishmael. Indeed, Leaming glowingly
described the "central communal dance hall" owned by Brook's son,
John Owens, as "the pride of the Ishmaelites." Not surprisingly, however, he omitted Wright's description of its proprietor as "a man of a
powerful frame, and of great strength, and in the days of slavery he had
been in demand as a slave whipper, because of his ability to do the work
in a scientific manner."[65]

The case of the Owens family clearly demonstrates the extent to
which Hugo Leaming selectively interpreted Wright's biographical
sketches in order to create a more sympathetic—and uniform—image of
the Ishmaelites. How, for instance, would the slavery-supporting Owens
family have viewed the racially integrated Ishmaels and vice versa?
Could a man like John Owens, supposedly infamous as a slave whipper,
have accepted Tom Ishmael, married to an octoroon, or Robert Chism,
a former slave himself, as his leaders? Yet this is precisely what Hugo
Leaming later suggested. Wright himself never raised these questions,
nor did he attempt to establish any direct links between the Ishmael and
the Owens families, even though, like Oscar McCulloch before him, he
identified both families as belonging to the Tribe of Ishmael.

Significantly, Wright devoted only the first quarter of his notes to
describing the Ishmaels and their in-laws. In the remaining pages, he
composed biographical sketches of literally hundreds of people who do
not appear to have been related by either blood or marriage to the
Ishmaels. Like the Ishmaels, however, all belonged to the economic
underclass of Indianapolis and most had originally migrated to the city
from the Upland South. They lived in the same neighborhoods, socialized

in the same bars, and engaged in the same set of marginalized economic activities as the Ishmaels. In these important respects, the people identified by Wright as Ishmaelites belonged to the same community, even though they no more constituted a tribe than did the residents of Indianapolis's tonier neighborhoods.

A typical example of the hardscrabble men and women defined as Ishmaelites was Jack Potter, whom Wright described as "poor white trash from North Carolina, or as he would say, 'de Kaliny state.'" In order to eke out an income of twenty-five to fifty cents a day, Potter would "scrape the ponds," a practice that Wright explained as follows: Even after municipal garbage collection was introduced, many residents of Indianapolis continued to throw their refuse, including dead dogs, cats, and, on occasion, a dead infant or an abortion "to save someone's reputation," into privy vaults that were later be emptied into low-lying ponds. As the sun heated the water, an oily film formed on the surface of the ponds, which enterprising scavengers removed with the help of old oyster cans attached to long poles. They then rendered out the grease by boiling the liquid on a makeshift stove of bricks and sheet iron. Once separated, the grease was sold to the city's soap factories or, according to one rumor, to the oleomargarine producers of Chicago.[66]

Many so-called Ishmaelites supported themselves by hauling away bones, ashes, and other trash to the city's dump, where the materials were sorted by other families who informally owned—in some cases for multiple generations—different areas of the dump. Instead of appreciating the invaluable public service and hard labor performed in filthy working conditions involved in this precursor to contemporary recycling, Wright had only contempt for Ishmaelite junkmen like James Logsdon, whom he dismissed with the sentence "Like his family he is principally animal."[67]

Wright refused to see marginalized activities like scraping the ponds or hauling and recycling trash as real work—no matter how much sweat they required. Nor did he express sympathy for those unfortunate enough to depend on public charity or private handouts for their meager subsistence. His stinging portraits of these individuals anticipate the popular stereotype of the "welfare queen" by a century. For example, when Mary Lawson, a mother of nine children, justified her application for charity by stating "I consider [it] my right, and it is no disgrace to ask for help if you really need it. We really need it," Wright responded by condemning her as a "dirty, lazy, shiftless" woman who spent whatever money she got on lottery tickets.[68]

Mary Lawson was married to a man named William Gideon. Because of this and her notable "breeding propensities," Wright explained that "she and her family were known as 'Gideon's Band,' in the circle of charity." In a harbinger of the welfare reform debates of the 1990s, Wright also observed that "a diet of pauper bread breaks down the best of poor families, and the greatest unkindness to the poor is to encourage them to ask and accept charity—something for nothing."[69]

Ultimately, Wright's research does not support Oscar McCulloch's portrait of a nomadic tribe of thousands of interrelated paupers and criminals centered around the Ishmael family. Rather than belonging to a closely knit tribe of urban "savages," the people identified by Wright as Ishmaelites belonged to what we would now simply call the socioeconomic underclass of the city of Indianapolis. Many so-called Ishmaelites did have important things in common—particularly those who originally came from the Upland South—but there is nothing in Wright's notes to suggest that they viewed themselves as forming a community distinct from the city's broader mass of poor and working-class residents.

Nor did Wright provide any evidence to justify Hugo Leaming's later claim that members of the Ishmael family functioned as hereditary leaders or "patriarchs" of a community. On the contrary, Wright even noted that one of the Ishmaels' own in-laws, Priscilla Ross, looked down on the family. According to Wright, Ross "admitted that her daughter Mary had 'disgraced the whole family by marrying into that Ishmael family; but that she did not want that put on the record against her (Priscilla) for she felt the disgrace, and had disowned the daughter because she had stooped below her level.'"[70] When Wright informed Kate Thornton Ishmael of Ross's snobbery, however, she reacted by turning the tables: "Kate Ishmael cooled her nose in fine scorn when the Ross family was mentioned, and told me that she did not understand why Henry [Ishmael] had condescended to marry Mary Ross, although she did not much blame Mary for wanting to marry in a grade above her family."[71] Of course, it is possible that both Priscilla Ross and Kate Thornton Ishmael merely told Wright what they thought he wanted to hear about their respective in-laws.

Although Wright's unpublished notes do not support the existence of a triracial, crypto-Islamic community, they do shed light on why the Ishmael family itself captured the attention of men like McCulloch and Leaming. According to Wright, despite persistent efforts to stigmatize them, the Ishmaels remained fiercely proud of who they were. For several generations after arriving in Indianapolis, they held on tightly to cultural values and traditions they had brought with them from Kentucky, including a belief in spirits and omens and a decidedly non-Victorian view of women's social roles. The Ishmaels resisted assimilating into the newly industrialized wage-labor economy that came to dominate Indianapolis in the second half of the nineteenth century. Instead, they continued to engage in a variety of increasingly stigmatized economic activities that allowed them to retain their independence. The family's frontier spirit and extended kinship ties—rather than the "wandering blood" suggested by McCulloch—also motivated them to engage in their most distinctive behavior: the annual migrations they undertook, apparently in search of odd jobs and in order to visit relatives in small towns throughout the Midwest. This, above all, had fired the imagination of Oscar McCulloch and inspired him to cast the Ishmaels as the central characters in a large tribe of wanderers, despite the fact that most people in Wright's notes do not appear to have participated in these peregrinations.

In constructing his version of the Tribe of Ishmael, McCulloch ignored a distinctive feature of the Ishmael family that does appear in Wright's notes, namely, its racially integrated character. Save for a single "half-breed" Indian ancestor, McCulloch depicted all of the Ishmaels as white descendants of Anglo-Saxon convicts and indentured servants. Yet, according to Wright, members of several generations of the Ishmael family in Indiana married individuals with African American or Native American ancestry. These mixed-race couples were apparently welcomed into the Ishmael family fold rather than shunned as pariahs. Significantly, however, Wright portrayed all of the African Americans who married into the Ishmael family as light-skinned, and it is possible that they passed as whites in order to avoid problems with the authorities. This may explain why McCulloch had failed to note the presence of individuals with African American ancestry in his published account of the Ishmaels.

On the other hand, Hugo Leaming later employed the existence of a handful of mixed-race individuals in the Ishmael family to justify his exaggerated claim that the entire Tribe of Ishmael was "'colored,' therefore 'Negro' or African-American (but including others, by marriage or adoption)," when, in fact, most of the Ishmaels, not to mention a vast majority of the so-called Ishmaelites, were Anglo-Saxon in origin.[72]

Both McCulloch and Leaming, therefore, argued from the part to the whole, extending certain distinguishing characteristics of the Ishmael family itself to a larger body of people whom they called the "Ishmaelites." Although they employed the same method, McCulloch and Leaming arrived at dramatically different conclusions. McCulloch's Ishmaelites were a wandering lot of paupers and criminals of Anglo-Saxon descent; Leaming's were a nomadic community of escaped slaves and their white and Native American allies.

The Charity Organization Society files on members of the Ishmael family and their "connections" reveal other important aspects of the Tribe of Ishmael's story. Along with newspaper articles, these files indicate the extent to which the Ishmael family was demonized in the city of Indianapolis by the late 1870s and early 1880s. Merely possessing the Ishmael surname during this period was enough to transform someone into a marked man or woman. Indeed, the case files reveal that some members of the Ishmael family employed pseudonyms—including Wishmeyer, Ishman, and Ashem—in order to avoid the stigma associated with their own name. Not only did Ishmael family members face prejudice from the COS and other institutions, but they must have encountered discrimination when searching for jobs and housing, thereby contributing to a vicious cycle of marginalization and poverty.

The case files also indicate that the number of so-called Ishmaelites who received charity was relatively small compared to the thousands of individuals who sought aid from the COS in Indianapolis during the last two decades of the nineteenth century. Those Ishmaelites who did come to the attention of the COS often did so because they were reported for begging, not because they directly applied for aid themselves. Frequently, such individuals would be denied aid on the grounds that they were "undeserving," despite their desperately poor living circumstances. These factors suggest not only that many Ishmaelites sought to support themselves independently, albeit by means that were scorned by middle-class society. but also that at least in some cases they did not expect to receive aid from the Charity Organization Society.

These files open a door onto the nature of poor relief in America at the end of the nineteenth century. Today, after decades of programs like Aid to Families with Dependent Children (AFDC or "Welfare"), Medicaid, Medicare, Social Security, and public housing, we are used to the idea of the federal government providing aid to our neediest citizens—the nation's poor, children, the elderly, sick, and homeless. Before the reforms of the New Deal, however, the most vulnerable members of society relied on local governments and private charities, like the COS in Indianapolis, for piecemeal handouts of food, clothing, shoes, and fuel. The most indigent were placed—sometimes forcibly— in draconian institutions like almshouses and poor farms. Meanwhile, those poor folk, like members of the Ishmael family, who were unlucky enough to be deemed "undeserving" by the "scientific" methods developed by Oscar McCulloch and his colleagues on both sides of the Atlantic, could frequently expect plenty of condemnation but little if any real help.

CHAPTER 4

The Ishmaelites and the Menace of the Feebleminded

Arthur Estabrook, the man who resurrected the Tribe of Ishmael in the early part of the twentieth century, was a native New Englander from a middle-class family. After receiving a B.A. and M.A. from Clark University—the training ground for many prominent eugenicists, including Henry Goddard, author of *The Kallikaks*—Estabrook worked there as an assistant zoologist from 1906 to 1907. In 1910, he completed his Ph.D. in biology at Johns Hopkins University. Later that year, he joined the newly established Eugenics Records Office, where he embarked on a series of family studies. Over the next two decades, Estabrook would become the most prolific eugenics field worker in the history of the movement.

Located in Cold Spring Harbor, New York, the Eugenics Records Office was founded in 1910, alongside the older Station for Experimental Evolution. Whereas the station had focused on the selective breeding of sheep, mice, trout, sow bugs, snails, and other creatures large and small, the Eugenics Records Office was "the first building to be erected and devoted solely to the study of human evolution or race biology."[1] Together, these constituted the Department of Genetics of the Carnegie Institution in Washington, D.C.

Among the prominent individuals who advised the Eugenics Records Office in its work were Alexander Graham Bell, better known today for his invention of the telephone than for his enthusiasm for eugenics; David Starr Jordan, a biologist and a friend and early admirer of Oscar

Figure 4. Arthur Estabrook, 1921. (The American
Philosophical Society)

McCulloch in Indianapolis, who went on to become the president of
Stanford University; and a host of other scholars from prestigious institutions, including Harvard, Johns Hopkins, Cornell, and the University
of Chicago. Funding for projects came from Mary Harriman (the widow
of the railroad financier E. H. Harriman), John D. Rockefeller, and other
important philanthropists. In short, the Eugenics Records Office did not
operate on the margins of American society during the first few decades
of the twentieth century, but at its very center.

   Under the directorship of Charles Davenport, a former professor at the
University of Chicago and secretary of the Committee on Eugenics of the
American Breeders' Association, the office trained field-workers to collect
genealogical data on both individuals and groups. While the field-workers
investigated the ancestry of so-called geniuses, they were particularly

interested in the family trees of "the submerged tenth, the socially inadequate persons who must be prevented from reproducing . . . the insane, the
feebleminded, the paupers, the epileptic, the criminals, and so on."[2]

For his first family study, Arthur Estabrook targeted a "highly inbred
rural community of New York State," which he nicknamed the "Nam
family." This seemingly innocuous pseudonym actually encoded a
deeply disturbing message, for "Nam" was "Man" spelled backwards.
According to Estabrook, the Nam came by their atavistic character naturally, since, like the Indianapolis branch of the Ishmael family, they
originally sprang from a union between a "roving" pioneer, in this case
Dutch, and "an Indian princess."[3]

In January 1912, after publishing his research on the Nam, Estabrook
began to work on his second family study, a follow-up to Richard
Dugdale's earlier investigation of the Jukes. Almost immediately,
Estabrook encountered difficulties in his research. On January 17, he
wrote a letter from Kingston, New York, to his supervisor, Charles
Davenport, in which he reported that he had visited some of the Jukes and
found their current situation to be problematic. Estabrook noted that in
contrast to the people Dugdale had first encountered, contemporary
"Jukes" were no longer concentrated in a single locale and were therefore
less isolated and more worldly. He also described them as much smarter
than the people Dugdale had described thirty years earlier and more reluctant to share personal details with outsiders likehimself.[4] Significantly, the
very factors that Estabrook identified as problematic—greater intelligence,
decreased social segregation, increased worldliness—indicated that the
Jukes had benefited from the environmental changes that had occurred in
the years since Dugdale first encountered them. Of course, for a eugenicist
like Estabrook, the positive transformation of the Jukes *was* a problem,
since it directly contradicted his hereditarian assumptions.[5]

Not surprisingly, Davenport was displeased with the findings of his
protégé. On May 16, he complained in a letter to Estabrook, who was
still in Kingston conducting research, that after reviewing the material
Estabrook had sent him, he was forced to conclude that almost none of
it was publishable in its present form and, in fact, would do a disservice
to both Estabrook and the Eugenics Records Office.[6] In fact, so many
changes were necessary before it could be published, that in Davenport's
view, their working relationship could be compared to that of someone
who provides a slab of rock to a sculptor who then shapes it into a statue.

For this reason, Davenport claimed, he, rather than Estabrook,
deserved to have his name listed as the study's primary author. He

assured his employee that he had absolutely no desire to claim work that rightfully belonged to someone else, especially to a junior colleague trying to make a name for himself. But Davenport also complained that while Estabrook hoped to raise his public profile by publishing the account, Davenport only sought to protect the reputation of the Eugenics Records Office. The chilly correspondence between the two men reveals fault lines beneath the preternaturally smooth surface that the eugenics movement sought to present to the public and confirms Mark Haller's rather ironic observation that Charles Davenport was haunted by "vague feelings of inferiority" throughout his life, despite the supposedly superior "germ plasm" that he possessed.[7]

These behind-the-scenes struggles over the Jukes remained hidden. When the study appeared in print, Estabrook was listed as its sole author, and Davenport contributed a preface in which he suppressed any hint of the problems that Estabrook had encountered at the beginning of his research. Instead of publicly acknowledging Estabrook's private admission that environmental changes had supposedly made the Jukes much smarter in the years since Dugdale's investigation, Davenport falsely claimed in his preface that they "still show the same feeble-mindedness, indolence, licentiousness, and dishonesty, even when not handicapped by the associations of their bad family name and despite the fact of being surrounded by better social conditions."[8] In the years to come, other eugenicists would follow this lead and suppress or manipulate evidence in order to paint more sinister portraits of their subjects—sometimes quite literally, as in the case of Henry Goddard's crude retouching of Kallikak photographs to create what one photographic expert at the Smithsonian later called "the appearance of dark, staring features, sometimes evilness, and sometimes mental retardation. It would be difficult to understand why any of this retouching was done were it not to give the viewer a false impression of the characteristics of those depicted."[9]

In retrospect, Estabrook's follow-up study of the Jukes confirms many of the problems endemic to the eugenics movement. At the time, however, eugenicists and their allies praised it wholeheartedly. For instance, Gertrude Hall, the inspector for the State Board of Charities of New York, gushed in a letter to Estabrook, "Your 'Jukes in 1915' is a masterpiece. It is delightful reading," a startling compliment for a mind-numbing litany of crime, disease, and degradation.[10] Emboldened by his success, Estabrook next set his sights on what would be his most ambitious undertaking yet: a follow-up study of the Tribe of Ishmael.

In the years after Oscar McCulloch's death, the state of Indiana had become a laboratory for the eugenics movement, thanks to advocates like John Hurty, the Indiana State Health Commissioner; Thurman Rice, a professor at the Indiana University School of Medicine; Amos Butler, the secretary of the Indiana Board of State Charities (later the Indiana Department of Welfare); and Harry Sharp, a physician at the Indiana Reformatory, who pioneered vasectomy surgery in the United States. On December 14, 1914, Hurty articulated the chilling ideology of these men in a talk entitled "Practical Eugenics in Indiana," delivered before the New York Academy of Medicine: "Now, at least, we realize that the human race is to be improved by applying exactly the same laws to man that will perfect the breed of the lower animals. Defective people generally curse the day of their birth. . . . I thoroughly believe that nine out of ten of those who suffer from inherited infirmities would rather be dead than alive."[11]

In 1905, Indiana was among the first states to pass a eugenics law forbidding the feebleminded, the insane, chronic alcoholics, and other undesirables to marry. Two years later, in 1907, the state passed the country's first compulsory sterilization law. Known as the Indiana Plan, this statute empowered a board of experts to order the sterilization of so-called idiots, imbeciles, rapists, and other criminals in state institutions. This statute represented the culmination of years of lobbying by Sharp, who, by his own account, had performed hundreds of vasectomies on inmates—without administering local or general anesthetic—since importing the operation from Europe in 1899. Like Oscar McCulloch before him, Sharp justified his actions by selectively interpreting the biblical commandment to "be fruitful and multiply." As he put it: "Shall we permit idiots, imbeciles, and degenerate criminals to continue the pollution of the race simply because certain religionists teach that 'marriages are made in heaven'; and that the 'function of procreation is divine'? . . . To me these are the most damnable heresies."[12]

Many Hoosiers saw a direct link between Oscar McCulloch's groundbreaking work on the Tribe of Ishmael and the state of Indiana's pioneering eugenical policies. As Thurman Rice, who had published *Racial Hygiene: A Practical Discussion of Eugenics and Race Culture,* observed: "To a considerable extent the pre-eminent position taken by the State of Indiana in the matter of eugenical legislation in 1907 can be traced to his [McCulloch's] studies."[13] Kate Parker, who served as the registrar of the Charity Organization Society and had produced a genealogical diagram of the Tribe of Ishmael for Oscar McCulloch during the 1880s, echoed this sentiment in a letter to McCulloch's son, Carleton.[14] On May 7, 1914,

Parker requested a photograph of the elder McCulloch that she could send to Harry Laughlin, a prominent eugenicist. According to Parker, Laughlin "speaks of your father, Dr. Dugdale and Dr. Graham Bell as the pioneers in Eugenics work in this country, and wants a little history of each, and I am glad to do what I can to preserve the record of your father's work, which marked him as the foremost man in the country in social work."[15]

By the time Arthur Estabrook arrived in Indianapolis in 1915, some preliminary research on the Tribe of Ishmael had already been conducted by Mary Ogden Dranga, one of the many young women employed as field-workers by the Eugenics Records Office. In *White Trash,* her excellent survey of eugenic family studies, Nicole Hahn Rafter has demonstrated that women were considered better eugenical field-workers than men for several reasons.[16] First, women were viewed as less threatening and, therefore, better able to glean embarrassing personal information from reluctant subjects. Second, women were seen as more acute observers than men; as Henry Goddard put it: "The people who are best at this work, and who I believe should do this work, are women. Women seem to have closer observation than men."[17] Many young women, in turn, took advantage of the opportunities for professional training offered by the eugenics movement at institutions like the Vineland (New Jersey) Training School for Feebleminded Girls and Boys—opportunities that were typically denied to them in the more established sciences. By 1916, the Eugenics Records Office had trained 131 women and only 25 men to be field-workers.[18]

Except for a brief stint in the army after the United States entered World War I, Arthur Estabrook devoted much of the next seven years to his study of the Ishmaelites. During the same period, he helped conduct a survey for the Indiana Committee on Mental Defectives, which provided him with complete access to the state's legal, hospital, and social service records.[19] The survey's goal was to count the number of so-called mental defectives—epileptics, the insane, and the feebleminded—living in Indiana. It was hoped that this would be the first step toward creating a national registry, something that Oscar McCulloch had first called for in his 1891 presidential address to the National Conference of Charities and Correction. In more ways than one, therefore, Arthur Estabrook had inherited Oscar McCulloch's mantle, though unlike his predecessor, he seems to have lacked any compassion for the people he studied.

As in his earlier fieldwork on the Jukes, Estabrook initially encountered difficulties when he tried to gather information on the Ishmaelites. In a letter to Davenport dated November 17, 1915, Estabrook complained from Indianapolis that several factors were hampering his research: many of the Ishmaelites had left Indianapolis and settled elsewhere, and those who remained dissembled when they spoke with Estabrook, often denying that they were related to their own family members, making it difficult for him to construct the kind of pedigrees that were the stock and trade of eugenics family studies.[20] A few months later, on February 16, 1916, Estabrook informed Davenport that the Ishmaelites had now spread to nearly every county in Indiana, as well as to other states throughout the Midwest, including Illinois, Iowa, Kansas, Missouri, and Nebraska.[21]

These letters reveal two important changes among the Ishmaelites since the days of Oscar McCulloch. Many so-called Ishmaelites appear to have become wary of investigators and were reluctant to share information with Estabrook that might later be used against them or their relatives. Although their suspicions were understandable, given the ongoing attempts to monitor them, Estabrook reacted angrily to what he saw as the Ishmaelites' deceit. In addition, the Ishmaelites, like the Jukes, had scattered around the country since first being identified by McCulloch. Rather than interpreting this as a sign that they no longer constituted a distinct community—if, in fact, they ever had—Estabrook would argue in his published and unpublished writings that the Ishmaelites had now become a nationwide problem.

In order to conduct his research more effectively, Estabrook asked Davenport to help him secure a car so that he could visit rural areas that lacked train service. The first research trip Estabrook undertook was to Kentucky, where he gathered information about the Ishmael family in that state. He informed Davenport in his letter of February 16, 1916, that one branch of the family included several medical doctors and others who owned land.[22] A short while later, on March 31, Estabrook wrote a letter from Indianapolis to Lewellys Barker, a member of the Eugenics Record Office's Board of Scientific Directors, in which he reported that the Ishmaels and Daniel Boone had known one another in Kentucky.[23] These discoveries indicated that at least some of the Ishmael family members had been hardworking pioneers and frontiersmen. Predictably, Estabrook would later downplay or suppress these details in his published writings on the tribe.

The war interrupted Estabrook's research on the Ishmaelites, as well as his correspondence concerning the community. We pick up the trail again at the beginning of 1920, when Estabrook wrote Davenport a letter from Staten Island—where he and his wife had settled—in which he requested financial support to complete his study of the Tribe of Ishmael.[24] When Davenport responded positively, Estabrook packed his things and moved back to Indianapolis, where for the next two years, he and female assistants such as Corinne Eddy conducted interviews, examined penal, hospital, and other records, and traveled to communities throughout the upper Midwest to track down members of the tribe.

On August 19, 1921, Estabrook complained in a letter to Davenport that many members of the Tribe of Ishmael had spent the war years traveling from city to city in search of the higher wages that World War I had ushered in for laborers.[25] This information troubled Estabrook for several reasons. The Ishmaelites' dispersion made it difficult to locate them and suggested that they no longer constituted a cohesive community or tribe. The mobility of the Ishmaelites during the war years was clearly motivated by the search for employment and therefore undermined the claim that they traveled because of a hereditary impulse to wander. The fact that many members of the tribe had become part of the wage-labor industrial economy also directly contradicted the standard portrait of the Ishmaelites as a community of criminals, beggars, and gleaners: that is, the undeserving poor.

Ironically, Estabrook's own preliminary research indicated that the Ishmaelites' chronic poverty had more to do with the unavailability of decent-paying jobs than it did with their supposed predisposition to laziness or constitutional inability to work. Indeed, he inadvertently confirmed this cycle later in the same letter when he noted, "With the present industrial depression and the return to unemployment on the part of some of the Ishmaels, the former low standards of living have again been reached." Rather than supporting a hereditarian interpretation, therefore, Estabrook's private observations to Davenport pointed to environmental explanations for the Tribe of Ishmael's changing economic fortunes.

Arthur Estabrook publicly presented his findings on the Tribe of Ishmael for the first time in the July–August 1921 edition of *Eugenical News,* the official organ of the Eugenics Research Association, established by Davenport and Laughlin in 1916. Despite the dispersal of the Ishmaelites, Estabrook was able to compile a pedigree of the tribe, if an incomplete one. His brief report, however, was basically a rehash of McCulloch's work on the nineteenth-century Ishmaelites, with one very important addition. Whereas Oscar McCulloch had omitted any discussion of intelligence in his published account of the Tribe of Ishmael, Estabrook emphasized that the ultimate source of the Ishmaelites' economic and social problems was their endemic "feeblemindedness."[26]

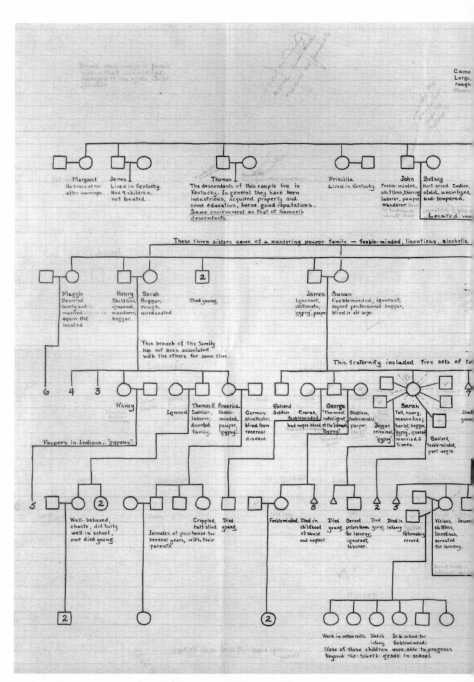

Figure 5. Arthur Estabrook's pedigree of the Tribe of Ishmael, circa 1921. (The American Philosophical Society)

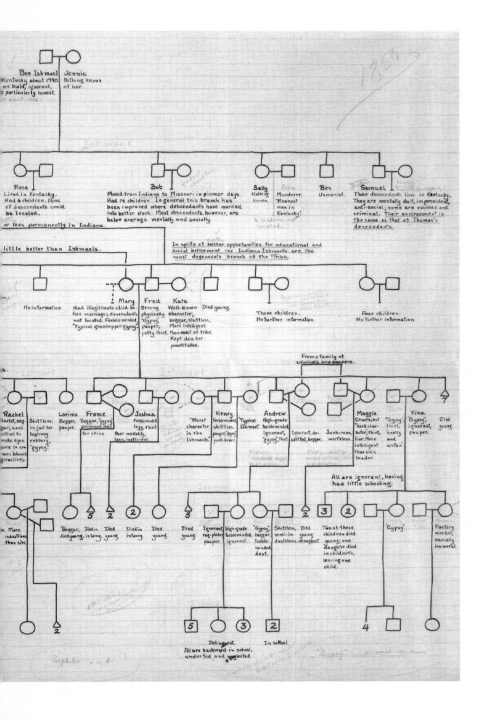

The possibility of a causal link between low intelligence, antisocial behavior, and poverty had already become a topic of discussion in the final decades of the nineteenth century. In 1884, for example, Isaac Kerlin, the superintendent of the Pennsylvania Training School for Feebleminded Children had asked: "How many of your criminals, and prostitutes are congenital imbeciles?"[27] But the idea that people of low intelligence constituted a national threat—a phenomenon that Mark Haller in his history of the American eugenics movement has called the "myth of the menace of the feebleminded"—did not take off until the beginning of the twentieth-century.

The so-called feebleminded were held to pose a far greater eugenical threat than "idiots" (those with a mental age of two years or younger) and "imbeciles" (those with a mental age of three to seven years), for the same reason that cacogenic native-born whites posed an even greater eugenical threat to middle-class America than blacks or immigrants from Southern and Eastern Europe. While idiots and imbeciles—like blacks and undesirable immigrants—were usually easy to identify and therefore to regulate, the feebleminded, as "high-grade" defectives with a mental age of eight to twelve years, could frequently pass as "normal." So much so, in fact, that until eugenicists and psychologists began to wage their campaign against the feebleminded, many Americans did not even know they existed. As Henry Goddard told a gathering of the American Association for the Study of the Feeble-Minded in 1910: "I presume no one in this audience, certainly none of the superintendents of institutions need to be reminded that the public is entirely ignorant of this particular group."[28]

More than any other eugenicist, Goddard spearheaded the efforts to identify and regulate the feebleminded in the United States. In 1908, he translated the work of the French psychologist Alfred Binet into English and began to employ Binet's intelligence scale at the Vineland Training School for Feebleminded Girls and Boys, where he was the director of research. Whereas Binet had never intended his scale to be used as the basis for a rigid social hierarchy, Goddard enthusiastically advocated this idea. Realizing that the term *feebleminded* was misleadingly ambiguous, Goddard even coined the new word *moron* (from the Greek word *moronia* or "foolish") to describe "persons who are incapable of adapting themselves to their environment and living up the conventions of society or acting sensibly."[29]

Not surprisingly, Goddard also championed the view that intelligence, in general, and feeblemindedness, in particular, were hereditary.

Morons were born not made, according to Goddard. Like other eugenicists, he enthusiastically embraced the rediscovery of the nineteenth-century geneticist Gregor Mendel's pioneering work on peas. Applying Mendel's conclusions to human characteristics, Goddard naively assumed that a single gene determined intelligence. This meant that "if both parents are feeble-minded all the children will be feeble-minded. It is obvious that such matings should not be allowed. It is perfectly clear that no feeble-minded person should ever be allowed to marry or to become a parent." Not only did environmental factors play an insignificant role in creating feeblemindedness, according to Goddard, but improving their surroundings did little to raise the intelligence of morons, a perspective that Stephen Jay Gould has described as "the equation of 'heritable' with 'inevitable.'"[30]

The efforts of Henry Goddard and others, including Lewis Terman, a native of Indiana who developed the Stanford-Binet exam in 1916, resulted in the wide-scale intelligence testing of millions of army recruits, immigrants, and others during the first few decades of the twentieth century. This testing produced some rather astounding results. For example, in one highly tendentious study of new immigrants to Ellis Island, Goddard concluded that 79 percent of the Italians and 83 percent of the Jews were feebleminded—notwithstanding the fact that they possessed enough intelligence to make the difficult journey to America. Eventually, even Goddard found it impossible to stomach his own dubious findings. By 1928, he had reversed himself and now asserted that feeblemindedness was "not incurable" and that most feebleminded individuals did not require institutionalization.[31]

Like Goddard, Arthur Estabrook was an early and committed convert to the new science of the feebleminded. At a January 6, 1916, meeting of the Indiana Committee on Mental Defectives, Estabrook emphasized the importance of specialists in the field: "An expert on feeble-mindedness will in many cases detect feeble-minded, where perhaps the physician who is not a specialist in that line, would not, and the social worker, on account of his sympathy, may hesitate to pronounce feeble-minded."[32] Estabrook added that physicians often knew the feebleminded members of their communities but "may not at that time be thinking of them as such." Feeblemindedness, therefore, was not a new phenomenon. On the contrary, it had always existed right under the noses of physicians and social workers. The problem was that members of these professions were typically unable—either by training or temperament—to diagnose the condition. What was required, therefore, was a new class of professionals, one that possessed the necessary skills and ideological orientation to identify the feebleminded. Estabrook saw himself as part of this important vanguard, and during his time in the army in World War I, he administered intelligence tests to army recruits in Georgia, as part of a broader initiative designed by Robert Yerkes, a prominent psychologist and primatologist, which resulted in the evaluation of 1.75 million recruits.

In September 1921, soon after his article on the Tribe of Ishmael appeared in *Eugenical News,* Estabrook traveled from Indianapolis to New York, to deliver a talk before the Second International Congress of Eugenics held at the American Museum of Natural History. Alexander Graham Bell presided over the week-long gathering, where papers were delivered by professional eugenicists from the Carnegie Institution, as well as scholars from Columbia University, Johns Hopkins, Princeton, the University of Michigan, the University of Texas, and a host of other institutions. The papers ranged from the "Individual and Racial Inheritance of Musical Traits" to "The Genetics of Fecundity in the Domestic Hen" to Estabrook's own "The Tribe of Ishmael."

As he had done in his earlier *Eugenical News* article, Estabrook described McCulloch's Tribe of Ishmael to his audience as a "large group of feeble-minded folk." He did not support this inflammatory claim with evidence from intelligence tests, however. Indeed, Estabrook even stated that "in a paper such as this, statistics and family histories are of little value to tell the story and are out of place." Instead, Estabrook cited the Ishmaelites' supposedly deviant behavior as conclusive proof of their collective feeblemindedness: "The men were shiftless; the women, immoral, and the children, ill-fed and clothed, the typical feeble-minded people who are so easily recognized today."[33] The clues provided by an individual's physical appearance and behavior were as reliable as the results of an intelligence test—that is, if they were properly interpreted by an expert on feeblemindedness such as Estabrook himself. In this regard, Estabrook was following the lead of Goddard, who had asserted in 1913, "After a person has had considerable experience in this work, he almost gets a sense of what a feeble-minded person is so that he can tell one afar off . . . [and] pick out the feebleminded without the aid of the Binet test at all."[34]

Yet unlike the feebleminded individuals referred to by Goddard, Arthur Estabrook was diagnosing Ishmaelites who had lived during the nineteenth century. How could Estabrook possibly identify people as feebleminded when he had never actually observed them? The answer is that Estabrook, like other self-styled experts in the field, firmly believed that he could identify someone as feebleminded on the basis of second-hand reports alone—in this case, Oscar McCulloch's account of the Tribe of Ishmael.

Estabrook's retrospective diagnosis of the Ishmaelites as feeble-minded represents the flip side of efforts by Francis Galton in *Hereditary Genius* (1869) and more contemporary eugenicists such as Lewis Terman and Catherine Cox, to measure and rank the intelligence of hundreds of deceased individuals, including Mozart, Cervantes, and Copernicus. These famous high achievers were not only evaluated on the basis of their own merits but also on the basis of their parents' pro-fessional and financial accomplishments. The son of a wealthy physi-cian, for example, gained more IQ points than did the son of a poor cobbler, even if their own achievements were comparable. Moreover, an individual's "fossil IQ"—as Stephen Jay Gould has called it—suffered if he or she had ever exhibited behavior that was deemed antisocial (e.g., not always doing what he/she was told in school). Similarly, in his talk before the Congress of Eugenics, Estabrook claimed that the Ishmaelites were feebleminded because they "did much as they wanted to do and cared little for the opinion of others."[35] These absurd criteria reveal how unscientific the new science of intelligence really was.

Almost all of Estabrook's remarks to the Congress of Eugenics con-cerned Ishmaelites who had lived during the nineteenth century rather than those of his own day. Estabrook relegated discussion of contempo-rary members of the tribe to his conclusion, where he grimly noted that they "are continuing to mate like to like, and are reproducing their own kind." He conceded that a "few branches" of the tribe had "mated into better stocks," but added that their numbers were so small that they were "hardly noticeable." By contrast, Estabrook warned, the mass of cacogenic Ishmaelites "have now spread through the whole middle west and are continuing to spread the anti-social traits of their germ plasm with no check by society."[36]

Following his talk, Estabrook fielded questions from the audience. In response to one query, Estabrook stated that the tribe currently num-bered "about fifteen thousand individuals," even though he had earlier declared that "today no estimate of the number of Ishmaels can be made . . . but the number would not be less than ten thousand." When another audience member asked whether "there are any good Ishmaels," Estabrook responded that: "In the last decade or two there are a few good Ishmaelites. I think of the whole group, approximately two or three per cent might be classed as average persons, socially and intellectually. . . . I can think of but two or three individuals who have become what we would call exceptionally good individuals, socially adequate, from among the Ishmaels."[37]

After returning to Indianapolis from New York, Estabrook spent the next year tracing the fate of the tribe's members since the days of McCulloch. On August 11, 1922, he sent a letter to Davenport triumphantly declaring that he was done with his study of the Tribe of Ishmael and that it was ready to be published.[38] It had taken seven years but Arthur Estabrook had finally achieved his goal of producing a definitive follow-up study of the Ishmaelites. All that remained was to publish these findings in book form, as he had already done with the Nam and the Jukes. Despite his many years of hard work, however, Estabrook's "final report" on the Ishmaelites would never see the light of day.

It is unclear why Estabrook's book-length study of the Tribe of Ishmael was never published. Save for another status report that Estabrook sent to Davenport on August 4, 1923, in which he mentioned giving his manuscript and charts on the Ishmaelites to Harry Laughlin and his original data on the group to the Eugenics Record Office archives, there is no extant correspondence concerning the fate of his study. Moreover, the extensive materials on the tribe that Estabrook apparently transferred to the Eugenics Records Office and its officials are now missing. However, one copy of Estabrook's unpublished manuscript on the Ishmaelites did survive and is currently located among his personal papers at the State University of New York in Albany.[39]

This nearly three-hundred-page document represents the apex and the nadir of the eugenical family studies. It is arguably the most ambitious and the most flawed of the works produced by Estabrook, Goddard, and their colleagues. Ambitious, because it sought to trace the histories of nearly twenty supposedly interrelated families rather than a single clan like the Jukes or the Kallikaks; flawed, because even more than the average eugenical family study, Estabrook's work on the Tribe of Ishmael was full of contradictions, spurious assertions, faulty statistics, and significant omissions. Indeed, these flaws may have inspired Charles Davenport to nix publication of the Ishmaelite manuscript, as he had earlier threatened to do with Estabrook's admittedly problematic follow-up study of the Jukes.

Estabrook's account of the Ishmaelites opens with a discussion of earlier sources on the community and then segues into a general survey of the tribe's history and current situation before focusing on several branches of the Ishmael family itself, as well as sixteen other families supposedly belonging to the tribe. Estabrook concluded his work with a map of the tribe's annual migratory route, statistical tables, and appendices analyzing the purported rates and causes of the Ishmaelites' licentiousness, pauperism, gypsying, insanity, epilepsy, alcoholism, mental abilities, industriousness (or lack thereof), criminality, and fecundity.

Estabrook had hoped to achieve three primary goals in his study. The first was to confirm the claims made by Oscar McCulloch concerning the Ishmaelites of the nineteenth century. The second was to demonstrate that the Ishmaelites of his own day were still engaging in a similar set of degenerate activities. This was critically important. If contemporary Ishmaelites no longer exhibited the negative characteristics attributed to their ancestors—including wandering, unemployment, pauperism, criminality, licentiousness—it would suggest that environmental factors, rather than defective germ plasm, had played the decisive role in shaping their ancestors' aberrant behavior. Finally, Estabrook set out to prove that genetically based feeblemindedness was the ultimate source of the Ishmaelites' poverty and antisocial activities.

The first serious problem with Estabrook's work concerned his use of sources. According to Estabrook, Oscar McCulloch and his coworkers had compiled fifteen thousand pages of data on the Ishmaelites that were stored in the office of the Charity Organization Society in Indianapolis. Yet in his published study McCulloch had actually claimed to have had collected only seven thousand pages on the tribe, a figure that was probably an exaggeration in itself. Estabrook further asserted that all of this original data—save for "two folio books, one giving the genealogical trees of the 400 different families, the other an index to the destroyed data"—had been "inadvertently thrown away about 1895," or, alternatively, "about 1892." For this reason, he noted: "the present study has practically started anew with only the genealogical trees from the earliest known ancestor (i.e. known to McCulloch) to 1890 as available data."[40] Estabrook also neglected to stress one extremely important source of information that he had employed: James Frank Wright's notes. It is clear that Estabrook had access to this material, since he frequently paraphrased Wright's observations and sometimes even quoted them directly in his own study. Indeed, the front cover of Wright's notes in the Indiana State Archives explicitly states, "These notes were loaned to A. H. Estabrook by Mr. Wright in 1917." By not including them in his list of primary sources, Estabrook created the false impression that he had reconstructed the early history of the Ishmaelites de novo.

Other problems arise when we turn to Estabrook's overview of the Ishmaelites' early history. One of Oscar McCulloch's central assertions was that the Tribe of Ishmael comprised several hundred interrelated families. Yet Estabrook revealed that "many of the families were distant from the central Ishmael family by eight or nine connections."[41] Nor did all of these barely connected—or, as Estabrook put it, "more or less remote"—families live together in Indianapolis or even in central Indiana. Instead, Estabrook admitted that it was enough for a single member to "come in contact with the Charity Organization Society of public officials or McCulloch's investigators," for the entire family to be included in the tribe, no matter where they lived. These revelations seriously undermine the very notion of the Ishmaelites as forming a distinct community or subculture within the city of Indianapolis during the nineteenth century.

Like McCulloch, Estabrook sought to establish genealogical links between the Ishmaelites and the indentured servants, criminals, and prostitutes shipped to America from England in the colonial period. If such links were proven, they would help Estabrook and other eugenicists to transform the Tribe of Ishmael into a potent symbol for the dangers of unregulated immigration. Despite having access to records unavailable to McCulloch, Estabrook was forced to admit that he could not establish an "actual lineage connection" between the Ishmaelites and the "paupers, criminals, and lewd women" who were shipped to the colonies.[42]

Instead of a single community of nomadic families, as McCulloch had suggested, Estabrook argued that the Tribe of Ishmael actually comprised two somewhat distinct, though still overlapping groups that he labeled "summer gypsies" and "winter gypsies."[43] The first group had been the focus of McCulloch's study; the second was much smaller in number and, as its name suggested, consisted of families who chose to wander around the countryside during the winter rather than the summer. This difference reflected the fact that most winter gypsies worked in brickyards that were idle during the colder months.

By admitting that the winter gypsies regularly performed "real" work, Estabrook severed the link between two of the Ishmaelites' defining characteristics: wandering and pauperism. Probably for this reason, he asserted that the winter gypsy "families were of a slightly higher mental level than the summer gypsies."[44] In other words, because the winter gypsies worked steadily in an industrial setting they must have been more intelligent than the other Ishmaelites, even though they still couldn't resist their inherited impulse to wander.

Estabrook made another observation about the winter gypsies that may inadvertently shed light on the cultural origins of at least some of the people identified as Ishmaelites. According to his account, the winter gypsies annually "went south from Indianapolis into southern Indiana at the beginning of fall, in wagons, swapping horses, gambling and living as best they could." Later in the manuscript, Estabrook described one of these Ishmaelites as "horse trading when on the road and junking and rag picking when settled for a longer or shorter period in some town or city."[45] These descriptions are potentially significant because horse trading was the chief occupation of the Travellers who, as noted in chapter 2, immigrated to America in the nineteenth century and later settled in the Upland South. As the scholar Jared Harper has written, "about the time of the American Civil War . . . they abandoned all other occupations . . . and specialized in the mule and horse trade." Like the winter gypsies, the Travellers "camped by the roadside in a friendly farmer's field, living in wagons and tents," and conducted their trade during the colder months, specifically "from the middle of September to the end of April."[46] While none of these factors in itself constitutes solid proof, taken together they strengthen the possibility that some of the families identified as Ishmaelites were actually Travellers.

Despite their supposed differences in intelligence and industriousness, winter and summer gypsies alike inherited a "pioneering or restless spirit" from colonial ancestors who had migrated in stages from the "seacoast to Kentucky and Indiana." Before the frontier was settled, the pioneering spirit of the Ishmaelites' ancestors had served a useful purpose. Once the wilderness had given way to farms and cities, however, the same nomadic behavior created social problems between the Ishmaelites and their settled neighbors. Of course, millions of Americans had traveled cross-country during the nineteenth century in search of land, work, gold, or (in the case of the Mormons) religious freedom. The critical difference between them and the Ishmaelites was that these pioneers had set out on their travels for rational reasons, whereas the Ishmaelites felt compelled to travel due to hereditary and, therefore, implicitly, irrational impulses.

Oscar McCulloch was the first to suggest that the Ishmaelites' wandering was hereditary, but he lacked the eugenical terminology that Estabrook later possessed. Employing the technical language of his profession, Estabrook wrote in his manuscript, "It is apparent then that Nomadism in the Tribe of Ishmael acts as a sex-linked, recessive mono-hybrid trait." Since this "wandering trait" was recessive, he claimed, it could skip a generation, as "is seen in several instances where the off-spring [of Ishmaelites] have been wanderers but neither parent has had the trait."[47] Although Estabrook went so far as to include elaborate sta-tistical tables concerning the supposed occurrence of nomadism among the Ishmaelites, he never cited any real evidence for a genetic predispo-sition to wander for one simple reason: it did not exist.

Indeed, contrary to his own assertions, Estabrook's descriptions of the Ishmaelites' travels actually suggested that they were inspired by rational motivations, rather than by an inherited, irrational inclination. For example, Estabrook wrote that some members of the Ishmael family regularly "traveled to Missouri or Kansas by train visiting relatives and friends . . . later returning to the land to again accumulate a little" (120). He described another member of the tribe as "still wandering here and there. . . . Most of these trips are to the 'homes' of her various children, where she makes short visits" (168). Another Ishmaelite nick-named "Napoleon" "has always been a gypsy and only last year, 1921, made a long trip in a wagon to Tennessee and northern Alabama 'visitin' kin folk'" (211). Once again, these descriptions indicate that many of the Ishmaelites traveled in order to maintain close kinship ties, a prac-tice that reflected their Upland Southern cultural roots.

Other Ishmaelites, like millions of migrant laborers around the globe, traveled from place to place in search of work. Concerning one such individual, Estabrook observed that he "hauls ashes and junks at times or works as a day laborer. He is continually wandering about 'looking for work' as he expresses it. He formerly traveled by wagon but the train or the traction lines are his modes of conveyance now" (169). Another Ishmaelite, nicknamed "Hugo" by Estabrook, brought his family along on his journeys, during which he performed odd jobs as well as seasonal agricultural work:

> An inquiry among friends of Hugo in Indianapolis as to his whereabouts, elicited a smile and the following: "Why they don't know where you can find Hugo; he is here today, gone tomorrow. They go in a wagon, regular gypsies, you know. Why, they'll come through here in a wagon, furniture, pans, 'kittles', and everything to cook with, an' his wife and children, he takes them right along with him. Why, it was last spring (1920) he came through here in automobile, bags, baggage, pots, kittles, wife, furniture, kids and all, on his way down to Greensburg. They came back in a wagon; he sold the automobile and bought a wagon again." Hugo works

at any odd job, such as fruit picking, window washing, laboring and junking. (172)

In contrast to "Hugo" and his family, Estabrook noted that most Ishmaelites had stopped traveling the countryside in gypsy caravans twenty-five years earlier, that is, about 1900. Despite the Ishmaelites' supposedly inherited predisposition to wander, therefore, the vast majority of them were now sedentary. Estabrook addressed this potential contradiction in several ways. He asserted that most Ishmaelites had abandoned the road "when the Illinois, Iowa and Missouri frontiers became thickly settled and the gypsying in wagons thus became too difficult and complex for this class of high grade mental defectives" (233). The Ishmaelites' supposed feeblemindedness, therefore, had trumped their inborn nomadism. In addition to this tortured explanation, Estabrook also suggested that the tribe's impulse to wander had recently been sublimated into the search for industrial jobs:

> In the last five years due to the extremely high wages, even for undependable, unskilled and casual labor many of the Tribe have been moving from the country to the city and from one big industrial center to another, on the least excuse or provocation. *The lure of higher wages combined with the inherent restlessness of these people* has transplanted many during this period and the slightly higher standard of living due to the higher wage has made it difficult to find them in their new habitats. This lure has resulted in many of the Tribe leaving Indianapolis for other places as Cleveland, Detroit, Toledo, Chicago, etc., and here they seem to be engulfed in the industrial whirlpool and lost for the time being. (33; italics added)

By admitting that numerous Ishmaelites had relocated around the upper Midwest in search of high-paying industrial jobs, however, Estabrook undermined his own claims concerning the tribe's "unindustriousness and laziness" (231).

Like McCulloch, Estabrook asserted that in addition to their nomadism, "the two distinguishing traits of the members of the Tribe of Ishmael are the pauperism and the loose marriage relations" (39). He defined a pauper as "one without means except such as come from charity, especially public charity" (229). According to Estabrook, poor relief inevitably led to pauperism "because the feeble-minded always take the line of least resistance in any situation presented to them for solution. It is easier to beg than to work" (231). For too long, well-intentioned but misguided social programs, including "indoor care in institutions," had encouraged the congenitally feebleminded, such as the Ishmaelites, to become paupers. Even the organized or scientific charity earlier endorsed by Oscar McCulloch was counterproductive, because "the root of the problem has not be[en] touched; i.e. the low intellectual and therefore, correspondingly low industrial capacity of the mental defectives, the recipients, mainly, of poor relief" (231).

Yet, according to Estabrook's own testimony, the Ishmaelites actually received very little public or private aid. During the final decades of the nineteenth century, the Charity Organization Society had begun to encourage residents of Indianapolis to call the police whenever anyone came begging at the door. This campaign was so successful that "by the year 1900 street and house begging had almost ceased to exist in Indianapolis" (44). In the same period, Estabrook admitted that township relief was "reduced greatly in the Ishmael areas, especially in Indianapolis," although he complained that "Tribe members are still being aided in coal, food, burials and school books for the children" (46).

In Estabrook's opinion, giving free school books to desperately poor students might be charitable, but it was also useless, because "the school reaction of the children of the Tribe has been typical of that of defective stocks" (255). He conceded that many Ishmaelite children performed poorly in part because of environmental factors such as undernourishment, frequent illness, and irregular attendance, but adamantly asserted that the chief cause of their dismal grades was "a low mental condition."

Although he had done the best he could, Oscar McCulloch had failed to diagnose the Ishmaelites' inferior intellectual ability because "scientific knowledge of feeble-mindedness was meagre and not at all common" in his day (252). Moreover, even Estabrook conceded that "very few [Ishmaelites] were very low grade mentally; the matter of a trip across a wilderness in the very early part of the nineteenth century would have been too difficult a problem for such a grade of mentality to solve." Instead, most members of the tribe supposedly belonged to the highly nebulous category of "just below the average" (252).

Even though Estabrook characterized the Tribe of Ishmael as a community of feebleminded paupers, in his study he actually portrayed most individual Ishmaelites as members of the working poor, others as middle-class professionals, and even a few as well-off landowners. Astoundingly, according to Estabrook's own findings, most Ishmaelites do not appear to have relied on charity. Instead, they engaged in one of many occupations, including hotel clerk, commercial photographer, laundry worker, physician, preacher, plasterer, factory worker, cobbler, dressmaker, coal miner, bootlegger, prostitute, petty thief, store owner, farmer, politician, laborer, pump repairer, photo engraver, stenographer, telephone operator, soldier, packing-plant worker, sign painter, truck driver, junkman, musician, painter, seamstress, house cleaner, and restaurant worker. Some Ishmaelite junk dealers had actually gained semiofficial status since the days of McCulloch; one was even made "caretaker of the dump" in Indianapolis and given a badge by the city "indicating that he alone has the right to pick junk from that particular dump in return for which privilege he agrees to keep the dump levelled and to prevent the dumping of refuse not permitted by the Board of Health. . . . He owns two small lots and a house on the dumps and maintains a poor standard of living" (211).

Similarly, Estabrook was unable to provide hard evidence for his third defining feature of the Ishmaelites, namely, their "loose marriage relations." Like pauperism, licentiousness was not, in itself, an inherited characteristic, according to Estabrook. Instead, it was the "natural result" of feeblemindedness combined with inadequate sex education. Estabrook reiterated McCulloch's assertion that a majority of the houses of prostitution in Indianapolis were once run by Ishmaelites but conceded that "the amount of prostitution and illicit sexual relations occurring in this Tribe can never be estimated" and, even more significantly, that "no figures as to the number of people married, divorced, children born in or out of wedlock, etc., are presented in this report as the official registration of such data is so meagre especially before 1890" (41–42). Despite his lack of reliable statistics for the tribe's overall birth rate, Estabrook referred to the Ishmaelites as an "extremely prolific feeble-minded people" (53). Later, however, he conceded that "the fecundity rate in all these families is gradually becoming lower . . . indicating that smaller families are being produced in the later generations" (268).

In his account, McCulloch had claimed that there was little intemperance in the Tribe of Ishmael; by contrast, we have seen that Wright portrayed most of the Ishmaelites as heavy drinkers. Estabrook ignored Wright's account in favor of McCulloch's, even though he admitted that the Ishmaelites' low rate of alcoholism surprised him. By way of explanation, Estabrook suggested rather implausibly that "the unindustriousness and low economic development of the Tribe members in Indiana have precluded sufficient wages in the great majority of the folk for the use and especially the abuse of alcoholic drinks" (251). In other words, the Ishmaelites were too poor to drink.

For a supposedly cacogenic community, the Tribe of Ishmael also exhibited very low rates of insanity, epilepsy, and crime. On the basis of newly researched penal records, Estabrook admitted that the "Tribe people have not been particularly criminal in behavior" (262), a view that contrasted dramatically with McCulloch's earlier assertion that "the criminal record is very large. . . . Nearly every crime of any note belongs here" (4, quoting McCulloch). Like pauperism and licentiousness, Estabrook claimed that crime did "not behave according to any law of heredity," but it was "closely associated with a defective mental make-up" (267). One would therefore expect many, if not most, members of the tribe to have been criminals, since a "great majority" of the Ishmaelites were supposedly "feeble-minded folk" (252). The fact that most members of the tribe were law-abiding citizens, according to Estabrook's own data, indicates that his entire set of assumptions was deeply flawed.

In addition to painting a general portrait of the Tribe of Ishmael, Estabrook attempted to reconstruct the particular histories of nearly twenty families. Despite the small size of his sample relative to his estimate of the total number of Ishmaelites—over ten thousand—Estabrook claimed that it "gives a true cross section of the Tribe and is indicative of the genetic make-up and behavior of the whole four hundred families of the Tribe" (223). Although Estabrook relied extensively on the earlier work of McCulloch and Wright to flesh out these portraits, he also conducted original research into the fates of some of the more colorful members of the Tribe of Ishmael.

For instance, Estabrook discovered that Thomas Williams entered the poor house in 1891 and died there in 1896, following an unsuccessful operation (217). George Williams, Maggie Ishmael's fiery, scragglybearded husband, met an ignominious end in 1903 after being hit by a car. Like Wright before him, Estabrook was both fascinated and repelled by Robert Chism, whom he characterized as "a pseudo-leader and petty boss of many of the Tribe members." According to Estabrook, Chism was "of a 'light coffee color, had a high forehead and in later years, a little white wool, with the face of a saint'" (189). After arriving in Indianapolis in 1848, Chism served four terms in the Indiana State Penitentiary, two in Ohio, and one in Iowa, for a range of convictions including burglary, grand larceny, and counterfeiting. Estabrook admitted that Chism had published several pamphlets "over his name," but claimed that he "could read and write only a little" and therefore had "furnished the subject matter and told 'what he wanted written.'" In contrast to Hugo Leaming's later assertion that these publications had caused quite a stir in Indianapolis, Estabrook stated that "they were never considered seriously by anyone." According to Estabrook, Robert Chism died of gangrene in 1899 at the age of ninety-three (190).

From the perspective of the eugenics movement, the most important contribution that Estabrook could make with his study of the Ishmaelites was to demonstrate that contemporary members of the Indiana branch of the Ishmael family itself had continued to exhibit degenerate behavior, presumably because of their inferior germ plasm. Indeed, this was the primary reason for undertaking a follow-up study of the Tribe of Ishmael in the first place. We would therefore expect the Ishmaels of Indiana to constitute the centerpiece of Estabrook's study.

The surviving manuscript does contain a few pages devoted to John Ishmael and his descendants. For example, Estabrook remarked that John Ishmael—who was supposedly known as "Granddaddy Ishmael" by his family—never owned any property and died around 1870 or so in the Fountain County Poor Asylum. Concerning his character, Estabrook claimed that John Ishmael was "lazy and never worked hard or steadily. He was never averse to begging and brought his children up as professional beggars. . . . That he was feebleminded there is no doubt" (84–85). Like her husband John, Betsy Harbet, a "half breed Indian" who died at ninety, was also "no doubt . . . feebleminded" (86). Predictably, Estabrook provided no evidence for his retroactive diagnoses of John and Betsy Ishmael. Besides these thumbnail sketches, Estabrook also provided a few new details about other members of the family, noting, for example, that George Ishmael—"somewhat keen and shrewd in his way"—had married the widow of his own stepson, Joel Tillberry, in 1920 (91).

What is most notable about Estabrook's treatment of the Indiana Ishmaels, however, is that almost all of the pages (93–103) that he devoted to the actual Ishmael family are now missing from the only surviving manuscript. Significantly, Estabrook must have removed these pages from the manuscript himself, before transferring it along with his other papers to the special archives collection of the State University of New York at Albany. Although Estabrook promised in a letter to the director of the archives that he would mail the missing manuscript pages later, he never did. Given the critical importance of these very pages, it is hard to avoid the impression that Estabrook did not wish this material to be seen.

Perhaps the Ishmaels of Indiana suffered from the same "problem" as did the Jukes, namely, that more recent generations of the family no

longer exhibited the same degree of degenerate behavior as their ancestors. This, of course, would undermine the eugenical premise of the
entire project and may be, as has been suggested, the reason that
Estabrook's book-length study of the Tribe of Ishmael was never published. Indeed, Estabrook alluded to this possibility in the manuscript,
when he admitted that the Ishmaels "do not seem to be as big a problem as formerly" (33) and even asserted that "the Ishmael family, on the
whole, including all branches, is better than the Tribe as a group. The
Ishmael family then is bettering itself slowly while improvement in
social reaction of the rest of the Tribe is only slightly noticeable" (269).

From a eugenical point of view, therefore, Estabrook's long-awaited
Tribe of Ishmael study could only be termed a failure. By his own admission, all of the implicated families were improving—if only "slightly"—
and the Ishmael family, the cornerstone of McCulloch's original
research, was clearly bettering itself. Although Estabrook claimed that
members of the Indianapolis branch of the Ishmaels were still displaying
degenerate behavior, the only surviving manuscript of the study lacks
precisely those pages that would document this assertion.

The central assumption of Estabrook's study was that feeblemindedness invariably led to higher rates of criminality, sexual promiscuity, and
pauperism. On the one hand, Estabrook argued—without the benefit of
intelligence tests and, in many cases, retroactively—that a large proportion of Ishmaelites were feebleminded. On the other hand, his own
research revealed that many families historically linked to the tribe were
currently engaged in "respectable" professions or, in some cases, were
involved in illegal (e.g., bootlegging) or extralegal (e.g., managing the
city dump) activities that required what Estabrook called a certain
"shrewdness." Either the Ishmaelites were not as feebleminded as
Arthur Estabrook claimed or the links between feeblemindedness, criminality, and pauperism were not as powerful as he asserted.

Estabrook was unable to provide any evidence that the Tribe of
Ishmael still constituted a distinct community—if it ever had. On the
contrary, all of his research pointed in an opposite direction, namely,
that the various families traditionally associated with the tribe had
ceased to exhibit any of the collective behavior that had formerly distinguished them from their neighbors in Indianapolis. Most notably,
Ishmaelite families had ceased to travel together on annual migrations
at least two decades before Estabrook completed his study in the early
1920s. While some individuals still traveled to visit relatives or search
for work, this behavior hardly constituted the veritable caravans

described during the nineteenth century and could not easily be called nomadism, even by the most enthusiastic eugenicist.

Since no correspondence on the subject appears to have survived, we do not know what Estabrook's colleagues at the Eugenics Records Office thought about his Tribe of Ishmael study. Undoubtedly the most damning evidence that the powerbrokers within the eugenics movement considered the work to be highly problematic is that it was never published, despite the fact that Estabrook and his supporters had invested several years and a considerable amount of money in the project. Moreover, this would have been the first eugenics family study to appear in print since 1919, when *Dwellers in the Vale of Siddem*, a study of the supposedly feebleminded "Yaks" family in Minnesota, was published.[48]

Although his Tribe of Ishmael study was never published, this would prove to be only a temporary setback for Arthur Estabrook. Indeed, he soon went on to play an important role in what would become the most notorious court case involving the eugenics movement: the state of Virginia's decision to sterilize a young, supposedly feebleminded woman named Carrie Buck.[49] In 1924, Arthur Strode, a lawyer representing the state of Virginia, asked Estabrook to investigate Carrie Buck and her mother, after local social workers failed to gather sufficient information regarding the two women's genealogical background and mental and moral character. Both Estabrook and his colleague Harry Laughlin, an expert in sterilization, then testified before the Circuit Court of Amherst County, Virginia. The men claimed that Carrie Buck was feebleminded, that her condition was inherited, and that it would likely be passed on to any offspring, including the infant she had already given birth to at the State Colony for Epileptics and Feebleminded. On the basis of this expert testimony, both the Circuit Court and the Virginia Supreme Court affirmed the state's right to perform involuntary sterilization. Several years later, in 1927, the *Buck v. Bell* case finally made its way to the United States Supreme Court, which ruled in favor of involuntary sterilization. As Justice Oliver Wendell Holmes, Jr., infamously declared: "Three generations of imbeciles are enough."[50]

More than half a century later, historians would uncover evidence that Carrie Buck's daughter, Vivian, had received above average grades in school, thereby giving lie to the claims that she was feebleminded. By that time, however, approximately sixty thousand Americans had been involuntarily sterilized. Despite the fact that the Supreme Court decision was never overturned, the practice was finally ended in the 1970s.

During the same period that he was testifying in the Carrie Buck case, Arthur Estabrook also conducted research for what would be his and, indeed, the entire eugenics movement's, last family study. In typical fashion, Estabrook and his coauthor, Ivan McDougle, a sociologist at Goucher College in Maryland, called their work *Mongrel Virginians: The Win Tribe*. Like the names of most cacogenic families or communities—indeed, the Tribe of Ishmael was the only exception—"Win" was a pseudonym. It reflected the purported "triracial" composition of the community and was an acronym standing for white, Indian, and Negro. Locally, however, the families in the Blue Ridge Mountains of Virginia studied by Estabrook and McDougle were known as "Isshies," an abbreviation of "Free Issues," a name given to slaves freed by their masters before the Civil War.

Mongrel Virginians presented itself as a "careful summary of the facts of history" rather than "as theory or as representing a prejudiced point of view." Despite this assertion, the study was predictably tendentious. Among the "facts of history" that Estabrook and McDougle recorded were the following:

> The persistency of Indian traits among the Wins appears remarkable when the remoteness of pure Indian blood is taken into consideration. When one sees a group of men walking along the county road they will always be found parading in single file and for the most part noncommunicative. . . . There is practically no music among them and they have no sense of rhythm even in the lighter mulatto mixtures. As is well known, the negro is "full" of music. . . . It would seem from these and many other observations that the negro temperamental characteristics are completely dominated by the Indian.[51]

Meanwhile, in their private correspondence, Estabrook and McDougle occasionally dropped even the thinnest veneer of scientific objectivity, revealing the crude racism that lay beneath the surface of their published work. For instance, in a letter dated May 3, 1924, McDougle wrote to Estabrook: "Miss Harned and I have interviewed and seen Silas Branham, Lottie Roberts and Rennie Johns over in the 'free love colony' since I last wrote. Lottie is as white as any white woman you ever saw while Silas is a typical coon although he has straight hair."[52]

Although Estabrook and McDougle focused their study on an obscure and geographically isolated community, their goal was anything but narrow. As they stated in the book's conclusion, "unquestionably the people covered by this study represent an ever increasing social problem in the South."[53] In addition to the so-called Wins, the authors provided a list of other triracial communities scattered throughout the southeast as far north as Delaware. These included the Pamunkey (called "Weromos" in the study), the Croatans (called "Rivers"), and the Chickahominies (called "Renabees"). Yet even these isolated mixed-race "tribes" were not the real problem that Estabrook and McDougle sought to tackle.

Instead, what they were really interested in was the contemporary threat of miscegenation between blacks and whites on a national scale. For this reason, Estabrook and McDougle added an unusual appendix to *Mongrel Virginians*, namely, a copy of the Virginia Racial Integrity Law of 1924, partially authored by Madison Grant, a racist ideologue whose work we will examine in the following chapter. This notorious piece of legislation, passed with the strong support of the eugenics movement, specified that "It shall be a felony for any person wilfully or knowingly to make a registration certificate false as to color or race." If found guilty of racially passing, individuals were subject to one year in a state penitentiary. Furthermore, in a section that became known as the "one-drop rule," the law prohibited "any white person in this state to marry any save a white person. . . . For the purpose of this act, the term 'white person' shall apply only to the person who has no trace whatsoever of any blood other than Caucasian."

The inclusion of the Virginia Racial Integrity Law in *Mongrel Virginians* hints at Arthur Estabrook's nefarious role in the law's implementation. Numerous letters between officials of Virginia's State Board of Health and Estabrook reveal how much the state relied on him to identify racially suspect individuals and potential cases of "miscegenation."[54] Arthur Estabrook's efforts in Virginia were only one part of a much broader war against racial passing and "race-mixing" fought by the eugenics movement and its allies during the 1920s. This war was fought on many fronts, including in the battle over immigration, a battle in which the Tribe of Ishmael would play a major role.

CHAPTER 5

The Tribal Twenties

Ishmaelites, Immigrants,
and Asiatic Black Men

In January 1924, Harry H. Laughlin, the superintendent of the Eugenics Records Office in Cold Spring Harbor, delivered an address to a London audience on the state of the eugenics movement in America. The talk was hosted by the Eugenics Education Society, whose first honorary president was Francis Galton, the man who originally coined the term eugenics in 1883. Following Galton's death in 1911, the society's mantle had passed to his younger cousin Leonard Darwin, son of Charles.

In one of the many ironies that marks the history of the eugenics movement, during this same trip to England, Harry Laughlin himself first began to exhibit symptoms of epilepsy. For the rest of his life, Laughlin would suffer from grand mal seizures, on one occasion almost driving his car into the ocean after suffering an attack.[1] Needless to say, Laughlin did not tell his English hosts about his newly discovered condition. Nor, when he began to draft model sterilization legislation, did his own condition prevent Laughlin from including epileptics among those who should be subject to involuntary sterilization.

In his speech before the Eugenics Education Society, Laughlin lavishly praised his English audience for providing America with "some of the finest stock in the world," but he added ominously, "We have received also some degenerate stock from the same nation. We should have sorted the human seed more carefully at the border." To illustrate his point, Laughlin cited the infamous case of the Tribe of Ishmael, the subject of the recent follow-up study by Arthur Estabrook:

Figure 6. Harry Laughlin, circa 1929. (The American Philosophical Society)

> Dr. A. H. Estabrook of the Eugenics Records Office has traced some families in the valleys of Indiana. They are descended from English stock, most likely from people dumped by the British penal authorities in Virginia. They travelled across the country to make way for better immigrants, and came finally to Indiana, where they spread over the state. They are known as the American gipsies. There are many hundreds of them. I do not know why they call these people the Ishmaels, but they are very numerous, and we can imagine a significant connotation for the name. America is suffering very much from them, but is waking to its danger. We shall have to provide some practical plan for getting rid of the stock.[2]

If even England could produce degenerates like the Ishmaelites, Laughlin argued, then other countries were liable to flood the United States with hordes of cacogenic immigrants unless strict quotas were enacted. Since the days of Oscar McCulloch, Laughlin claimed, the Tribe of Ishmael had grown into a national threat that required immediate and drastic attention. Laughlin did not spell out his own recommendations for "getting rid of the stock." Yet his audience would have already known the most effective option: sterilization, an area in which Laughlin was an expert.

Harry Laughlin's lecture before the Eugenics Education Society in London was only one salvo in a broader and ultimately successful campaign to limit immigration to the United States. In 1920, 1922, and 1924, Laughlin testified as an expert witness before the House of Representatives Committee on Immigration and Naturalization. He had come a long way from his modest childhood in Oskaloosa, Iowa, where he was one of ten children born to George Laughlin, a clergyman and teacher, and Deborah Laughlin, a supporter of women's suffrage and activist in the Women's Christian Temperance Society.

On April 16–17, 1920, Harry Laughlin delivered his first testimony, entitled "Biological Aspects of Immigration," before the committee, which was chaired by Albert Johnson from Washington State. Under questioning by Representative John Box from Texas, Laughlin emphasized that "immigrants ought to be made out of such stock that when they come to this country . . . [they] would develop into desirable citizens." Then, to illustrate what could happen if immigrants were not screened eugenically, Laughlin again invoked the terrible specter of the Tribe of Ishmael:

> You have all doubtless heard of the Jukes and Ishmaels; our field workers went to Indiana to study degenerate families, and found a certain name (now called the Ishmaels) so common that they said there must be something wrong with that family. They began to study it scientifically. To the first questions people would respond: "Poor things, they have never had an opportunity." But on further investigation it was found that they were the kind who would steal the bishop's silver if they got the chance; they were in institutions, in prison, and in the poorhouse. They were traced back into Kentucky and found to be about the same there, and then traced back to Virginia, where the clue seems to indicate that they had been deported from England, as was the former custom in that country. . . . That is one sort of study our association is making in immigration; we want to prevent any deterioration of the American people due to the immigration of inferior human stock.[3]

Nearly fifty years after Oscar McCulloch first discovered the Ishmael family, Harry Laughlin had transformed these descendants of the earliest pioneers into poster children for the dangers of unregulated immigration, one of the chief obsessions of the American eugenics movement during the 1920s. Despite their Anglo-Saxon background, the Ishmaelites were seen as forerunners of the Southern Italians, Eastern

European Jews, Syrians, and other supposedly inferior groups that Laughlin and his allies hoped to keep out of America. Indeed, the Tribe of Ishmael served as a particularly potent symbol precisely because most of its members were from the same stock as the eugenicists themselves. By citing the example of the Ishmaelites, eugenicists could argue that they held Anglo-Saxons to the same rigorous standards that they applied to other, far more numerous—and in their minds, more cacogenic—immigrant groups.

As far back as 1898, the pioneering biologist and eugenicist David Starr Jordan had identified the Tribe of Ishmael as the most striking evidence that "no race is so perfect that judicious weeding out could not improve it." Jordan insisted that eugenically inspired immigration restriction was not based on cultural bias but on objective, scientific criteria or, as he put it, "The essential danger of unrestricted immigration is not in bringing in an alien population strange to our language and customs. Language and customs count for little if the blood is good." Ironically, the best proof of this argument lay in early Anglo-Saxon immigrants like the Ishmaelites, who shared the same cultural background as other old-stock white Americans, but who nevertheless possessed bad blood: "Every family of 'Jukes' and 'Ishmaels' which enter at Castle Garden carries with it the germs of pauperism and crime." Such people, whether they were Anglo-Saxon, Jewish, or Italian, undermined the democratic principles of American society, since "the immigration of poverty, degradation, and disease make government by the people more and more difficult."[4]

Despite the evenhanded rhetoric of eugenicists like Jordan and Laughlin, in reality, the Ishmaelites were the exception that proved the rule. Eugenicists worked hard to identify cacogenic Anglo-Saxon groups like the Tribe of Ishmael that were already in the United States, but they also assumed that the vast majority of potential immigrants from England and other Northern European countries were eugenically desirable. By contrast, the same eugenicists categorized Jews, Italians, and Asians en masse as possessing inferior germ plasm. In the eyes of the eugenicists, therefore, most immigrants were potential Ishmaelites until proven otherwise by intelligence tests and other forms of screening. As Harry Laughlin stated in a work entitled *Immigration and Conquest*, "Racially the American people, if they are to remain American . . . can successfully assimilate in the future many thousands of Northwestern European immigrants. . . . But we can assimilate only a small fraction of the number of other white races; and of the colored races practically none."[5]

It would not take long for the efforts of Harry Laughlin and his colleagues to bear legislative fruit in Washington. Only a few months after Laughlin delivered his address to the Eugenics Education Society in London, the U.S. Congress passed the Immigration Restriction Act of 1924 (the Johnson Act), which set quotas of immigrants from each nation according to their percentage in the 1890 census—in other words, at the levels before the full force of the giant waves of immigration from Eastern and Southern Europe began to arrive at America's shores. In the following decades, this fateful decision would have tragic consequences. America closed its doors to increasingly desperate—and ultimately doomed—eastern European Jews, even as more generous quotas for immigrants from western and northern Europe went unfilled. Concerning this act, Stephen Jay Gould has written, "The eugenicists battled and won one of the greatest victories of scientific racism in American history."[6]

The eugenicists' use of the Ishmaelites in their successful campaign to restrict immigration exemplifies what John Higham, in his seminal study of American nativism, has called the "Tribal Twenties."[7] In the years following World War I, the United States experienced the Red Scare, the revival of the Ku Klux Klan and its spread to states outside of the South (including Indiana, where it became immensely powerful for a time), and the rise of scientific racism as an influential ideology. Many native-born whites, and some blacks as well, embraced essentialist identities that pointedly excluded and typically denigrated others on the basis of race, religion, and/or nationality.

The eugenicists' savvy decision to resurrect the Tribe of Ishmael at the height of this period tapped into America's burgeoning tribalism in several ways. The Ishmaelites were explicitly linked to a tribal identity that was only alluded to vis-à-vis other communities. Their name's powerful Arabic and Islamic associations evoked the looming Asiatic menace that, according to influential racists, was threatening to destroy the United States from both within and without. Indeed, one of the reasons that the Ishmaelites were chosen to represent the dangers of unrestricted immigration is that, although Anglo-Saxon themselves, they could signify the Asiatic threat. Thus, as in McCulloch's day, the Tribe of Ishmael's symbolic value during the 1920s was intimately linked to contemporary developments in American Orientalism.

The Asiatic menace was one of the chief obsessions of Madison Grant and Lothrop Stoddard, the two most influential racist ideologues in America between the world wars. Not surprisingly, both men took an active interest in eugenics and were members of the Galton Society (est. 1918), an elite forum that included David Starr Jordan, Charles Davenport, and Harry Laughlin. They also played prominent roles in the anti-immigration movement. Grant, in particular, was a close friend of Congressman Albert Johnson, and together they served on the eugenics subcommittee of the United States Committee on Selective Immigration.[8]

A patrician New Yorker and lifelong bachelor, Madison Grant belonged to a host of important organizations, including the American Museum of Natural History, the American Geographical Society, the New York Zoological Society (which he helped to found), and the Boone and Crockett Club, a gentlemen's hunting organization established by Teddy Roosevelt. In 1916, Grant published the work that catapulted him to fame: *The Passing of the Great Race,* a polemic against the decline of America's Nordic heritage, the "great race" of the book's title.

Following the lead of William Ripley, author of *The Races of Europe* (1899), Grant subdivided Europeans into three races: Nordics, Alpines, and Mediterraneans. Whereas aristocratic Nordics had long dominated America, the country was now being overrun by hordes of inferior Alpines and Mediterraneans, including Slavs, Jews, Italians, and Greeks. From Grant's perspective, the problem with the Alpines and Mediterraneans was that they were fundamentally Asiatic, with only an overlay of Nordic (i.e., purely European) blood: "We have shown that the Mediterranean race . . . forms part of a great group of peoples extending into southern Asia, that the Alpine race came from the east through Asia Minor. . . . Both of these races are, therefore, western extensions of Asiatic subspecies, and neither of them can be considered exclusively European. With the remaining race, the Nordic, however, the case is different. This is a purely European type."[9]

While Madison Grant emphasized the threat to Nordics from "Asiatic-European" immigrants entering the United States, his protégé Lothrop Stoddard stressed the growing danger posed by Asiatics abroad. In his highly popular 1920 work *The Rising Tide of Color: Against White World-Supremacy,* Stoddard clarified his ideological position at the outset: "a better reading of history must bring home the truth that the basic factor in human affairs is not politics, but race."[10] According to Stoddard, the devastating demographic impact of World War I and generations of low birth rates had made the Nordic race around the globe vulnerable to the growing dangers of immigration, Bolshevism, Pan-Islamism, and what his fellow racist Henry Ford called the "International Jew."

Instead of emphasizing the sociopolitical or religious dimensions of these seemingly disparate phenomena, Stoddard viewed them all through a racial lens and, even more specifically, as manifestations of a centuries-long "conflict between the East and the West—Europe and Asia." Concerning the Jews, for example, Stoddard noted that "the majority of the Jews of eastern Europe, the round-skulled Ashkenazim," who were then entering the United States in large numbers, were actually descendants of "Tatar and Mongoloid tribes settled in southern and eastern Russia. Chief among these were the Mongol Chazars."[11] In short, the Jews were Asiatic rather than European.

Likewise, the Red Scare was justified by portraying an Asiatic campaign against Nordic-dominated Europe and America: "Bolshevism in Russia means the elimination of the Nordic aristocracy and the dominance of the half-Asiatic Slavic peasantry. . . . Asia in the guise of Bolshevism with Semitic leadership and Chinese executioners, is organizing an assault upon western Europe."[12] Of course, if Ashkenazi Jews like Leon Trotsky (né Lev Bronshtein) were really descendants of "Mongol Chazars," then they could not constitute a "Semitic" Bolshevik vanguard, but this kind of inconsistency did not bother Stoddard.

Even more than the International Jew or the Bolsheviks, however, Stoddard saw Pan-Islamism as potentially the greatest future threat to Nordic hegemony. Stoddard wrote about Islam with some insight—he perceptively compared the rise of the Wahabi movement to the Protestant Reformation, for example—and even with some respect, although he also repeated tired canards about the Islamic world's decadent and violent character. In *The Rising Tide of Color,* Stoddard argued that Pan-Islamism did not presently pose a danger to white power but that this situation could easily change since "Islam is militant by nature, and the Arab is a restless and warlike breed. Pan-Islamism once possessed of the Dark Continent and fired by militant zealots might forge black Africa into a sword of wrath, the executor of sinister adventures."[13]

The threat posed by Islam, therefore, was that it could unite the peoples of Asia and Africa under a single banner opposed to Nordic Europe and America. So convinced was Stoddard of the potential Islamic danger that in 1921, he even published an entire work on the subject, entitled *The New World of Islam.* After devoting nearly four hundred pages to the topic, Stoddard concluded that "The 'Immovable East' has been moved at last—moved to its very depths. . . . The world of Islam, mentally and spiritually quiescent for almost a thousand years, is once more astir, once more on the march."[14]

Unlike the Chinese, Japanese, and other inhabitants of East Asia, the more proximate Asiatics of the Near East shared much of the same religious and cultural heritage as Europeans, as well as centuries of political, social, and economic connections. Moreover, in some cases, their physical appearance was indistinguishable from that of Europeans. Grant and Stoddard acknowledged that Levantines had more in common with white Europeans and Americans than did East and South Asians. Yet they also believed that these proximate others could serve as the vanguard of an Asiatic assault on the Nordic race, whether in the form of Pan-Islamism or via immigration and race-mixing. As Stoddard put it, "there is a very imminent danger that the white stocks may be swamped by Asiatic blood."[15]

Within the United States itself, the number of immigrants from the Ottoman Near East had gone from almost none during the 1870s to nearly two hundred thousand by 1910, according to statistics from the Department of Labor, Immigration and Naturalization Service.[16] This population included Turks, Syrians, Palestinians, Armenians, and others, belonging to Muslim, Christian, Jewish, and Druze religious communities. Immigrants from the Ottoman Empire had begun to arrive as refugees following the Russo-Turkish War of 1877. Their ability to enter the country and eventually become citizens was predicated on the assumption that they were white, since an 1870 law directed at Asians had specified that only free whites and aliens of "African descent or African nativity," were eligible to become naturalized citizens of the United States.[17]

Not surprisingly, given the climate of the country, the racial status of Near Eastern immigrants became an increasingly contested issue during the first few decades of the twentieth century. In 1910, for example, the U.S. Census Bureau began to classify people from the Eastern Mediterranean as "Asiatic."[18] This did not settle the question of whether Syrian, Armenian, and other Levantine immigrants were white for the purposes of immigration and naturalization, however. Nor did a series of state court cases (among them, *Halladjian*, 1909; *Mudarri*, 1910; *Shahid*, 1913; *Dow*, 1913) concerning the right of individual Levantine immigrants to become naturalized citizens come to any conclusive decision about their collective racial identity.

Indeed, these cases typically raised more questions than answers. For instance, in deciding that four Armenian immigrants had the right to citizenship, the court in the Halladjian case declared, "If 'the aboriginal peoples of Asia' are excluded from naturalization . . . it is hard to find a loophole for admitting the Hebrews" since "their origin is Asiatic." In 1915, the Syrian community used this same logic to successfully appeal the case of George Dow, a Syrian immigrant initially denied citizenship by a South Carolina court on the grounds that he was not white.[19] The message from the Syrian community was clear: if Jews are white, then so are we. Needless to say, this tenuous claim to whiteness did not prevent the Oriental Exclusion Act of 1917 from closing the door to laborers from an "Asiatic Barred Zone" that included many countries in Near, South, and East Asia. Nor did it stop the Johnson Act of 1924 from limiting immigration from Syria to an annual quota of one hundred people, just as the same legislation ended the flow of Jewish arrivals from eastern Europe.[20]

While Syrian, Armenian, and other Levantine immigrants were busy trying to become white—at least for the sake of citizenship—their neighbors were enjoying the "brown face" performances of Theda Bara, Rudolph Valentino, and T. E. Lawrence, "Lawrence of Arabia."[21] All three revealed the permeability of racial categories and, more specifically, the ability of people to move between European and Levantine identities, despite the efforts of eugenicists, racial ideologues, and the courts to reify those same categories.

Less famous today than her male counterparts, Theda Bara illustrates that race in the Tribal Twenties had as much to do with fantasy and performance as it did with genetics and geography. Born Theodosia Goodman in Cincinnati to a Jewish father and Swiss mother, the actress adopted the name Theda Bara to appear more exotic. Her savvy handlers at Fox Studios spread the story that Bara was the daughter of a European artist and an Arab courtesan and was raised on the banks of the Nile in the "shadows of the pyramids." Titillated observers who watched Bara vamp her way through Orientalist films like *Cleopatra* and *Salomé* pointed out that her name was an anagram of the words "Arab Death."

Although this was apparently a coincidence, it was no accident that blatantly Orientalist films like *The Sheik* and *Cleopatra* became immensely popular at precisely the same historical moment that racists like Madison Grant and Lothrop Stoddard were warning of the Asiatic menace. As in earlier periods of American Orientalism, during the 1920s there was a romantic flip side to the more crudely negative portraits of white racists. Just as the Shriners, "Mohammaden" Mormons,

Street Arabs, and the Ishmaelites had all represented different faces of late-nineteenth-century American Orientalism, so the Tribal Twenties were populated by celluloid sheikhs and vamps, the Asiatic menace, and, once again, the Tribe of Ishmael.

In their second incarnation, the Ishmaelites performed a symbolic role in an Orientalist drama directed by the eugenicists and their allies. The Tribe of Ishmael represented a community of whites that, because of their inferior germ plasm, had essentially taken on the behavior, if not the physical appearance, of Arabs and other Levantines. Indeed, it is extraordinary how much popular stereotypes of Near Eastern immigrants during the first quarter of the twentieth century overlapped with contemporary accounts of the so-called Ishmaelites of Indiana. In an exhaustive survey of sources from this period—including such august publications as *The Atlantic Monthly* and *The New York Times*—Helen McCready Kearney has summarized these pernicious attitudes: "Arabs in the United States were generally perceived in the same negative terms as their cohabitors of the Levant: the Christian Armenians and Muslim Turks. The earlier undifferentiated perception of the Nearer Orientals displayed a remarkable tenacity within the American consciousness. . . . All Levantines were essentially alike: physically dirty, ignorant, semi-civilized, superstitious, indolent, parasitic, cunning, shrewd, mercenary, fractious and violent."[22]

While Lawrence of Arabia could return to being an English gentleman simply by removing his Bedouin robes, the Ishmaelites of Indiana were doomed to act like Arabs because of their inherited predisposition towards wandering, economic parasitism, violence, thievery, and licentiousness. Similarly, if Anglo-Saxon members of the Tribe of Ishmael had failed to enter middle-class society after several generations of trying, then Levantine immigrants were even more likely to remain unassimilated, despite their own efforts in court and elsewhere to lay claim to a white American identity.

One of the goals of eugenicists and racial ideologues during the Tribal Twenties was to reveal the Asiatic character of groups that might otherwise pass as white. It was essentially a form of racial outing. Being Asiatic signified more than just a racial or a geographical designation, however; it also represented an inherited set of behaviors that did not conform to middle-class American norms. Asiatics were particularly dangerous because they were neither black nor white, racially or culturally. Their betwixt-and-between identity meant that they could lay waste to Nordic hegemony in a way that blacks never could.

Most dangerous of all from a eugenical perspective were those Asiatics whose physical appearance allowed them to pass as white; those who laid claim to a white legal identity for the purpose of naturalization; those who possessed hybrid Asiatic-European ancestry, and those who were racially European but whose behavior was Asiatic. In practical terms, this spectrum included Levantines, Jews, "Alpines," Mediterraneans, and Anglo-Saxon "Asiatics" like the Ishmaelites of Indiana. The Tribe of Ishmael, therefore, represented a branch of the Asiatic menace that had taken root right in America's heartland. Is it any wonder, therefore, that Harry Laughlin singled them out during his testimony before the Congressional hearings on immigration?

Significantly, there was one group of Americans that enthusiastically adopted an Asiatic identity during the Tribal Twenties. This was the newly emerging African American Islamic community. Not coincidentally, the Moorish Science Temple and the Nation of Islam, the two oldest and most important African American Islamic organizations, were established during the same period of intense American Orientalism that gave rise to *The Sheik,* the resurrected Ishmaelites, and the Asiatic menace. Indeed, although the Moorish Science Temple was founded immediately before World War I and the Nation of Islam in the early 1930s, both groups may be seen as African American manifestations of the Tribal Twenties.

By adopting an Asiatic-Islamic identity, the Moorish Science Temple and the Nation of Islam became symbolic Ishmaelites at a time when American eugenicists had succeeded in transforming the Tribe of Ishmael itself into a symbol for the dangers of unrestricted immigration and the looming Asiatic-Islamic menace. The creation of the "Asiatic Black Man" and the "Moors" during this period represents a kind of mirror image to the construction of the Tribe of Ishmael. Whereas white eugenicists considered it a profound insult to label other whites "Ishmaelites," black members of the Moorish Science Temple and the Nation of Islam proudly took on Asiatic-Islamic identities of their own invention. Instead of signifying degradation, as "Tribe of Ishmael" did for middle-class whites, for black members of the Moorish Science Temple and the Nation of Islam, titles like "Asiatic Black Man" and "Moor" pointed to a noble heritage that whites had obscured from African Americans since they had landed on Plymouth Rock.

The Moorish Science Temple was founded by a black North Carolina native named Noble Drew Ali. Born Timothy Drew in 1886, Noble Drew Ali inaugurated a pattern of self-invention that would be repeated over and over again within the different branches of African American Islam in the following decades. During his short lifetime, various legends were spread by followers and detractors about the "Prophet, who was to bring the true and divine Creed of Islam," as Noble Drew Ali described himself in his 1927 work, the *Holy Koran,* also known as the *Circle Seven Koran.*[23]

Some contemporaries claimed that Ali was a descendant of Bilali Mohammet, a well-known African Muslim slave who had lived on one of the Gullah-speaking islands off the coast of Georgia during the nineteenth century. Others said that he had been raised by Cherokee Indians or by a wandering band of Gypsies, before traveling to Egypt, Morocco, and Mecca, where the local sheikhs encouraged him to spread Islam to the United States. Still others asserted that Ali had adopted his Eastern persona after apprenticing with a Hindu fakir in a touring circus.[24]

Whatever the truth regarding his early years, by 1913 Noble Drew Ali was living in Newark, New Jersey, where he established the first Moorish community or, as he initially called it, the Canaanite Temple. Ali claimed that European Americans had distorted the true racial and religious identity of African Americans for centuries. Rather than being "Negro, colored, or black," Ali claimed that African Americans were actually "olive-skinned" members of the "Asiatic nation of North America."[25] Originally, according to Ali, African Americans had lived in Mecca until they migrated to Morocco, where they established a Moorish empire before being conquered and enslaved by Europeans.

Along with other "Asiatic" peoples such as Egyptians, Arabians, Japanese, Chinese, Indians, South and Central Americans, Turks, and Persians, African Americans were descended from the biblical figures Ham and Canaan (hence the name "Canaanite Temple"). Like all of their fellow Asiatics, Noble Drew Ali claimed, African Americans (or "Moors") were Muslim before their identity was obscured by whites, or as Ali put it, "Islam was the religion for the Asiatics." Significantly, Ali sometimes referred to Asiatics as "descendants of Hagar" or the "seed of Hagar"—in other words, as Ishmaelites.[26]

Ali expounded many of his beliefs in the *Holy Koran,* a sixty-four-page English text that, despite its name, actually had little connection to the Arabic Quran employed by orthodox Muslims. Although Ali appears to have had some first hand knowledge of Islam (perhaps via Ahmadiyah Muslim immigrants), his *Holy Koran* borrows more heavily from romantic Orientalist texts like *The Aquarian Gospel of Jesus Christ,* written by white Theosophical and Masonic authors, than it does from any Muslim work.[27] The influence of contemporary Orientalists on Noble Drew Ali went far beyond literary borrowing. Ali probably adopted his Arabic sounding name, as well as many of the Islamic symbols and clothes (e.g., turbans and fezzes) favored by the Moors from the Shriners, who had earlier incorporated these same elements as part of their own identification with Islam.[28]

Over the following decade, Noble Drew Ali succeeded in spreading his message to approximately thirty thousand followers in several cities, including Milwaukee, Chicago, Cleveland, Philadelphia, Pittsburgh, and Baltimore. As a sign of their new Moorish identity, members were instructed to add a "national name"—either Bey or El—to their surnames (e.g., John Givens-El; Ira Johnson Bey) and to give up alcohol and pork. Noble Drew Ali transferred the rapidly growing movement's headquarters to Chicago in 1923, and he officially renamed it the Moorish Science Temple of America in 1928. Within a year after that, Ali was embroiled in a deadly power struggle with other members of his organization. After being arrested following the murder of one of his opponents in March 1929, Ali was released from jail and died under circumstances that remain unclear.

Noble Drew Ali left behind a complex legacy. After his death, the Moorish Science Temple split up into competing factions and, in the 1930s, came under the intense scrutiny of the FBI for purportedly anti-American activities, beginning a pattern of government surveillance and harassment that would continue for decades. Despite these internal and external problems, the Moors continued to open temples—many in small Midwestern and Southern towns—and to attract new followers to their movement. Just as significantly, the Moors prepared the soil for the rise of another, more influential African American Islamic community: the Nation of Islam.

W. D. Fard (aka Fard Muhammad), the enigmatic founder of the Nation of Islam, may have been a disciple of Noble Drew Ali in Chicago before beginning his own mission in Detroit in the summer of 1930. Upon arriving in the Motor City, Fard became a peddler of silks and other goods to poor and working-class African American residents. Although this was a common activity for newly arrived immigrants from the Middle East, Fard's origins are shrouded in mystery. Various sources have suggested that he was a Palestinian, Turkish, Persian, or South Asian Muslim immigrant. The FBI, which created a large file on Fard in order to discredit him, claimed that he was really a white ex-con named Wallace Dodd Ford from either Portland, Oregon, or New

Zealand, who had served time in San Quentin during the 1920s for a narcotics conviction.[29]

The Nation of Islam, by contrast, depicted Fard as a native of Mecca whose mother was a Russian Jew from the Caucasus Mountains named Baby Gee and whose father was a black man named Alfonso from the Meccan tribe of Shabazz. According to *Message to the Blackman in America,* the Nation of Islam's most important text, Fard "had to have a body that would be part of each side (black and white), half and half. Therefore, being born or made from both people, He is able to go among both black and white without being discovered or recognized."[30]

While in Detroit, Fard's teaching attracted the attention of a young laborer from Georgia named Elijah Poole. Like other black migrants, Poole had come north in search of economic opportunities and to escape the violent racism of the Deep South. Poole quickly distinguished himself as one of Fard's most devoted and talented followers, taking on the new name Elijah Muhammad as a sign of his conversion. In his *Message to the Blackman,* Muhammad describes asking Fard, "Who are you, and what is your real name?" To which Fard responded, "I am the one that the world has been expecting for the past 2,000 years. . . . My name is Mahdi; I am God."[31] Fard's startling response contained elements of both Christian and Muslim eschatology. He implied that he was both the second coming of Christ and the Mahdi, who heralds the messiah's arrival according to traditional Islamic sources. Most strikingly, Fard also asserted his own divinity, a provocative—and by orthodox Muslim standards heretical—claim that would nevertheless be accepted by Elijah Muhammad and other members of the Nation of Islam.

Fard's missionary activities in Detroit soon attracted the attention of local law enforcement officials. According to Detroit Police Department records, Fard was arrested three times between 1930 and 1933 for "teaching Islam."[32] In the spring of 1933, after one of his arrests, Fard was driven out of Detroit for good. He made his way to Chicago, where Elijah Muhammad had earlier established a branch of the Nation of Islam. In 1934, Fard disappeared without a trace, and following a fierce power struggle within the movement, Elijah Muhammad emerged as the sole leader of the Nation of Islam. From his headquarters on the South Side of Chicago, Muhammad would head the Nation for nearly half a century, until his death in 1975.

Like the Moorish Science Temple, the Nation of Islam developed its own distinctive interpretations of traditional Muslim teachings. Members of the Nation referred to God as Allah, quoted from the

Quran, and eschewed pork. Yet they transformed these elements in ways that frequently drew the ire of orthodox Muslim critics. Thus, for example, the Nation claimed that Fard was Allah incarnate—"We believe that Allah (God) appeared in the Person of Master W. Fard Muhammad"— and that Elijah Muhammad was his prophet.[33] Both beliefs were anathema to orthodox Muslims, who affirm the unity of God and believe that Muhammad was the final "seal" of the prophets. These and other differences (calling houses of worship temples rather than mosques, referring to religious leaders as ministers instead of imams) were enough to place the Nation beyond the pale for many orthodox Muslims, although others sought to encourage the Nation's members to accept more traditional beliefs.

In addition to radically reinterpreting Islamic teachings, Fard and Elijah Muhammad also promoted the Moorish Science Temple's view that African Americans were Asiatic or, as *Message to the Blackman in America* put it, "so-called Negroes [are actually] 'lost-found members of the Asiatic nation.'"[34] This claim was so central to the Nation of Islam's identity that one of the first newspaper accounts to discuss the group, a *Detroit News* article from November 22, 1932, referred enigmatically to "an Asiatic trend among Negro dole recipients of the Elmwood district."[35]

During World War II, Elijah Muhammad's strong sense of kinship with the Japanese, whom he described as "Allah's Asiatic Army," even inspired him to refuse military surface. In a series of speeches delivered in August 1942, Muhammad justified his decision by telling his followers, "The Japanese are brothers of the black man" and "The Asiatic race is made up of all dark-skinned people, including the Japanese and the Asiatic black man. Therefore, members of the Asiatic race must stick together. The Japanese will win the war because the white man cannot successfully oppose the Asiatics."[36] Several decades later, this same ideology would inspire another member of the Nation, the boxer Muhammad Ali (né Cassius Clay), to refuse to serve in Vietnam. Ali's declaration before a group of reporters in Miami, "Man, I ain't go no quarrel with the Viet Cong," became famous.[37] Less publicized was the view he espoused on a Louisville radio show in the same period: "I am not a negro. . . . I am an Asiatic black man."[38]

African American Muslims identified themselves as Asiatic during the 1920s and 1930s for a host of complex reasons. Like many other Americans of the day, Noble Drew Ali, Elijah Muhammad, and their followers were drawn to Orientalist fantasies of the Islamic Near East.

Yet their interest went much deeper than that of the average filmgoer who went to see *The Sheik* or who read T. E. Lawrence's 1926 account of his adventures in Arabia. In certain respects, early African American Muslims had more in common with white members of the Noble Order of the Mystical Shrine, who playfully but painstakingly constructed an imaginary Islamic identity for themselves by dressing in fezzes, greeting one another in Arabic, and gathering in temples possessing Islamic names and architecture. Yet even the Shriners fell short of the kind of existential identification that the Moors and members of the Nation of Islam embraced.

As blacks in a profoundly racist country, devotees of the Moorish Science Temple and the Nation of Islam viewed the so-called Asiatic menace through the lens of their own very different experience. Instead of being threatened by the prospect of a worldwide alliance between Asiatics and Africans, which Lothrop Stoddard had warned about in *The Rising Tide of Color,* many African American Muslims were intrigued and inspired by the idea. Unlike Madison Grant, they did not lament the "passing of the great race," they welcomed it.

The view that Asia could lead the so-called colored peoples of the world in a victorious struggle against white power emerged in both Asian and black nationalist circles in the first few decades of the twentieth century.[39] Japan's resounding victory in the Russo-Japanese War of 1904–5 had encouraged a sense of pride among Asian and black observers alike. Sun Yat-Sen, the father of Chinese nationalism, commented that "since the rise of the Japanese, the Caucasians dare not look down upon other Asiatic peoples."[40] Lajpat Rai, an Indian nationalist, composed an essay entitled "An Asiatic View of the Japanese Question," in which he argued that Japan had "vindicated the honor of Asia and proved to the world that, given equal opportunities, the Asiatics are inferior to none—in any sphere of life, military or civil."[41] Most importantly for black nationalists in America, the Japanese victory inspired Marcus Garvey to warn, "The next war will be between the Negroes and the whites unless our demands for justice are recognized. . . . With Japan to fight with us, we can win such a war."[42]

In the years following World War I, this sentiment was echoed by Asian immigrants preaching a message of Asiatic-African unity in America's black ghettos. For instance, Satokata Takahashi (né Naka Nakane) told supporters like Elijah Muhammad, "I come here to promote international unity between the dark people of Japan and the dark people of America to lead them to a better and fuller life," and Muhammad

A. Kahn, a South Asian immigrant, told audiences in Detroit, "the white man has been lying to you ever since Lincoln saved you. . . . You dark races had better wake up and organize."[43]

It was also in Detroit that Duse Mohammed Ali, a Sudanese-Egyptian native, founded the Universal Islamic Society and America-Asia Society in the mid-1920s. Duse Mohammed Ali was an important ally and mentor to Marcus Garvey. From 1910 to 1920, Ali had published a London-based journal called *The African Times and Orient Review,* in which he united African, Asian, and Islamic interests under a single umbrella.[44] In 1921, he also became a columnist for the *Negro World,* the journalistic organ for Marcus Garvey's Universal Negro Improvement Association (UNIA). There he helped to introduce a Pan-Islamic, Asiatic-African perspective to the black nationalist movement in America. As one article in the *Negro World* put it, "With the stirring events in India and elsewhere, Mohammedanism, dormant for centuries, is suddenly seizing the center of the stage in world politics. . . . All these things are part of a Pan-Islamic movement intended to restore Mohammedan power."[45]

Another influence on the African American adoption of an Islamic-Asiatic identity was the Ahmadiyah movement, a sectarian branch of Islam founded in South Asia during the 1880s. In 1920, Mufti Muhammad Sadiq, the first leader of the Ahmadiyah mission in America, arrived in Philadelphia, where he was promptly jailed for violating immigration acts that excluded polygamists and those who believed in or advocated the practice of polygamy from entering the country.[46] Several months later, under pressure from influential Ahmadiyahs abroad, the U.S. government relented, after securing a promise from Sadiq that he would not advocate polygamy while in the United States.

Soon after his release, Sadiq made his way to the Midwest, where he established his base of operations. The Ahmadiyah message of universal brotherhood attracted Muslim immigrants from the Middle East, the Balkans, and Russia, as well as a few native-born whites. Most new converts, however, were African Americans from Midwestern cities like Detroit, Chicago (where the movement had its headquarters beginning in 1922), and Gary, Indiana.[47] Because the Ahmadiyah movement and its representatives in the United States were Asian in origin, it was natural for many of these converts to associate Islam with that region. Sadiq himself encouraged this sense of identification by stressing that American converts would find "allies" among the Muslim peoples of Afghanistan, Turkey, China, India, and other Asian countries.[48]

Although he continued to preach that Islam was colorblind, as Sadiq grew more and more disillusioned with America's racist climate, he began to encourage his largely black audiences to view Islam as an antidote to the white power structure and the Christian religion that oppressed them. Significantly, he also informed blacks that Islam had been their original religion in Africa, a fundamental belief of both the Moorish Science Temple and the Nation of Islam. In the pages of his publication *The Moslem Sunrise,* Sadiq angrily lambasted "the Christian profiteers [who] brought you out of your native lands of Africa and in Christianizing you made you forsake the religion and language of your forefathers—which were Islam and Arabic. . . . Christianity cannot bring real brotherhood to the nations. Now leave it alone. And join Islam, the real faith of Universal Brotherhood which at once does away with all distinctions of race, color and creed."[49]

Not all the African Americans who came under the influence of the Ahmadiyahs accepted their colorblind view of Islam. Some, like the members of the Moorish Science Temple and the Nation of Islam, preferred to see Islam as solely a religion for non-white peoples, whom they identified collectively as "Asiatics." By embracing an Islamic-Asiatic identity, African Americans from impoverished and segregated communities reinvented themselves both religiously and racially. The adoption of an Asiatic identity enabled members of the Moorish Science Temple and the Nation of Islam to see themselves as part of a broader spectrum of "colored" peoples opposed to white rule, but it also suggested a deep ambivalence towards their own African heritage and what it signified.

Noble Drew Ali, who had traced the roots of African Americans to Morocco (which he saw as an "Asiatic" area) rather than to sub-Saharan Africa, even went so far as to describe them as "olive-skinned" rather than black. Within the context of the Tribal Twenties, the Moors' olive-skinned Asiatic identity, complete with Arabic names and clothing, may be seen as a kind of "brown face" performance, though one done for different reasons than those of their white contemporaries. Whites played with an Asiatic identity because it allowed them to enact a more exotic, sexual, and dangerous persona than they were used to embodying. For American blacks, by contrast, becoming Asiatic signified an escape from the even worse stereotypes associated with being African.[50] At the same time, adopting an Asiatic identity did not mean that one was "acting white," a serious accusation among black nationalists. Thus, the intermediary status of the "Asiatic" allowed both whites and blacks to break out of the dichotomous racial hierarchy that straitjacketed everyone in America. For both groups, then, becoming Asiatic—if only temporarily or symbolically—was a form of racial escapism.

In an era when a pygmy named Ota Benga from the Belgian Congo was displayed in the monkey cage of the Bronx Zoo before thousands of gawking visitors, no place was more denigrated in the American imagination than sub-Saharan Africa. So primitive were the inhabitants of "black Africa" considered to be that in *The Rising Tide of Color*, Lothrop Stoddard had not even treated them as a serious threat to Nordic power, except as potential pawns of the Asiatics; as he put it: "We must conclude that black Africa is unable to stand alone. The black man's numbers may increase prodigiously and acquire alien veneers, but the black man's nature will not change. . . . No black 'renaissance' impends, and Africa, if abandoned by the whites, would merely fall beneath the onset of the browns."[51]

Unlike Noble Drew Ali, Elijah Muhammad did not claim that African Americans were olive-skinned rather than black. Indeed, although some accused the Nation of Islam of being dominated by a light-skinned elite, Muhammad declared to his followers that "your black skin is the best, and never try changing its color."[52] He did, however, refer to Africa itself as "East Asia" and to the Middle East as "the best parts of our planet to live on." Moreover, he and others in the Nation of Islam sometimes articulated crudely negative stereotypes of sub-Saharan Africa. One of the movement's publications, for instance, stated that "ignorance and savagery here and there in Africa must be removed and replaced with the modern civilization of Islam."[53] In a work called *The Fall of America*, Muhammad declared: "The Black man in America accepts the jungle life, thinking that they would get the love of Black Africa. Black Brother and Black Sister, wearing savage dress and hairstyles [i.e., dashikis and afros] will not get you the love of Africa. The dignified people of Africa are either Muslim or educated Christians."[54]

The focus on an Asiatic identity and the concomitant transformation of Africa into a part of Asia contrasted with the more explicitly Africa-oriented views of other black nationalists.[55] Over the years, some of these Afrocentrists took issue with the idea that black Americans were actually Asiatic. In 1934, for instance, Charles James, the head of the UNIA branch in Gary, Indiana, complained that "simple minded Negroes were turning Moors, Arabs, and Abyssinians," while several decades later, Carlos Cooks, the leader of the African Nationalists Pioneering Movement, criticized Elijah Muhammad for a "lack of understanding that the so-called Negroes are Africans and not Muslim Asiatics or Arabs."[56]

Notwithstanding these charges of false consciousness, members of the Moorish Science Temple and the Nation of Islam initially adopted an Asiatic identity at least in part because they found it empowering to be part of a broader Islamic-Asiatic movement that could challenge European-Christian hegemony. Ironically, in so doing, they actually confirmed the worst nightmares of Lothrop Stoddard, who viewed the possibility of a Pan-Islamic Asiatic-African alliance as the greatest potential challenge to Nordic rule.

The Nation of Islam would turn the tables on contemporary white racists in yet another way. Among the most important teachings that Fard Muhammad bequeathed to his chief disciple and prophet, Elijah Muhammad was a creation story that dramatically inverted the standard racial hierarchy of the day. What became known in some circles as the Yakub myth, after its central character, did not accomplish this reversal by repudiating eugenics but rather by harnessing its ideology to a different horse, that of black racial superiority. In order to understand the broader context for the Nation of Islam's own brand of eugenics, we must first turn briefly to the relationship between black progressives and eugenics.

Between the wars, some black progressives, like their white counterparts, expressed eugenical viewpoints, while generally rejecting the coercive methods of men like Harry Laughlin and Charles Davenport. Most notably, in June 1932, the entire issue of the journal *Birth Control Review* was devoted to the black community. The journal was not an official organ of the eugenics movement, but in this period it viewed the relationship between birth control and eugenics as an important part of its mission. As the issue, entitled "The Negro Number," stated in its introduction: "Thus the question arises to what extent birth control has had a eugenic effect upon the Negro race. The social history of the Negro affords unique laboratory material in a study of this aspect of the birth control problem."[57]

One of the things that made the "The Negro Number" significant was that it invited black leaders to voice their opinions on birth control and eugenics within their own community, rather than simply reiterating the viewpoints of white experts on the so-called race problem. Advertisements on the back of the journal from the NAACP and the Urban League indicate that the most powerful progressive black institutions of the day approved of the volume.[58]

In an essay entitled "Eugenics for the Negro," Elmer Carter, the editor of *Opportunity*, the journal of the Urban League, and the first chairman of the New York State Commission Against Discrimination, lamented, "Negroes who by virtue of their education and capacity are best able to rear children shrink from that responsibility and the Negro who, in addition to the handicaps of race and color, is shackled by mental and social incompetence serenely goes on his way bringing into the world children whose chances for mere existence are apparently becoming more and more hazardous. . . . The probabilities are that the race problem in America is infinitely aggravated by the presence of too many unhappily born sub-normals, morons, and imbeciles of both races."[59]

In another essay, a black physician named M. O. Bousfield, who served as chairman of the Public Health Committee of the National Negro Insurance Association, called for "some colored woman to become the Margaret Sanger of her race" and stressed that "it is important that colored physicians, especially women practitioners, and colored nurses and social workers," become involved in birth control. Walter Terpenning, a black sociologist at Western State Teacher's College, in Kalamazoo, Michigan, noted that "as among whites, there are cases of degenerate Negroes whose propagation will be checked only by sterilization or institutionalization."[60]

Most importantly, W. E. B. Du Bois, who saw himself as representing a black elite he called the "talented tenth," also argued that the black lower classes should not reproduce in large numbers for eugenical reasons. In his contribution to "The Negro Number," Du Bois, a friend and political ally of Margaret Sanger, the pioneer of birth control in America, complained that:

> the mass of ignorant Negroes still breed carelessly and disastrously, so that the increase among Negroes, even more than the increase among whites, is from that part of the population least intelligent and fit, and least able to rear their children properly. . . . Moreover, they are quite led away by the fallacy of numbers. They want the black race to survive. They are cheered by a census return of increasing numbers and a high rate of increase. They must learn that among human races and groups, as among vegetables, quality and not mere quantity really counts.[61]

Matthew Pratt Guterl has pointed out that Du Bois and Lothrop Stoddard, who sat on the board of directors of the American Birth Control League, "shared an aristocrat's faith in the power of birth and heredity: in eugenics. . . . As the most supremely evolved representatives of their races, Stoddard and Du Bois believed that they shared obligations of privilege and social responsibility."[62] Because of their common sense of noblesse oblige and their fierce disagreements concerning race, Du Bois and Stoddard eventually conducted a series of debates in print, on the radio and in person. Du Bois was so impressive in these confrontations that even a died-in-the-wool racist like Stoddard couldn't help but develop a strong sense of respect for his supposedly inferior opponent.

While members of the African American elite advocated birth control for poor blacks, the Nation of Islam angrily rejected such efforts as nothing short of genocide. *Message to the Blackman in America* warns its readers to reject "the lie (that you are not able to feed and clothe your children and that you should not have many children)," to recognize "that the devils [whites] are tricking you into birth control in order to sterilize the so-called Negroes of America" (parentheses in original). Despite their strident opposition to birth control among poor African Americans, the Nation of Islam nevertheless shared the white eugenicists' obsession with racial purity and their vehement opposition to race passing and miscegenation. Elijah Muhammad further warned that some whites possessed a physical appearance that allowed them to pass as non-white: "There are certain climates which seem to change the white race into a 'red' or 'brown' color." However, just as white experts claimed to be able to identify any black who sought to pass, so Muhammad noted that "by carefully watching their [such whites'] behavior, you can easily distinguish them from our people (dark, brown, yellow, or red)."[63]

Flipping the stereotypes of white racists, the text explained that the children of even the darkest-skinned whites inevitably revealed their true racial identity because these "devil children, whenever they are around . . . talk filth; sing filthy songs, filthy dancing; and games; and will not leave the original [black] children without starting a fight." By contrast, "black people are by nature the righteous. They have love and mercy in their hearts." Because of whites' predisposition to violence, promiscuity, and deceit, it was incumbent upon blacks to avoid mixing with them. Like racial separatists on the other end of the color spectrum, the Nation of Islam opposed miscegenation, even singling out liberal whites for trying "to destroy the black man by pretending to be their friends and allow intermarriage."[64]

In short, the Nation of Islam rejected white eugenicists' claims of black racial inferiority while accepting the basic assumptions underlying eugenics itself. Indeed, the Nation employed these very assumptions in formulating the so-called Yakub myth and, in so doing, hoisted the white eugenicists on their own petard. As Malcolm X testified in his autobiography, the Yakub myth has been one of the most fundamental and enduring beliefs of the Nation of Islam since the group's inception. Indeed, after Elijah Muhammad's death in 1975, the Nation of Islam split into two factions, one led by Warith Muhammad, the leader's son, and one led by Louis Farrakhan, the group's national spokesman, in part because the former rejected the Yakub myth while the latter continued to affirm it.

The basic narrative of the Yakub myth is as follows. A little more than six thousand years ago, a renegade black resident of Mecca named Yakub, known as "big head scientist," because of his impressive cranium, decided to conduct an elaborate eugenics experiment. At that time, blacks were the only inhabitants of the planet, but Yakub "started studying the life germ of man to try making a new creation. . . . He learned, from studying the germ of the black man, under the microscope, that there were two people in him, and that one was black, the other brown. He said if he could successfully separate the one from the other he could graft the brown germ into its last stage, which would be white. With his wisdom, he could make the white, which he discovered was the weaker of the black germ."[65]

For a while, Yakub preached the merits of his plan on the streets of Mecca, meeting some success. When the authorities got wind of his activities, however, they exiled him and his followers from Mecca to the island of Patmos in the Aegean Sea. There, Yakub began to put his experiment into practice. He selected "doctors, ministers, nurses and a cremator for his top laborers," and instructed them to prevent dark-skinned blacks from reproducing. First, the doctors administered phony blood tests to dark-skinned couples seeking to marry. The doctors would then lie, declaring that the couple was incompatible. If dark-skinned children were born anyway, Yakub commanded the nurses to kill them as soon as possible "by pricking the brain with a sharp needle." If a child somehow managed to survive, he or she was fed to wild animals or cremated. Brown-skinned couples, by contrast, were encouraged to reproduce, and a brown-skinned baby was considered a "holy child" and treated with great care. As a result of these draconian methods, "after the first 200 years, Mr. Yakub had done away with the black babies, and all were brown. After another 200 years, he had all yellow or red. . . . Another 200 years . . . Mr. Yakub had an all-pale white race of people on this Isle. . . . This lie was born into the very nature of the white baby; and, murder for the black people also born in them."[66]

In response to Yakub's experiment, the black rulers of Mecca decided to exile the inherently murderous whites to the "hills and caves of West

Asia (now called Europe)." There, they lived as "savages" while a few ambitious and lucky ones "got as far as what you call the gorilla. In fact, all of the monkey family are from this 2,000 year history of the white race in Europe."[67] Out of sympathy for their wretched condition, Allah sent the whites several prophets who raised their level of civilization but could not eliminate the murderous impulses that eventually enabled whites to enslave the naturally superior and more peaceful black race.

Practically every aspect of the Yakub myth betrays the influence of the eugenics movement. A number of elements seem to respond directly to essays in the "Negro Number" of *Birth Control Review*. This is not unlikely, since the special issue was published in 1932, around the same time that Fard Muhammad began to disseminate the Yakub myth. Even Yakub's odd-sounding nickname, "big head scientist," makes sense when we see it as a nod to craniometry, the belief that an individual's intelligence is directly proportional to the size of his/her head.

The Yakub myth substitutes "germ" for the standard "germ plasm," and instead of dominant and recessive genes it refers to stronger (black) and weaker (brown) "germs" or, as it also calls them, "people." It also explicitly compares Yakub's methods with contemporary medical practices, noting, for example, "The doctors of today hold the same position over the people [as Yakub's doctors did]. You go to them to get a blood test to see if you are fit to be married." Finally, the myth contains clear references to euthanasia, sterilization, segregation in colonies, and selective breeding—all important features of the eugenics movement during the 1920s.

Despite these parallels, the message of the Yakub myth was completely at odds with the standard racial assumptions of the eugenics movement. According to the Nation of Islam, it was a brilliant but misguided black native of Mecca named Yakub, not the Englishman Francis Galton, who invented eugenics. In the myth, whites were now the apelike savages while blacks were scientists, doctors, nurses, and even "Gods," as Elijah Muhammad frequently referred to the original inhabitants of Mecca. Instead of blacks being experimented on by white scientists (as in the now infamous Tuskegee syphilis tests), whites were the misbegotten product of an experiment conducted by blacks. The Nation of Islam also reversed the positions of Ota Benga and the supposedly more evolved white audiences that had gawked at him in the Monkey House of the Bronx Zoo. In the Yakub myth, the apelike whites imprisoned in "Western Asia" were now the subjects of a mocking black gaze.

Ironically, the Nation of Islam's description of savage whites living in the "hills and caves" of Europe closely resembled the eugenics movement's standard portrait of a cacogenic community. Indeed, almost all of the eugenics family studies focused on poor whites dwelling in hills or in the isolated valleys that lay between them. At first glance, the largely urban Tribe of Ishmael appears to run counter to this tendency, but it should be recalled that in his 1924 speech before the London Eugenics Education Society, Harry Laughlin mistakenly but tellingly referred to Ishmaelite "families [living] in the valleys of Indiana." Apparently, Laughlin was so invested in the eugenicists' stereotype of mountain and valley dwelling white primitives that he didn't realize—or decided to ignore the fact—that the region of Indiana where the Ishmaelites lived was as flat as a pancake.

In the Yakub myth, its own version of the eugenics family study genre, the Nation of Islam transformed *all whites* into cacogenic savages living in hills and caves. Whites, in general, rather than isolated cacogenic clans like the Jukes or Ishmaelites, were the result of a process of devolution or degeneration. Like white eugenicists, the Nation of Islam even coined an ominous sounding name for its cacogenic community: "devils." The white devils of the Yakub myth thus took their place alongside the Jukes, the Ishmaelites, the Win, the Kallikaks, the Zeros, and other groups of supposedly degenerate whites with exotic, dangerous-sounding titles. Against the wider backdrop of the eugenics movement, therefore, the Nation of Islam's myth of Yakub may be read as a kind of family study in which the entire white race has become an extended Tribe of Ishmael.

The Nation of Islam's enthusiastic, if highly idiosyncratic, embrace of eugenics adds a profoundly ironic twist to Hugo Leaming's later speculation that some Ishmaelites who survived the "war" waged against them by the eugenics movement may have helped to establish African American Islamic groups like the Nation of Islam during the 1920s and 1930s. We have already established that when they were first "discovered" in the final decades of the nineteenth century, the Ishmaels and their associates in Indianapolis were not members of an underground Islamic community. Nevertheless, did some of the individuals identified as belonging to the Tribe of Ishmael join the Moorish Science Temple and Nation of Islam in the first few decades of the twentieth century, perhaps, in part, because of their stigmatization as "Ishmaelites"? It is to this question that we now turn.

CHAPTER 6

Lost-Found Nation

How the Tribe of Ishmael Became "Muslim"

Although the eugenicists did not know it at the time, the Chicago world's fair of 1933 would prove to be the last public hurrah of the eugenics movement in the United States. Ironically, the decline of American eugenics was precipitated by one of its greatest—and most dubious—achievements. In 1933, while eugenicists were trumpeting the threat of the Ishmael family in Chicago, their German counterparts across the Atlantic were employing Harry Laughlin's model sterilization law as a blueprint for their own draconian legislation. For his significant contributions "to the science of race cleansing," Harry Laughlin received an honorary degree in 1936 from the Nazi-run University of Heidelberg.[1] By this time, Laughlin had become a rabid propagandist for the Nazi regime. His anti-Semitic pronouncements and unscientific research methods finally convinced the Carnegie Institution to sever its links with him in 1939. On December 31 of that year, Laughlin formally retired, and the Eugenics Records Office closed its doors for good.[2] Given the links between Harry Laughlin and the Nazis, Hugo Leaming later wrote, "The trail runs straight, from the war on the Tribe of Ishmael, through the Indiana Plan, to the extermination of . . . at least six million Jews."[3]

In the aftermath of the Holocaust, eugenics declined in the United States as an organized movement, but it did not disappear completely. Many eugenicists now joined the rapidly expanding field of genetics, which, for both scientific and political reasons, distanced itself from its eugenical roots. Other eugenicists and their sympathizers remained active, albeit in a diminished capacity. Most notably, the American Eugenics Society continued to function after World War II under the leadership of Frederick Osborn, a nephew of Henry Fairfield Osborn, who had presided over the Second International Congress of Eugenics where Arthur Estabrook presented his findings on the Tribe of Ishmael. The society continued to publish *Eugenical News* (renamed *Eugenics Quarterly* in 1954) until the late 1960s, when the journal was renamed *Social Biology* and the organization itself became the Society for the Study of Social Biology.[4]

Even more significant than the activities of postwar eugenicists was the ongoing impact of the public policies formulated by their predecessors during the heyday of American eugenics in the 1920s. Eugenically inspired laws concerning miscegenation, immigration, and compulsory sterilization remained on the books until the 1960s and 1970s. Congress finally overturned restrictive national quotas in 1965, thereby opening the door to a wave of previously barred immigrants from Asia and the Middle East. It took until 1967 for the Supreme Court to strike down state laws banning mixed-race marriages.

Despite years of dire warnings by eugenicists that the Tribe of Ishmael would damage the moral and genetic fabric of the United States if left unchecked to breed "like to like," the decline of the eugenics movement did not result in the Ishmaelite conquest of America. Indeed, once the Tribe of Ishmael was no longer subject to surveillance by eugenicists, it simply disappeared, both from public discourse and, apparently, from the streets of Indianapolis. This indicates that the Ishmaelites had never existed as a cohesive "tribe" distinct from the poor white underclass of Indianapolis, except in the fertile imaginations of observers like McCulloch, Estabrook, and Laughlin. As the entry on the Ishmaelites in the *Encyclopedia of Indianapolis* put it in 1994: "There was no Tribe of Ishmael; there were only the poor of Indianapolis."[5]

Once decried as a national menace, the Ishmaelites were now almost completely forgotten, except by local Indiana historians. In 1952, for example, Thurman Rice, a public health official and prominent eugenicist, published a history of medicine in Indianapolis in which he discussed the Tribe of Ishmael—"a sordid story . . . we have been loath to record." Rice recalled that when he was a medical student in Indianapolis from 1917 to 1921, "we would often have a person pointed out as an 'Ishmaelite,' or would see the word written on a case history." According to Rice, the Ishmaelite "colony was scattered and they were no longer often recognized as a group" after "the Negro population increased in the area," and Ishmaelite dwellings were razed to clear land for the construction of the Riley Hospital for Children in 1922. So complete was the disappearance of the Tribe from the streets of Indianapolis, Rice noted, that "medical students now tell us that they have never heard the term 'Ishmaelite' used. The same statement holds for some two decades in the past."[6]

Rice's account indicates that health officials in Indianapolis viewed the Ishmaelites as a distinct community until the early 1920s. This is not surprising given the strong links between members of the Indiana medical establishment and the eugenics movement. Yet Rice gave no indication that the so-called Ishmaelites were anything but desperately poor white residents of a particularly run-down neighborhood in Indianapolis. Significantly, Rice's recollections undermine both the eugenicists' and Hugo Leaming's competing views of the Tribe of Ishmael. On the one hand, Rice's chronology suggests that the Ishmaelites were no longer recognized as a distinct community in Indianapolis after 1922. This directly contradicts the claims made by eugenicists that the Tribe of Ishmael was still a cohesive social unit well into the 1930s. On the other hand, Rice's suggestion that an influx of blacks inspired the Ishmaelites to abandon their old neighborhood gives lie to Leaming's claim that the Tribe of Ishmael was a harmoniously integrated, predominantly African American community.

By the early 1970s, the Tribe of Ishmael had even ceased to be a memory in Indianapolis. As an article in *Indianapolis Magazine* from 1972 put it: "The Ishmaelites have become a forgotten segment of local history."[7] The article, sardonically entitled "The Tribe of Ishmael Came and Multiplied," simply rehashed the earlier work of McCulloch and Estabrook, casting the Ishmaelites in a crudely negative light. Yet just when it seemed that the Tribe of Ishmael would disappear forever, the community was dramatically rediscovered.

Hugo Prosper Leaming, the man who saved the Ishmaelites from the dustbin of history, was born in Providence, Rhode Island, in 1924. Soon after his birth, Leaming and his family moved to Richmond, Virginia, where he spent the first two decades of his life.[8] Leaming's father, Silas, was an upper-middle-class Unitarian from Nebraska; his mother, Lillian (née Allen), was a native of Richmond whose family had lived in the city for generations. They were married at the First Unitarian Church of Richmond. In later life, Hugo Leaming would proudly assert that his mother came from poor white stock, although he appears to have exaggerated his mother's poverty because it helped him to construct a new identity as a man of the people.[9]

Figure 7. Hugo Leaming, undated. (Unitarian
Universalist Inactive Minister Files, bMS 1446,
Andover-Harvard Theological Library, Harvard
Divinity School, Harvard University)

After graduating from the University of Richmond in 1944, Leaming
spent two years in Lebanon, where he taught history at the American
University of Beirut and first became fascinated by Islam.[10] It would
prove to be an abiding interest. Upon returning to the States, Leaming
enrolled in the Meadville Theological School in Chicago, where he was
ordained as a Unitarian minister in 1951. He initially served as religious
education director for the Free Religious Fellowship in Chicago, an integrated church with many middle-class African American members. The
Fellowship was founded by Lewis McGee in 1947, a year before the
First Unitarian Society of Chicago was desegregated.

Despite their liberal tradition, not all of Leaming's fellow Unitarians
were as open to racial integration as he was. When some members of
the Chicago community gave the Fellowship a hostile reception,
Leaming became frustrated and left for a ministerial position in New

Jersey. Over the next few years, he lived a peripatetic existence, moving from position to position and even working as a department store salesman for a while before becoming the pastor of a church in Fort Wayne, Indiana, in 1956.

Politically and personally, Leaming underwent a major transformation during the 1950s. After initially flirting with communism in the late 1940s, he became increasingly convinced that the most pressing moral issue in the United States was the ongoing oppression of African Americans. As he became more involved with the nascent civil rights movement, Leaming grew close to an African American activist from New Jersey named Grace Thompson (1919–85). In the early 1960s, after returning to Chicago to assume the pulpit of the All Souls First Universalist Society, Leaming divorced his first wife, Marjorie, and married Thompson. During the next few years, Leaming was arrested twice for participating in civil rights protests, first in Chicago and later in Albany, Georgia, at a demonstration led by Martin Luther King, Jr.

In 1968, having become disillusioned with the ministry, Leaming left All Souls and entered a graduate program in American history at the University of Illinois at Chicago Circle. For the next decade, Leaming worked on his dissertation, "Hidden Americans: Maroons of Virginia and the Carolinas," which he completed in 1979. The work explored the largely forgotten—or suppressed—history of triracial communities in the southeastern United States. Leaming argued that in the late 1500s, white survivors from the Roanoke colony joined with Native Americans and Africans from earlier Spanish explorations to form a new community that rejected the strict racial hierarchy then emerging in mainstream colonial society. Over the next three hundred years, white indentured servants and radical Quakers, remnants of Native American tribes, and, most significantly, escaped slaves colloquially known as maroons, who had taken refuge in a region called the Dismal Swamp, added to this nucleus.

Like the Tribe of Ishmael, this triracial community was traditionally viewed "with great distaste. They are called outlaws, and placed in the context of ordinary, if dramatic, criminality not social revolt." Yet, Leaming added, this "viewpoint is that of the slaveholders and public opinion they so successfully created. To arrive at a history closer to the facts, values must be reversed." Thus, for example, "'Outlaws plundering farms and enticing slaves away' must be translated into 'Maroons engaged in guerilla warfare and freeing slaves from the plantations.'" This, in a nutshell, was Hugo Leaming's historiographical approach, one that he also applied in his study of the Tribe of Ishmael. To reconstruct the true history of America's oppressed and marginalized peoples, one had to subvert or even invert the standard historical narrative, a process that he likened to recovered memory: "Perhaps a sick nation, like a sick person, can obtain health through an awareness of . . . memories long suppressed."[11]

Significantly, Hugo Leaming concluded his dissertation by praising "maroon society" as an example of "'the Other America'—the America that might have been,—no, the America that *was* for a time, in certain places."[12] This idiosyncratic use of the phrase "the Other America," to describe poor but harmonious triracial communities who had resisted the standard "caste system" of the United States situated Leaming's work squarely within the unfolding debate about the culture of poverty and the underclass. Leaming had borrowed the phrase from Michael Harrington's groundbreaking book of the same name published in 1962. Like Oscar Lewis before him, Harrington had argued that desperately poor people—his Other America—possessed a different culture that prevented them from just "pulling themselves up by their bootstraps." A socialist, Harrington proposed that only massive government intervention could undo the influence of generations of this culture of poverty, thereby helping to inspire the War on Poverty of the 1960s.

By contrast, Leaming rejected the very notion of a pathological culture of poverty. Instead, he argued that those people historically identified as paupers, the undeserving poor, or, more recently, the underclass, actually possessed a legitimate culture of their own, one that typically ignored or intentionally subverted hegemonic ideas of race, culture, and religion. While Harrington originally coined the phrase "the Other America" to draw attention to the national crisis of endemic poverty that he thought could be ameliorated through governmental programs, Leaming redeployed the same phrase to refer to poor but proud triracial communities that were essentially written out of American history because of their threatening nature. Rather than a phrase signifying shame, therefore, Leaming offered "the Other America" as a badge of honor.

Hugo Leaming first became interested in the Tribe of Ishmael during the period that he was working on his dissertation. How he initially heard about the Ishmaelites is unknown. What is clear, however, is that he soon became obsessed with the subject. He read the published accounts of McCulloch and Estabrook and traveled to Indianapolis, where he uncovered Wright's unpublished manuscript and searched the city for any surviving traces of the tribe. Leaming also traveled throughout

Indiana and Illinois, interviewing residents of small towns about the Tribe of Ishmael. Even though he was unable to locate a single individual who remembered the Ishmaelites or who even recalled hearing any stories about them, Leaming was not discouraged. Instead, he took this as striking confirmation of his theory of repressed memory: "Mass social amnesia, produced by local or regional social trauma, is suggested to explain this phenomenon."[13]

The more he learned about the Tribe of Ishmael, the more Leaming became convinced that the group's true identity and significance had been erased from the historical record. Ultimately, he would argue that the Ishmaelites, like the maroons, represented a classic case of the Other America: a harmonious community of social outcasts and rebels that rejected traditional hierarchies based on race, religion, and gender. Because of the profound challenge that their very existence had posed to mainstream society, the Ishmaelites were demonized by a succession of observers, beginning with Oscar McCulloch. Moreover, McCulloch and his successors were so focused on the alleged depravity of the Tribe of Ishmael that they had missed signs pointing to a discovery of great historical significance. For the Ishmaelites, according to Leaming's daring hypothesis, were not only a triracial group, they were also an Islamic community that had served as the conduit between Islam in Africa and twentieth-century African American Islamic groups like the Moorish Science Temple and the Nation of Islam.

Not surprisingly, Leaming was determined to distance himself from his predecessors in the study of the Tribe of Ishmael. Concerning Oscar McCulloch, Leaming wrote critically that he was the "social engineer" of the "third stage of the war on the Tribe of Ishmael." He was responsible for "the creation of an ideology, system, and unity for the crusade."[14] And yet even Leaming realized that there was more to McCulloch than this negative portrayal suggested. Thus he added that McCulloch was "a pioneering Modernist, or Liberal, Protestant, who placed social reform ahead of doctrinal orthodoxy." What Leaming did not or, perhaps, could not, openly acknowledge were the many parallels between himself and the man who had discovered the Ishmaelites. Like McCulloch, Leaming was a liberal clergyman who attended seminary in Chicago and served congregations in the upper Midwest, including Indiana. Both men sympathized with socialism and devoted their professional lives to helping the downtrodden. Both became fascinated with Islam and with eugenics, though these interests took them in very different directions. And, of course, both were convinced that they had discovered the real Tribe of

Ishmael. In short, despite their differences, in many ways Hugo Leaming and Oscar McCulloch were kindred spirits.

In his revisionist account, Leaming proposed a number of intriguing connections between the Tribe of Ishmael and Islam. Yet many of these claims, such as the Ishmaelites' supposed aversion to alcohol, formalized polygamy, and uniform rejection of Christian worship are explicitly contradicted by his own primary sources, most notably James Frank Wright's unpublished manuscript. Another potential link, the annual journeys taken by some families identified as Ishmaelites to visit kin and search for seasonal work, are better explained by an Upland Southern cultural background than by any supposed connection to African Muslim nomads like the Fulani, as Leaming suggested.

Besides these easily refuted assertions, Leaming made three other claims in support of his Islamic hypothesis. The first was that a number of towns along the Ishmaelite migration route possessed Islamic names. Leaming himself admitted that towns with similar names—along with those of Greek, Roman, Chinese, and other "exotic" origins—could be found throughout the United States. "But," he noted, "when a community lies on the Ishmaelite route [and] has an Islamic name . . . it is worthy of comment."[15] Leaming's second claim was that Ishmaelites may have helped to establish the Moorish Science Temple and the Nation of Islam in the 1920s and 1930s, respectively. The third and perhaps most provocative and compelling suggestion was that Ben Ishmael, the founder—or "first patriarch," as Leaming dubbed him—of the Tribe of Ishmael, was an "Islamic saint or Imam" whose Arabic sounding name indicated an African Muslim origin.

Not coincidentally, Leaming's interest in reconstructing an Islamic identity for the Tribe of Ishmael arose at a time when Islam had dramatically reentered the American popular imagination after several decades of relative absence. A century before, Oscar McCulloch had first discovered the Tribe of Ishmael during an earlier phase of American interest in Islam and the Near East, one marked by the appearance of "street Arabs" in American cities, the rise of the Shriners, and the Chicago world's fair of 1893. Likewise, Arthur Estabrook's rediscovery of the Ishmaelites coincided with another stage, one that combined a romantic obsession with celluloid sheiks, the emergence of groups like the Moorish Science Temple, and the Immigration Restriction Act of 1924. Like his predecessors, Hugo Leaming encountered and reimagined the Tribe of Ishmael during a new and important phase in the ongoing history of American Orientalism.

From the 1930s to the 1950s, Muslims, both native-born and immigrants, had maintained a foothold in the United States. Yet, in a number of important ways, the 1960s ushered in a new era for Islam in America. As in earlier periods, dramatic events in the Near East helped to spur Americans' engagement with Islam. Over the course of two decades, a series of military conflicts between Israel and the Arab nations, the rise of the Palestinian independence movement, and the oil crisis of the 1970s all directed America's gaze towards the historical heart of the Muslim world. These events revived old stereotypes and helped to create new ones, such as the oil-rich sheikh and the Arab terrorist. Meanwhile, the repeal of national immigration quotas in 1965 meant that for the first time since the 1920s, Americans began to encounter growing numbers of Muslim immigrants from Asia, Africa, and the Middle East. Perhaps more significant than any of these factors, however, was the extraordinary rise to public prominence of African American Islam.

Following their emergence in the 1920s and 1930s, groups such as the Moorish Science Temple and the Nation of Islam had continued to attract new followers, as well as the unwanted attention of the FBI. A majority of Americans, however, remained unaware that Islam had become a significant feature of the African American landscape. This changed dramatically in 1959, when a young television journalist named Mike Wallace and a writer named Louis Lomax produced a five-part TV documentary on the Nation of Islam entitled *The Hate That Hate Produced,* which ran July 13–17. In the same year, national publications such as *Time, Reader's Digest, Life,* and *Newsweek* all covered the group.[16] African American Islam was now on the national radar screen. Thanks to the efforts of prominent members of the Nation of Islam like Malcolm X and Muhammad Ali, it would remain so throughout the 1960s.

While many Americans dismissed the Nation of Islam as a hate group during this period, others viewed it as a legitimate religious organization that sought to liberate African Americans from a sense of false consciousness produced by centuries of physical and mental oppression. An important part of this message was that African Americans had forgotten—or, more accurately, had been compelled to forget—their original identity as Muslims, a phenomenon referred to as "the lost-found nation."

It is important to note that neither the Nation of Islam nor its predecessor, the Moorish Science Temple, had invented the idea that African

Muslims were brought to America as slaves. Indeed, the fact that some African slaves were Muslim was known since at least the first half of the eighteenth century. In 1734, the life of a Muslim slave named Job Ben Solomon (an anglicized version of Ayuba boon Salumena or Ayuba Suleiman Diallo) was published in England. This account of Job Ben Solomon's sojourn in Maryland would become the first of a series of popular works that chronicled the experiences of Muslim slaves in America. Among the individuals whose stories were recorded for posterity, either by others or in their own hand, were Ibrahim Abd ar-Rahman, Umar ibn Said, and Muhammad Ali ben Said (aka Nicholas Said). The latter eventually gained his freedom, worked as a teacher in Detroit, and served in the Union army during the Civil War, ultimately publishing an account of his remarkable life in *The Atlantic Monthly* in 1867, as well as a book-length autobiography in 1873. Taken together, these slave narratives constitute a little known but significant chapter in America's ongoing encounter with Islam.[17]

By the first few decades of the twentieth century, the fascinating stories of these Muslim slaves had largely been forgotten save in a few scholarly journals. During the 1930s, however, new light was shed on the subject by researchers with the Georgia Writers' Project of the Work Projects Administration (WPA), who interviewed black residents of the Georgia Sea Islands. Elderly individuals on Sapelo Island still recalled Muslim slave ancestors with Arabic names like Fatima and Medina. At the center of their recollections was a nineteenth-century figure named Bilali, who passed on Islamic traditions, including prayers, sayings, and ritual foods, to his many children. During his lifetime, Bilali had attracted the attention of white observers, who referred to him as "Ben Ali" in their written descriptions.[18]

In 1940, the interviews conducted on Sapelo were published under the title *Drums and Shadows*. A decade and a half later, in 1955, the recollections of residents from nearby St. Simon's Island were also published. These focused on a Muslim slave ancestor named Salih Bilali, whose white master, John Couper, had described him as "a strict Mahometan; abstains from spiritous liquors, and keeps the various fasts, particularly that of Rhamadam."[19] The Georgia Writers' Project interviews confirmed the existence of practicing Muslim families well into the nineteenth century. Yet they also suggested that Muslim traditions had disappeared from the Georgia Sea Island communities by the time the interviews were conducted during the 1930s—unless, of course, some residents had purposely concealed Muslim practices from the interviewers.

Despite the newfound awareness of the Nation of Islam, the 1960s did not witness an explosion of public interest in the history of these Muslim slaves in America. Nevertheless, a few significant works were published on the topic, including an essay that explicitly addressed the question of whether African Muslim traditions such as those preserved on the Georgia Sea Islands during the nineteenth century had influenced the development of groups like the Nation of Islam and the Moorish Science Temple. The essay's author, Morroe Berger, acknowledged the possibility of such a link but ultimately answered this question in the negative: "the religion of twentieth-century Negro Muslims seems to have been imported from abroad, rather than to derive from any vestiges of earlier Islamic groups among slaves. It is quite possible that some of the various Muslim groups of the past half-century or so had their roots in these vestiges, that the tradition was handed down in a weak chain from generation to generation. But there is no evidence to support this."[20]

Later in the decade, the Africanist Philip Curtin published an important collection of African narratives from the period of the slave trade, including a number of accounts by Muslims brought to America, such as Job Ben Solomon and Salih Bilali.[21] Then, in 1976, one year before Hugo Leaming's essay on the Tribe of Ishmael appeared in print, a broader American audience finally learned about the existence of Muslim slaves via Kunte Kinte, the central character in Alex Haley's *Roots.* Although Haley did not depict Kunta Kinte's religion in detail either in his book or in the blockbuster miniseries that aired in 1977, he did explicitly identify him as a Muslim.[22] The same year that Americans were glued to their television sets watching *Roots,* Toni Morrison wove Muslim slave names from Sapelo Island into her classic novel *Song of Solomon,* and Terry Alford published *A Prince among Slaves,* a well-received biography of Ibrahim Abd ar-Rahman, an enslaved Muslim who became the "most famous African in America" during the 1820s.[23]

Against this backdrop, Hugo Leaming's Islamic portrait of Ben Ishmael ceases to stand out as an anomaly and, instead, takes its place alongside contemporary efforts to recover the important but largely forgotten Islamic dimension of early African American history. In his essay on the Ishmaelites, Leaming acknowledged this wider historiographical context and explicitly referred to Philip Curtin's book in support of his Islamic hypothesis. Indeed, from a number of perspectives, Leaming's seemingly daring reconstruction of the Tribe of Ishmael makes sense within the broader history of Muslim slaves in America. The image of

Ben Ishmael as a Muslim of African descent who passed on Islamic traditions to his extended family recalls the histories of Muslim patriarchs
on the Georgia Sea Islands. And although Muslim slaves like Bilali and
his descendants were typically found in Southern coastal areas, the
former slave Muhammad Ali Ben Said traveled as far north as Detroit, a
veritable stone's throw from Indiana.

Likewise, Ben Ishmael's name jibes with the names of a number of
well-documented African Muslim slaves in America, including Job Ben
Solomon, Ben Said, and Ben Ali (aka Bilali). Indeed, a federal census list
from the end of the nineteenth century reveals tens of African Americans
with the family name "Ishmael" (along with many more white
Ishmaels). Although the census does not indicate the religion of these
individuals, most black Ishmaels are listed as living in Georgia,
Louisiana, and South Carolina, precisely the states where the largest
number of Muslim slaves settled. Ironically, however, Hugo Leaming
was unaware of these southern black Ishmaels and erroneously asserted
that "Ishmael does not seem to appear as a family name in America
except among the Tribe of Ishmael . . . [and] only along the tribal migration route. [i.e., in the upper Midwest]."[24]

Despite the many problems with his Islamic hypothesis, Hugo
Leaming deserves credit for being aware of the possibility of Ben
Ishmael's African Muslim ancestry. Phrased differently, he deserves credit
for correctly realizing that there *could* have been an African Muslim
patriarch named Ben Ishmael in nineteenth-century America. In this
regard, Leaming was a pioneer—albeit an ultimately misguided one—in
a broader historiographical movement to recover the stories of Muslim
slaves and freed people of African descent in the United States, a group
that Michael Gomez has evocatively labeled "Founding Mothers and
Fathers of a Different Sort."[25] Had Leaming conducted more research
into Ben Ishmael's life, however, he would have discovered a very different but equally compelling story. For Ben Ishmael was neither African
nor Muslim. Instead, he was a poor white man of European background
who spent his whole life trying to scrape out a living for himself and his
large family. Along the way, he served with honor in the Revolutionary
War and was among the first European Americans to settle Kentucky,
along with his fellow pioneer Daniel Boone.

Two elements of Hugo Leaming's Islamic hypothesis still remain to be
addressed. The first is his suggestion that the Muslim names of several
towns in Indiana and Illinois may reflect the Islamic influence of the
Ishmaelites who passed through them on their annual journeys. Local

legends concerning the origins of Mahomet, Illinois, and Morocco and
Mecca, Indiana, reveal no links to the Tribe of Ishmael. In the case of
Mecca, however, they do suggest a possible connection to Islam.
According to one local story, in the 1890s a tile plant was built in the
vicinity of the town, "and they needed cheap workers, so they sent over
to the Near East and got these Moslems. . . . When they got paid, they'd
come to town and say it was almost like coming to Mecca, and so they
called the town Mecca." Another local tradition traced the genesis of
the town's name to the 1880s, when Arab workers from the Middle East
were supposedly brought in to train Arabian horses.[26]

Even though the names of Midwestern towns like Mahomet,
Morocco, and Mecca do not teach us anything about the Ishmaelites,
they do teach us something important about the presence of Islam in
Middle America. Such names should be seen as part of the broader flowering of romantic Orientalism in America's heartland during the second
half of the nineteenth century. Residents of towns like Morocco and
Mecca were attracted to these names for the same reasons that they
joined the Ancient Order of the Nobles of the Mystic Shrine, visited the
simulated streets of Cairo at the Chicago world's fair of 1893, and
smoked cigarette brands called Camel, Mecca, and Medina.[27] As formerly rugged places like Indiana and Illinois ceased to mark the
American frontier, residents began to turn their gaze from the Middle
West to the Middle East in search of a new frontier—one to be imagined
and consumed rather than physically settled.

During the same period that Shriners with names like Johnson and
Kelly were donning fezzes and meeting in places like the Mohammed
Temple in Peoria, Illinois, Arab immigrants from the Middle East were
beginning to arrive in significant numbers in the United States. In the
1880s and 1890s, Muslim, Christian, and Druze Arabs established
substantial communities throughout the Midwest, both in large cities
like Detroit and Chicago and in smaller towns like Fort Wayne,
Indiana, and Spring Valley, Illinois.[28] We will probably never know
whether Mecca, Indiana, received its name from Muslim laborers who
settled in the town during this period, but more importantly, the local
legends that suggest such an origin for the name Mecca point to the
broader phenomenon of Muslim settlement in rural towns across the
Midwest. Once again, therefore, in his effort to establish an Islamic
identity for the Ishmaelites, Leaming inadvertently shed light on a significant but largely forgotten chapter in the history of Islam in the
United States.

Leaming's final claim about the Tribe of Ishmael was that members of the community had helped to establish African American Islamic groups during the first few decades of the twentieth century. Although he linked this assertion to his overall hypothesis concerning the Ishmaelites' Islamic identity, the two claims are not necessarily interdependent. In other words, even though the Ishmaelites did not form an Islamic community in their own right, it is still possible that some individuals associated by others with the Tribe of Ishmael did actually join African American Islamic groups.

The evidence that Leaming presented in support of his claim consisted of a handful of recollections by African American Muslims in Chicago and Detroit, the two oldest centers of the movement. Several of these individuals told Leaming that a group known as the "Midwestern Tribe of Ishmael" was a topic of conversation in the period between the 1920s and World War II among various "black nationalists"—including "Black Hebrews" and "Black Muslims"—who viewed the Ishmaelites as "pioneers for black identity and self determination." Most significantly, an elderly member of the Moorish Science Temple told Leaming that when he joined the group in 1930, he encountered a woman named Mrs. Gallivant, "who had joined Moorish Science at Detroit around 1920, when it was first introduced to the Midwest. She had come from downstate Indiana or Illinois and called herself an Ishmaelite. She spoke of the Tribe of Ishmael as a people who dwelled downstate, and who after moving north were among the first to assist in the establishment of Moorish Science in the Midwest."[29] To these memories, Leaming added his own observation that Pembroke and Kankakee, Illinois, the smallest towns in America to have branches of the Moorish Science Temple and Nation of Islam, respectively, were also located on the route of the Tribe's annual migrations.

Leaming's findings raise several intriguing possibilities. In the decades between the world wars, some African American Muslims may have become interested in the Tribe of Ishmael simply because of the group's Islamic-sounding name and its apparent connection to the biblical figure of Ishmael. The belief that African Muslims were descended from Ishmael was common in such circles. A 1927 article in the *Chicago Defender,* for example, described four men from Aden who claimed "descent from Abraham through Ishmael, his son, and Hagar, his wife, commonly known as the forerunner of the Ethiopian race."[30]

Members of the Moorish Science Temple or the Nation of Islam could have easily learned about the Tribe of Ishmael simply by visiting the eugenics exhibit at the Chicago world's fair in 1933. Had they done so, they would have encountered photographs of Ishmaelites who appeared to be white but who were described with the kind of contempt typically reserved for African Americans. Perhaps they concluded that the photographs were of mixed race individuals who could pass as white. After all, Fard Muhammad, the purportedly half-white-half-black founder of the Nation of Islam, had also been light enough to pass as white, a fact confirmed by widely seen photographs. Thus, even if they had never actually met any so-called Ishmaelites, the "black nationalists" mentioned by Leaming may still have viewed them as kindred sprits.

It is also possible that some individuals identified as Ishmaelites did join groups like the Moorish Science Temple and the Nation of Islam during the 1920s and 1930s. In this period, individuals who had been stigmatized as Ishmaelites may have begun to claim this designation as a badge of honor rather than a mark of Cain. Perhaps the rise of African American Islam even influenced some people identified as members of the Tribe of Ishmael to question the significance of the name attributed to them. In other words, rather than Islamically identified Ishmaelites helping to establish groups like the Moorish Science Temple, as Hugo Leaming suggested, groups like the Moorish Science Temple may have helped to establish Islamically identified Ishmaelites. In this regard, it may be worthwhile revisiting George Ishmael's words to James Frank Wright concerning his family's origins: "I reckon ours is the oldest family in the world. I have heard tell of one of our family [i.e., Ishmael] being named in the Bible." Over time, this identification with the biblical figure of Ishmael may have developed into an identification with Islam, perhaps especially among some mixed race members of the Ishmael family itself.

Unfortunately, we do not know enough about how those designated as Ishmaelites saw themselves to do more than conjecture. Yet the possibility that some Ishmaelites became members of the Moorish Science Temple or the Nation of Islam is no stranger than the real transformation of Timothy Drew into Noble Drew Ali, Malcolm Little (aka Detroit Red) into Malcolm X, Elijah Poole into Elijah Muhammad—or Hugo Leaming into Hugo Leaming Bey.

Although Leaming did not succeed in establishing a definitive link between the Tribe of Ishmael and the Moorish Science Temple or the Nation of Islam, in his effort to do so, he did reveal two important and, sometimes, competing tendencies within the history of African American Islam. The first tendency is the desire to recover an unbroken chain of Islam in the United States, stretching back from the first slaves brought from Africa to the first members of the African American Islamic communities founded in the twentieth century. The second, equally powerful tendency is the desire for self-invention that has motivated numerous African Americans to abandon the religion of their childhood, change their names, and embrace an Islamic identity. It is precisely this ongoing interplay between roots and radical innovation that has made African American Islam so dynamic and, arguably, so American.

In the 1960s, Hugo Leaming embarked on his own remarkable journey of self-invention or, as he preferred to see it, self-discovery. By the time he published his revisionist account of the Tribe of Ishmael in 1977, Leaming had assumed a radically new identity. After living half a century as a white man, Hugo Leaming now claimed that he also possessed Native American and African American ancestry and was therefore "tri-racial."[31] In the coming years, he would also undergo a profound religious metamorphosis; as Graham Hodges has written, "during the 1980s, Leaming sought acceptance as an African American in a Black Muslim temple. Eventually he was received and permitted to wear a fez, which he combined with his Unitarian robes."[32]

In 1989, James Koehnline visited the All Souls First Universalist Society in Chicago, where Leaming was pastor emeritus. For the first time since suffering a stroke several years earlier, Leaming delivered a sermon before the congregation. Koehnline remembered that Leaming, "proudly wearing the fez of the Moorish Science Temple, . . . stood before us, a pale-skinned man of 'tri-racial' Chickhahominy Indian stock, and delivered his moving sermon, 'My African Ancestry.'"[33] Leaming's identification with the Chickahominy Indians adds yet another ironic twist to his story, for the Chickahominies were one of the triracial "Isshie" communities discussed by Arthur Estabrook in *Mongrel Virginians* and were also part of Leaming's own research on the maroons of Virginia and the Carolinas. Racially and religiously, therefore, Hugo Leaming had recreated himself in the image of "the Other America" he wrote about so passionately.

By the time he died in 1993, Hugo Leaming had fully embraced his new identity as a Chickahominy Indian–African American–Anglo-Saxon member of the Moorish Science Temple. Like other members, he had even added the honorific "Bey" to his name, becoming Hugo Prosper Leaming Bey. It was an extraordinary transformation for a man who had been raised as a white middle-class Unitarian in segregation-era Virginia.

Hugo Leaming's recovery of his own "lost-found" identity closely resembles his historical reconstruction of the Tribe of Ishmael. When he began his research, Leaming was confronted by a ragtag collection of primarily white Upland Southern Christian families who had settled in Indiana during the nineteenth century. By the time he was done, he had almost alchemically turned them into a triracial Muslim community consisting of freed and escaped black slaves and their Native American and white allies. It is unclear which came first, Leaming's own transformation or his transformation of the Tribe of Ishmael. Perhaps over time the two processes cross-pollinated one another in his fertile imagination. In the Tribe of Ishmael, Leaming had discovered what he called a "lost-found nation in the wilderness of North America." During that same search in the wilderness, he also discovered himself.

CHAPTER 7

The Ishmaels

An American Story

The Ishmaels were not a tribe of moral degenerates, a congenitally feeble-minded clan, or a triracial Islamic community. Perhaps the most profound irony in the saga of the Ishmaels is that their real story is as compelling and, in terms of the history of the poor in the United States, as revealing as any of the fantasies spun around them, beginning with the family patriarch, Benjamin Ishmael. Some of the most basic details of Benjamin Ishmael's remarkable life, including the date and place of his birth, remain a mystery. Despite their best—or worst—efforts, the eugenicists were never able link him to the thousands of criminals whom the British shipped to the American colonies. Between 1718 and 1775, around forty-five thousand felons were transported from Britain to the colonies, primarily to Maryland and Virginia, constituting about 20 percent of all British immigrants during this period.[1] Yet Benjamin Ishmael does not appear in any of the extant ship manifests or other colonial records that have preserved some trace of these largely forgotten individuals.

Hugo Leaming proposed that the name "Ben Ishmael" was Arabic in origin and therefore parallel to the names of well-documented African Muslim slaves in America such as Job Ben Solomon, Ben Ali (Bilali), and Nicholas Ben Said. In fact, however, "Ben" was simply an abbreviation for "Benjamin"—something Leaming either did not know or simply ignored—nor is there any other evidence to suggest that Benjamin Ishmael had any connection to Africa or Islam. Who, then, was Benjamin Ishmael?

Documents suggest that Benjamin was born in either 1736 or 1739, possibly in Pennsylvania. The Ishmael surname, which has inspired so much misguided speculation over the years, may hint at Benjamin's origins before he and/or his family arrived in the colonies. The eugenicists were fond of speculating that the Ishmaels had received their unusual surname because of their purported proclivity for thievery, violence, and wandering—in other words, because of a resemblance to the biblical figure of Ishmael and his descendants. Hugo Leaming, by contrast, interpreted the name as a sign of African Muslim origin. In fact, a number of African Americans possessing the surname Ishmael do appear in nineteenth century census lists, and some of these African American men and women, in particular those who lived in the Gulf and South Eastern states, may have had Islamic roots.

By contrast, in order to understand how Benjamin Ishmael probably received his unusual and evocative surname, we must take a brief detour to Wales. During the sixth century, a figure who became known as Saint Ishmael was a helper to, and perhaps nephew of, Saint David, the patron saint of Wales. Today, the latter's memory is preserved in St. David's, a cathedral town in western Wales overlooking the gray waters of the Irish Sea, now a favorite of tourists. Less known are two smaller Welsh towns named after St. Ishmael, one in Pembrokeshire and the other in Camarthenshire, not far from Dylan Thomas's old haunts.

In addition to the names of these towns, the two saints also inspired generations of Welsh parents to call their sons David and Ishmael, respectively. Until the eighteenth century, children in Wales received their father's first name as their own surname (i.e., as a patronymic). Thus, Benjamin, the son of Ishmael, became "Benjamin Ishmael," while Benjamin's own son, John, would be known as "John Benjamin" or "John ap [son of] Benjamin," and so on. By the 1700s, most people in Wales had begun to abandon patronymics and to adopt fixed surnames like Davis (an alternate form of David) and, far less commonly, Ishmael.[2] People with the Ishmael surname still live in Wales, some in the area of St. Ishmael's.

From the founding of Pennsylvania in 1681 until 1700, the Welsh constituted the largest single group of immigrants to William Penn's "Holy Experiment." By 1700, they formed fully one-third of the colony's estimated population of twenty thousand. The Welsh continued to play a significant role in Pennsylvania until 1730, after which their demographic and social influence declined. On the eve of the American Revolution, there were some twelve thousand individuals of Welsh ancestry in Pennsylvania out of a quarter million people, and most had assimilated into the much larger English and Scotch-Irish population.[3]

The earliest Welsh immigrants to Pennsylvania were Quakers who settled an area known as the Welsh Tract in Philadelphia and its environs. Later arrivals included Welsh Baptists, Anglicans, and Presbyterians. As early as 1700, pioneers from Wales had also begun to settle the frontier lands that would officially become Lancaster County in 1729. Some of these immigrants belonged to the gentry, others were yeoman farmers, and still others were laborers, many working in the iron industry. In 1729, the Welsh Society of Philadelphia was founded to aid poor immigrants from Wales then living in the colony.

Extant ship manifests from this period do not mention any Ishmaels arriving in the port of Philadelphia, whether from Wales or elsewhere.[4] Nevertheless, Benjamin Ishmael's family probably arrived in the colonies from Wales at some point in the late seventeenth or early eighteenth century and made their way to eastern Pennsylvania, where they joined the substantial Welsh community. Official documents reveal that Benjamin and at least one brother eventually settled in Cumberland County, a backcountry territory that was carved out of Lancaster County in 1750.

The earliest document that appears to mention a member of Benjamin Ishmael's family is a 1769 tax list from Antrim Township, Cumberland County (in an area that then became part of Franklin County in 1784; Antrim had been incorporated in 1741 as part of Lancaster County, taking its name from the place in Northern Ireland where Benjamin Chambers, the first European settler in the region, originally hailed from). The Antrim Township tax list from 1769 includes a Thomas Ishmael under the category "freemen."[5] In Pennsylvania during this period, the term "freeman" designated any free man (i.e., not a slave or indentured servant), white or black, who was over twenty-one years old, unmarried, and did not own property.

Thomas Ishmael later moved westward to Washington County (est. 1781), a frontier area that was claimed by both Virginia and Pennsylvania until the Baltimore Agreement of 1780 awarded it to the latter. In 1782, he was recruited at Castile Run to serve as a private in the First Battalion of the Frontier Rangers, a hardscrabble militia formed in western Pennsylvania to fight a "hinterland war" against Delaware, Shawnee, and other Indians considered hostile to the European settlers.[6] In 1794, Thomas Ishmael was awarded a land grant of two hundred acres in a part of North Carolina that would later become Greene County, Tennessee, where he settled with his family. The possibility that Thomas Ishmael was Benjamin's brother is strongly suggested by several factors: their extremely rare surname, common presence in Cumberland County, Pennsylvania, during the same period, and the fact that both men's immediate descendants (including Thomas' eldest son, Benjamin) shared the same set of first names.[7]

In January 1776, the same month that Thomas Paine's impassioned pamphlet *Common Sense* caused a sensation among the American colonists, Benjamin Ishmael enters the historical record, volunteering to serve a term of one year in the Continental Army.[8] At the Conecocheaque Creek settlement in Cumberland County, Benjamin joined the newly formed Sixth Battalion of the Pennsylvania Line under the command of Colonel (later General) William Irvine. Along with other men from Cumberland County, including Hugh Drennon and John Rannels, who would later testify on Ishmael's behalf in his military pension application, Benjamin became a private in a company commanded by Captain Abraham Smith.[9]

In the absence of his own testimony, it is impossible to say why Benjamin Ishmael decided to enlist. Like many other volunteers in the early period of the conflict, he may have been swept up in the popular war sentiment.[10] Most residents of the Pennsylvania hinterland, including Cumberland County, supported the rebellion, although records also describe some individuals as "going to the enemy" (i.e., becoming loyalists).[11] Perhaps, back in 1775, Benjamin Ishmael had joined a "large audience" in Cumberland County to hear Robert Cooper deliver a rousing sermon in which he preached:

> Those who have endeavored to maintain a character for piety, ought now to endeavor to distinguish themselves as brave soldiers. . . . To draw back, if you were even before the cannon's mouth, would fix both awful guilt and indelible disgrace upon you. . . . If then you would escape deep guilt before God, and lasting contempt among men, forward you must go, wheresoever the drum shall beat, and the trumpet sound for battle. You have, in a word, no alternative, but either to venture your lives bravely, or attempt to save them ignominiously; to run the hazard of dying like heroes, or be certain of living like cowards.[12]

Whether Benjamin Ishmael was caught up in the *rage militaire* that swept through Cumberland County or whether he had enlisted for other reasons, in March 1776 he and the rest of the Sixth Battalion received orders to march to New York. As the troops departed in their blue coats and breeches, Chaplain William Linn prayed, "May your summer's campaign be great and glorious, and may you be returned in safety to the bosom of your country, and meet the congratulation of your friends."[13] In the coming months, the Sixth Battalion would experience little of the glory hoped for by William Linn. Indeed, many would never return to the bosom of Cumberland County or hear the congratulation of their friends. Benjamin Ishmael, however, was one of the lucky ones.

After spending several months in New York, the Sixth Battalion was dispatched to join other American forces in an attack on the British garrison at Three Rivers in Quebec. It would turn out to be a fool's errand. The surprise assault, which began in the early morning of June 8, 1776, quickly degenerated into one of the worst American military disasters of the young campaign. Betrayed by a guide, the American soldiers spent hours wandering up to their waists in a bog that Colonel (later General) Anthony Wayne remembered as "the most Horrid swamp that ever man set foot in." Colonel Irvine, Benjamin Ishmael's commanding officer, observed, "Nature, perhaps, never formed a place better calculated for the destruction of an army." Shot at by British patrol boats, ambushed by hostile Indians, and attacked by mosquitoes that one soldier later described as of "monstrous size and innumerable numbers," the woefully outnumbered American troops were either killed, captured, or forced to retreat.[14] Among those taken prisoner was Irvine, who later wrote in his diary that "Generals Carleton and Burgoyne [the British commanders] . . . treated us very politely, they ordered us refreshments immediately; indeed, General Burgoyne served us himself."[15]

Needless to say, the American enlisted men did not fare as well. Unlike the officer class, regular soldiers like Benjamin Ishmael did not benefit from any sense of noblesse oblige. Concerning their fate in this and other battles, the historian Charles Henry Jones wrote in 1882:

> Small-pox, famine, raggedness, defeat, and disorder had broken the spirit of this little army. . . . The patriots of whom it was composed had patiently and perseveringly suffered every privation and physical hardship they were able to bear. . . . But everything had been against them from the first. . . . If anyone was responsible for the loss of Canada the blame could not be laid to the charge of these suffering troops. They had been sent . . . without credit, without supplies either of money, provisions, clothing, or munitions of war.[16]

With what was undoubtedly a combination of luck and toughness, both physical and mental, Benjamin Ishmael escaped the carnage at Three Rivers in one piece. He served out the rest of his term and was discharged at Albany, New York, in 1777. After returning to Cumberland County, Ishmael spent several months at home before reenlisting in the Continental Army in 1778. This time, he served in a company commanded by Captain Peter Bentalou in Casimir Pulaski's Independent Legion.[17]

The context for Benjamin Ishmael's second enlistment in the Continental Army differed dramatically from that of his first. By 1778, the *rage militaire* had given way to what Gregory Knouff has called "later war apathy."[18] As growing numbers of people grew tired of the conflict, it became increasingly difficult to fill the ranks of the military. The state of Pennsylvania responded by offering monetary and land bounties to potential recruits. In 1777, Pennsylvania also passed a law making all free white men between the ages of eighteen and fifty-three liable for draft into the militia, with the notable and ultimately controversial caveat that well-off individuals could pay for substitutes to serve in their place. Unlike units of the Continental Army, such militias were typically employed for local defense or, in frontier areas, to combat Indians. The Pennsylvania militia law served to reinforce local ties and to create a sense of white identity among the soldiers, since blacks were essentially excluded from serving, producing a "localist white male nation."[19]

The possibility of receiving a land bounty or of being paid to serve in someone else's stead dramatically increased the economic incentive for poor men in Pennsylvania and elsewhere to enlist in the military after 1777. Like many other soldiers during this period, Benjamin Ishmael may have reenlisted in the Continental Army at least in part for economic reasons. Benjamin was a poor man after serving in the American Revolution, and he was almost certainly a poor man before he went in. Given his likely economic situation in 1778, he may have seen reenlistment as a chance to improve his station in life.

Scholars of the American Revolution have demonstrated that most enlisted soldiers in the Continental Army were "under twenty-three years old and owned little or no property"; in short, they were poor young men.[20] From this evidence, some have concluded that the enlisted troops represented "the 'dregs of society'" and that the Continental Army's privates "acted overwhelmingly out of self-interest."[21] By contrast, others have argued that the fact that enlisted men possessed economic incentives did not necessarily preclude them from also sharing the ideological motives that influenced many in the officer class.[22]

Significantly, most poor men avoided serving in the military altogether. Moreover, those who did serve could have fought with the

British, who also offered financial incentives, or joined a local militia, where the duty was typically lighter and closer to home than in the Continental Army. In the case of Benjamin Ishmael, in particular, there are additional factors to consider. Ishmael was poor when he enlisted in the army but, according to his later military pension application, he was not young. In fact, he was apparently about forty when he reenlisted in 1778.[23] Remarkably, at a time when forty-seven was the average life expectancy for men in the American colonies, Benjamin Ishmael volunteered to serve as an underfed, poorly clothed, middle-aged private. Whether this testifies to the intensity of his patriotism, the depth of his economic desperation, or some combination of the two factors, is impossible to know.

What is certain, however, is that Benjamin Ishmael's decision to enlist was fairly unusual for any resident of Cumberland County in 1778, young or old. Unlike Pennsylvania's eastern counties, which faced the threat of British invasion, or its western ones, which were engaged in an ongoing guerilla conflicts with Native American tribes, Cumberland and other central countries were relatively secure. After an initial burst of enthusiasm for military service, by 1778 most residents preferred to stay at home and raise grain to sell to the Continental Army or, increasingly, to whiskey distillers.[24] In fact, in 1778 the state government upbraided Cumberland County for not providing enough troops. In the same year, John Carothers, an officer in the Cumberland County militia, tried to shame the men of Cumberland into serving, saying that he was "honestly sorry that . . . this county in particular should be found so extremely backward in marching out . . . when one manly effort would in all human probability, work out our political salvation."[25]

Despite his years, and for whatever reasons, Benjamin Ishmael was willing to make one more "manly effort" on behalf of the young country. After he reenlisted, he saw combat against the British at the Battle of Egg Harbour, New Jersey, and elsewhere. In 1779, he was discharged from the Continental Army for the second time, at Williamsburg, Virginia. Ishmael then returned to Cumberland County, where in 1780, he enrolled in the First Battalion of the local militia. Once again, economic factors may have motivated Benjamin Ishmael's enlistment. By 1780, General William Irvine (Ishmael's former commander in the Sixth Battalion) was complaining that growing numbers of men in Cumberland County were paying to have others—perhaps Benjamin Ishmael included—serve in the militia in their place. As Irvine put it in a letter to General Anthony Wayne, "the Monied & luke warm [of Cumberland County] are beginning to procure Men. . . . This goes down hard with people who are fond of militia."[26]

In the same year that he joined the local militia, Benjamin Ishmael also appeared in the Washington Township tax rolls as a "freeman," paying the lowest rate of five pounds.[27] Significantly, out of thirty-seven freemen on the township tax list, only four others paid such a low rate. This indicates that Benjamin Ishmael was poor, even compared to other freemen, who, by definition, did not own any land. The fact that Ishmael appears as a freeman in 1780 is significant for another reason. Since those listed as freemen were supposed to be unmarried, this either means that Benjamin Ishmael had never been married or that he was a widower at the time of the tax assessment.

To remain unmarried until one's fourth decade was unusual in colonial America. However, it is possible that Benjamin Ishmael did not marry before the war because he was an indentured servant. This would also explain why his name does not appear on tax rolls before that time. In Pennsylvania, indentured servants required the consent of their masters in order to marry, lest they incur a heavy financial penalty or an additional year of labor.[28] For this reason, servants might delay or put off marrying during their indenture, which was typically for several years but could extend to seven years or even more under certain circumstances. There is a good possibility that Benjamin Ishmael was a bound laborer, since between one-half and two-thirds of all white immigrants to the colonies arrived as indentured servants.[29] Given that records exist for only a very small percentage of these hundreds of thousands of individuals, the fact that Benjamin Ishmael does not appear in extant registration lists does not mean that he was never a bound servant, especially since during the eighteenth century, colonial Pennsylvania was an important site of indentured labor.[30]

If Benjamin Ishmael was an indentured servant before the American Revolution, it might not only explain why he appears to have been unmarried in 1780 but also why he enlisted in the military. In September 1776, the Council of Safety passed a resolution that required indentured servants and apprentices in Pennsylvania to get the "Consent of their Masters in writing," before serving in the military. Half a year later, in May 1777, a committee in Cumberland County called on the state's Assembly to reaffirm servants' status as property and condemned "the violation of the constitution and laws of the state by enlistments by servants."[31] In March 1778, the Assembly responded by passing an act that compensated masters for servants who had enlisted in the military. These legislative moves indicate that despite the efforts of Pennsylvania officials to prevent the phenomenon, significant numbers of indentured servants were seeking freedom via enlistment in the military. Indeed, at least one officer in the Pennsylvania Line openly recruited indentured servants and "encouraged them to return to him if their masters attempted to correct them . . . [promising that] he would protect them.'"[32]

In 1783, the same year that the United States and England signed the peace treaty ending hostilities, Benjamin Ishmael reappeared in the tax lists for Washington Township as a "freeholder."[33] Technically, this meant that he was a married landowner. However, like several other men listed as freeholders in the tax rolls, Ishmael did not own any land. It is probable, instead, that he was a tenant farmer who rented and worked on someone else's property. If so, then he would have belonged to the growing ranks of tenant farmers (those who rented farm land) and "inmates" (landless wage laborers who were married or widowed) in Pennsylvania during the second half of the eighteenth century.[34] Strengthening this possibility is the fact that the Washington Township tax lists do not possess a separate category for tenants. Therefore, it is likely that the tax assessor listed tenant farmers as freeholders and left the column for acreage blank for these landless individuals, including Ishmael.[35]

More concretely, this document reveals important information about Benjamin Ishmael's relative wealth—or, more accurately, his relative poverty. Although Ishmael was wealthier than the 30 freemen (all taxed at a one-pound rate) who lived in Washington Township in 1783, he was poorer than all but 11 of the 198 freeholders. To give some sense of the range of wealth among the township's freeholders, on one end of the scale, William Smith owned one cow and was taxed at a three-pound rate, while at the opposite end of the scale, Samuel Royer, Esquire, owned 870 acres, six horses, eighteen cows, thirty sheep, two stills, one lanyard, and one "Negro" for a total of £1,478.5. By comparison, Benjamin Ishmael owned one horse and one cow and was taxed at an eight-pound rate.

All the extant evidence indicates that Benjamin Ishmael's life in Pennsylvania was marked by hard work, brave military service, and grinding poverty. In dramatic contrast to the negative portrait later conjured up by the eugenicists, however, nothing suggests either that he was shipped to the colonies as a convict or that he ever committed a crime, let alone was a career criminal. He does not, for example, appear in a list of indictments for Cumberland County, Pennsylvania, from 1750 to

1800.[36] Yet, after years of farming and fighting for the fledgling nation, Benjamin Ishmael had only a pair of animals to his name.

Later census lists show that Benjamin Ishmael and his wife (whose name was apparently not recorded for posterity) had seven children between 1780, when they presumably married, and 1790. The strain of supporting his rapidly growing family appears to have inspired Ishmael to make a dramatic decision around the time that Cumberland County erupted in riots during the Whiskey Rebellion of 1794, an agrarian uprising that the historian Gary Nash has described as growing out of "rural poverty and stunted ambition."[37]

Like thousands of other fortune seekers from Pennsylvania, Virginia, and elsewhere, Benjamin Ishmael and his family set out for Kanta-ke, as the Iroquois originally called it, or, as it became known in English, Kentucky. For a man used to struggle and hardship, this fabled place must have seemed like the Promised Land. In fact, this is how Ishmael's contemporaries, including John Filson, described it: "Kentucke," Filson wrote, was "the land of promise, flowing with milk and honey . . . where you shall eat bread without scarceness, and not lack any thing." One frontier minister even described heaven to his congregants as "a Kentucky of a place."[38]

Before we follow Benjamin Ishmael down the Ohio River or through the Cumberland Gap to this fabled land of plenty, however, it is important to pause and ponder the wider significance of his hardscrabble life in Pennsylvania. Benjamin Ishmael's early biography not only gives lie to the competing claims of the eugenicists and Hugo Leaming, it also raises important questions about a number of persistent myths surrounding the founding of the nation. The first of these myths is that America in the eighteenth century was "the best poor man's country in the world," to quote William Moraley, an indentured servant who arrived in the 1720s.[39]

Over the years, Moraley's widely misinterpreted statement has helped to justify the view that colonial America, in dramatic contrast to Europe, was a kind of poor man's heaven.[40] Supporting this rosy outlook were two other myths: that the American Revolution largely eliminated any class divisions that existed under British rule and that the opening of the frontier made available a nearly limitless supply of cheap but fertile land to anyone who wanted it. Together, these views combined to form a picture of extraordinary upward mobility, which in the nineteenth century would take the form of the Horatio Alger myth.

Against the backdrop of these enduring myths, Benjamin Ishmael's impoverished life in Pennsylvania appears to be an aberration. Yet seen from the perspective of recent scholarship on the persistence of poverty in the revolutionary period, Benjamin Ishmael ceases to look like an anomaly and begins to resemble a kind of early American everyman. Poverty was much more widespread and far more intractable in early America than previously acknowledged. As Nash has written in one of his probing studies of the phenomenon, "every society needs its myths, and the great myth of early American history is that scarce labor in a land-rich environment eliminated poverty."[41] Even the historian Jackson Turner Main, who emphasized "the importance in the American creed of equality of opportunity," acknowledged that "the long-term tendency [of revolutionary America] seems to have been toward greater inequality, with more marked class distinctions."[42]

In support of this conclusion, Main cited a wide range of statistics and documents, including a 1786 editorial from the *Carlisle Gazette*, a newspaper published in the seat of Cumberland County, then home to Benjamin Ishmael. "A great inequality, as to wealth, already takes place among the citizens of this state," the writer soberly observed; "It did so at the declaration of independence . . . yet this very circumstance is not a little contrary to the nature of popular government; and the native influence of it, if not carefully counteracted, will, one day, produce a revolution."[43] Several years later, Thomas Paine echoed this sentiment in a series of works (including *Agrarian Justice* and *Rights of Man*) that condemned "the problem of a 'hereditary' poverty that was the off-spring of commercial society."[44]

Contrary to the Horatio Alger myth, many freed indentured servants and tenant farmers in early America did not achieve much in the way of upward mobility.[45] Among the most destitute were a class of people then known colloquially as the "strolling poor," who wandered from place to place in search of work, shelter, and basic sustenance.[46] For these and other poor folk, the frontier did not always promise salvation. Instead, "the land-rich trans-Appalachian West . . . while attracting thousands of down-and-out in search of better opportunities . . . seems to have shifted the scene of poverty for many while it solved it for others."[47]

In response to the growth of lifelong and inherited poverty during this period, private and public forms of charity (e.g., almshouses and poor farms) expanded, and distinctions between the deserving and undeserving poor became more important. In short, many of the socioeconomic factors that would later play a significant role in shaping the story of the Tribe of Ishmael were already in place at the end of the eighteenth century when Benjamin Ishmael decided to take a leap of faith and move his growing family from Pennsylvania to Kentucky.

By the time Benjamin Ishmael arrived in Kentucky sometime around 1795, European settlers had already been present for several decades. When the first white men set foot in the territory, scores of buffalo, elk, deer, and other game large and small made it a hunter's paradise. Years later, Daniel Boone, one of the first and certainly the most famous of the early white settlers, recalled, "you would not have walked out in any direction for more than a mile without shooting a buck or a bear. There were then thousands of Buffaloes on the hills in Kentucky; the land looked as if it never would become poor; and to hunt in those days was a pleasure indeed."[48]

Kentucky was also home to powerful Native American tribes whose members grew to resent and eventually to resist the advance of European settlers. As the pace of white migration increased in the wake of the American Revolution, so did the intensity of the conflict between Native Americans and settlers. On August 19, 1782, in the Battle of Blue Licks (in what would later become Nicholas County), Native American warriors routed a force of white militiamen, including Daniel Boone and his son Israel, who was killed in the battle.

As would so often be the case in the coming decades, however, the Native American victory at Blue Licks was short-lived. Boone and others soon led a series of reprisal attacks on Shawnee villages, and within a decade, European settlers had completely overwhelmed the Native inhabitants, both militarily and demographically. In 1882, a century after the Battle of Blue Licks, a history of Nicholas County, Kentucky, would observe, "The Indians sought to hold their favorite hunting-grounds, and for years held in check the tide of immigration . . . [but] the line of settlements . . . began to advance, and, with every step, slowly pressed back the Indian race to extinction."[49]

Benjamin Ishmael was almost sixty, already an old man by the standards of the day, when he and his family settled not far from where the Battle of Blue Licks had unfolded. Within a year of their arrival, Benjamin and his wife had their eighth child, a daughter named Prisceilla. Ishmael's wife apparently died during labor or soon after, since he married a second woman named Jane (nicknamed "Jenny") sometime between 1795 and 1800. Among the Ishmael family's new neighbors was Daniel Boone, who, after settling elsewhere for a few years, had returned to the area in 1795, building a one-room cabin on Brushy Fork Creek.

It is impossible to know whether Benjamin Ishmael and Daniel Boone knew one another during the three years that they were neighbors. As we have already seen, more than a century later, Arthur Estabrook would assert in private correspondence with a fellow eugenicist that the Ishmaels had known Daniel Boone in Kentucky.[50] Estabrook made this claim in 1915 after conducting research in Nicholas County, where he probably heard oral traditions linking the two men. Regardless of whether they were personally acquainted, however, the intersection of their stories provides us with an opportunity to see Benjamin Ishmael in a new and revealing light.

Even during his own lifetime, Daniel Boone was transformed into a folk hero and symbol of the frontier. As early as 1784, for example, John Filson had immortalized Boone in his immensely popular account *The Adventures of Col. Daniel Boon.*[51] Benjamin Ishmael, by contrast, lived and died in obscurity. Yet decades later, Ishmael, like his famous neighbor, was mythologized, albeit to a dramatically different end. Daniel Boone's biographers portrayed his rugged lifestyle as virtuous, while the eugenicists condemned Benjamin Ishmael's hardscrabble existence as primitive and savage. Whereas Boone's peregrinations were depicted as embodying the pioneer spirit that built America, Arthur Estabrook portrayed Benjamin Ishmael's journey from Pennsylvania to Kentucky as demonstrating an inherited and degenerate impulse to wander, one that he passed on to his descendants in the so-called Tribe of Ishmael.

In spite of these discursive differences, the two men actually had some important things in common. Like Benjamin Ishmael, Daniel Boone was born in the mid-1730s (1734, to be exact) and originally hailed from southeastern Pennsylvania. Both men were exceptionally tough individuals who survived difficult frontier conditions, long journeys, and multiple military engagements that took the lives of many of their less hardy—and less lucky—peers. Indeed, it is easy to imagine the two grizzled natives of Pennsylvania swapping war stories when they were neighbors between 1795 and 1798. Finally, after raising large families, Boone and Ishmael both died at the ripe old age of eighty-six, in 1820 and 1822, respectively.

Of course, there were also significant differences between the two men. Daniel Boone had received a basic education and could read and write, while Benjamin Ishmael was apparently illiterate. Born to a landowning family, Boone served as a colonel in the military, was elected to the Virginia assembly, and, at different points in his life, owned large tracts of land and slaves to work them. Ishmael, by contrast, may have toiled as an indentured laborer before serving as an enlisted soldier, and once the Revolutionary War ended, he barely eked out a living as a farmer.

Benjamin Ishmael was supposedly a congenital wanderer, but he actually stayed put in one place for long periods of time. Daniel Boone, on the other hand, spent years traveling along the shifting American frontier in search of adventure, better hunting grounds, and profit. Over the years Daniel Boone was accused and then acquitted of collaborating with the British, lost thousands of acres of land due to unpaid taxes, was the defendant in numerous lawsuits, and, in 1798, even became the subject of an arrest warrant issued by Mason County, Kentucky.[52] Ironically, although he was later demonized as the founding father of a supposedly cacogenic clan, there is no evidence to suggest that Benjamin Ishmael ever ran afoul of the law or was even accused of a crime.

Unlike Daniel Boone, Benjamin Ishmael did not lead the kind of life that lends itself easily to legend. He was not a great adventurer, military leader, politician, or rogue. Instead, he was one of the many early Americans whose largely undocumented and now forgotten lives intersected with the widely mythologized lives of "great men" like Boone. Despite their anonymity, ordinary people like Benjamin Ishmael were the mortar that held together the foundation of the young nation. Whatever faults he may have had, Benjamin Ishmael did not deserve to become a pawn in the game of the eugenicists.

In 1799, soon after Daniel Boone abandoned Kentucky for Missouri, the area around Blue Licks became Nicholas County. Nestled between the Appalachian foothills to the east and the rolling Blue Grass to the west, Nicholas County was, in the words of one nineteenth-century observer, "like the little Republic of San Marino . . . small in extent of territory, and nearly as rough and hilly. . . . In point of numbers, area, mountainous surface, and a lofty, chivalrous hospitality, the two sections are very much alike." The same historian described the earliest residents of the county as "a hardy, fearless and self-reliant people . . . simple in their habits and accomplishments, and devoid of all extravagance. Fresh from the scenes of the Revolutionary struggle—a free people—their manhood elevated, they shrank from no difficulty, but, with a stern, unflinching purpose, they went forth to subdue the wilderness and subject it to the use of man."[53]

Many of the early inhabitants of Nicholas County—there were 2,925 in 1800—had received bounty lands in return for service during the American Revolution. These flinty men and women cut down oak, ash, poplar, maple, walnut, hickory, and other trees and carved out farms, where they raised livestock, grew wheat, hemp, rye, corn, and tobacco, and distilled whiskey.[54] Along with the white settlers, in 1800 there were also 248 black slaves in Nicholas County, who farmed the land under white overseers and worked as servants in the wealthier homes. That year the county possessed 1,427 acres of "first-rate land" (prime farming land), 15,526 acres of "second-rate land," 30,334 acres of "third-rate land," four stud horses, and two tavern licenses.[55]

It is possible—though his name does not appear in extant Bounty Land Warrant records—that Benjamin Ishmael received a bounty grant to settle in Kentucky and then either sold or lost ownership of the land in some other way. Unfortunately, many poor and financially unsavvy veterans quickly lost hard-earned bounty land to speculators following the American Revolution. In any case, by the beginning of the nineteenth century, it appears that Benjamin Ishmael was once again toiling as a tenant farmer.

The Nicholas County tax rolls from 1801 to 1806 list Benjamin Ishmael among voting white males over twenty-one years of age and describe him as owning a couple of mares but no land.[56] Starting in 1804, Ishmael's eldest son, James (b. 1781/82), begins to appear in the tax rolls alongside his father, and several years later, two younger sons, Thomas (b. around 1787) and John (b. July 25, 1789) are also listed, indicating that they had reached the age of twenty-one. Benjamin Ishmael, himself, disappears from the Nicholas County lists after 1806 but reappears in the tax rolls for neighboring Fleming County in 1810, where he is listed as owning three mares. Significantly, the Fleming County tax rolls from this year also state that Ishmael owned 186½ acres of third-rate land along the Licking River watercourse.[57]

For perhaps the first time in his life, Benjamin Ishmael could lay claim to some land of his own. It may have taken him seventy-four years but he was now officially a property owner. Although the acreage would fluctuate (reaching a low of 116 acres in 1813 before returning to 186 acres in 1814), Ishmael would hold on to his land for the next few years.[58] In 1815, Benjamin and his sons (now including Robert, b. 1790) once again appeared in the Nicholas County tax rolls. Yet the elder Ishmael was no longer listed as owning any land, a situation that would remain constant until his death. He may have lost it because of debt, or he may have transferred it to one of his sons.[59]

During Benjamin Ishmael's brief tenure as a property owner, he decided to write out—or, more accurately, to have written out for him— a last will and testament. At the time, as the document suggests, Ishmael may have been suffering from a serious illness. Perhaps he was just worn out after nearly eighty years of hard living, or maybe he felt that he finally owned something worth passing on to his heirs. Whatever the reason, on November 13, 1813, Benjamin Ishmael affixed his mark on the following will:

> In the name of God, Amen. I, Benjamin Ishmael of the County Fleming, and State of Kentucky, being in a sick and low condition of health, but of sound mind and memory and calling to hand the mortality of this body, it being appointed once for all men to die, doth ordain and establish this to be my last will & Testament in manner and form following, viz: first I recommend my soul to Almighty God who gave it, and my body to be buried with decent Christian-burial; and next I allow all my just and lawful debts to be paid; and first Item in the legacies is, I give and bequeath to my daughter Margaret Wheeler, the sum of fifty cents, 2nd I give to my son James Ishmael, fifty cents, 3rd I give and bequeath to my son Thomas Ishmael, fifty cents, 4th, I give and bequeath to my daughter Sarah Ervin, fifty cents, 5th I give and bequeath to my son John Ishmael, fifty cents, 6th I give and bequeath to my daughter Rosey Myers, fifty cents, 7th I give and bequeath to my son Robert Ishmael, fifty cents, 8th I give and bequeath to my daughter Presay Ishmael, fifty cents, 9th I give and bequeath to my son Benjamin Ishmael, fifty cents, 10th I give and bequeath to my son Samuel Ishmael, fifty cents, 11th and lastly, I give and bequeath to my dearly beloved wife Jenny Ishmael all the balance and remainder of my estate, real and personal for her own proper use so long as she remains in her widowhood and to be disposed of at her death as she thinks proper, but provided she should think proper to enter into a married State and not live single, then and in that case I do not allow her anymore of my estate then the one third of my personal estate and the third of the proceeds of my real estate during her natural life or other words in the land of the County should entitle her to and for putting this my last will and testament in full force and execution I do hereby appoint my son James Ishmael Executor of this my said last will and testament revoking all others. In Testimony Where as I have unto set my hand affixed my seal this 13th day of November in the year of our Lord One Thousand Eight hundred and Thirteen.[60]

Despite its formal tone—the same introductory religious phrases appear in other wills from Nicholas County, for example—this document gives us a glimpse into Benjamin Ishmael's character. He comes across as a proud family man, determined to pass on what little he owned to his wife and many children. Indeed, the very act of creating a will suggests that Benjamin Ishmael, despite his material poverty, sought to leave behind a legacy to his descendants. Ishmael gave all of his living children—even his oldest son James, whom he named as the executor of his estate—the same amount of money. Perhaps he did not want to favor any child over another or to cause any divisions among his children once he was gone. As it turns out, however, Benjamin Ishmael was not yet on death's door. Instead, he would continue to struggle with declining health and mounting financial difficulties for nearly a decade.

Far from being anomalous, Benjamin Ishmael's hand-to-mouth existence was becoming increasingly common among the thousands of Revolutionary War veterans who had managed to survive into the first few decades of the nineteenth century. In 1818, the United States Congress sought to address the desperate circumstances of these men by passing the Revolutionary War Pension Act. This pioneering legislation granted $240 a year to officers and $96 annually to enlisted men who had served at least nine months (or until the war ended) in the Continental Army and were now "in reduced circumstances" and "in need of assistance from [the] country for support."[61]

The Revolutionary War Pension Act was a dramatic turning point in a number of respects. Following the American Revolution, people often made a sharp distinction between men who had served in local militias and those who had fought for the Continental Army. The militiamen were portrayed as brave individuals who embodied the noble ideals of the young democracy, while the veterans of the Continental Army were depicted as mercenary "vice-ridden rabble," belonging to a military institution whose very existence was "antithetical to republican ideals."[62] In the patriotic afterglow of the War of 1812, however, the nation began to adopt a more sympathetic attitude towards Continental Army veterans, many of whom were now living in dire financial circumstances. And so was born the powerful image of the "suffering soldier," who deserved the country's gratitude and help.[63]

The positive reevaluation of the Continental Army and its soldiers was not the only radical element of the Revolutionary War Pension Act. Of even greater long-term significance is the fact that the act was also "the first federal effort to aid some of the nation's poor; the 1818 pension act combined features of a pension plan and poor-law provisions to reward and assist impoverished Continental army veterans . . . [and] was the largest federal relief effort until the twentieth century."[64] Before the pension act was implemented, indigent war veterans, like other poor people in America, depended on aid from financially solvent family members (who were legally expected to support needy kin), private charities, and local governments. Rather than money, this aid typically took the form of fuel, food, clothing, and shelter.[65] It was also intended to be temporary. Those who could not escape the cycle of poverty after receiving such aid were classified as paupers and, in some localities, could be institutionalized in poor farms and almshouses. In addition, both the so-called deserving and undeserving poor were subject to surveillance to make sure that they were using aid properly and that they did not have relatives who could support them.

Despite its great significance as the first federal relief program, the Revolutionary War Pension Act did not fundamentally change the way that most aid to the poor was distributed in America. Indeed, as the story of the Tribe of Ishmael dramatically illustrates, private charities and local governments continued to dominate poor relief throughout the nineteenth century. Instead, what the Revolutionary War Pension Act did was to create a new category of deserving poor who, for the first time, could receive aid from the federal government.

In fact, some of the strongest opposition to the act came from critics concerned that needy veterans who received pensions would be stigmatized as paupers. For this reason, the act emphasized that veterans had earned their pensions as a result of the heroic service that they had rendered to their county as young men. In this way, the act marshaled the "moral sentiment" of the American people, exemplified by Congressman Josiah Cushman's remarks that veterans "suffered, they fought, and bled . . . in the cause of justice and humanity . . . [and now their] poverty, wretchedness and scars . . . invoke our justice as well as our gratitude."[66] Just as importantly, the act also established a radical new legal principle: the responsibility of the federal government to provide aid to at least some of its neediest citizens. As the *Federal Republican and Baltimore Telegraph* newspaper put it at the time: "If a patriot when dead deserves a marble monument at the expense of his country, how much more does he deserve during life, a subsistence from his country?"[67]

In 1818, Benjamin Ishmael joined thousands of other poor and not-so-poor veterans in applying for a pension. On October 1, he presented himself before a circuit court judge in Nicholas County and took an oath that he had served in the Continental Army for two years. Describing himself as eighty-two years old, Ishmael testified that he was currently in "reduced circumstances and . . . in need of the assistance of his country for his support."[68] He also acknowledged that he did not possess any official documentation of his military service. This was not an uncommon situation, particularly since fires in 1800 and 1804 had destroyed many of the relevant federal records. In the absence of any evidence beyond his own testimony, Benjamin Ishmael's initial application for a pension was denied by the War Department. As it turns out, however, even had he received a pension in 1818, Benjamin Ishmael would have had to reapply a few years later because the entire program was revamped in the wake of a scandal that forced all pensioners to resubmit their applications.

When the pension program was first implemented in 1818, the government expected only several thousand individuals to apply "at a cost of $115,000 for the first year."[69] And yet, within a few months, it became clear that an enormous number of applicants would soon swamp the local and federal infrastructure as well as the program's relatively small budget. Within two years of its implementation, the cost went from 1.5 percent to 16 percent of the entire federal budget. At this rate, the total cost of the program (projecting a time span of fifteen to twenty years) would end up being $75 million and "require a direct tax to pay for it."[70] Making matters worse, critics began to complain that the program was rife with corruption and fraud on the part of applicants and local officials alike. Not only did imposters pay off judges and clerks to certify falsely that they were veterans, but real veterans who were far from destitute, and in some cases actually wealthy, received pensions.

In response to the growing scandal, the government passed a second version of the pension act in 1820. Applicants like Benjamin Ishmael, who did not appear in extant military records could now demonstrate their service by securing the testimony of two "disinterested" witnesses. The integrity of these witnesses, as well as of the local officials who processed the applications, had to be verified by other witnesses in sworn affidavits. Moreover, all applicants were now required to provide a list of all their assets, both real and personal, and to pass a means test. Under the new legislation, veterans who possessed assets of less than two hundred dollars received pensions, those who had between two hundred and four hundred dollars were evaluated at the "discretion" of the War Department, while those worth more than four hundred dollars were denied aid.[71]

On March 23, 1822, Benjamin Ishmael reapplied for a pension. This time he listed his age as eighty-three, although, according to his earlier pension application, he should have been eighty-six. At the time, however, it was not uncommon for ages to fluctuate in official documents. On his list of assets (which the court certified as accurate), Ishmael reported "two horse creatures, at $65, six head of cattle at $30, fifteen head of hogs some small at $15. Farming utensils, plough hoes at $6. Amounting in all to $116."[72] In addition to listing these meager possessions, Ishmael noted, "My occupation is that of a farmer and am too old and infirm to pursue it. My wife is about fifty years of age; neither of us is able to work to support me. I live on the bounty of my friends. I have no other family." As with his last will and testament, Ishmael affixed an "X" in place of a signature at the end of the application.

One of the most striking things about Benjamin Ishmael's pension application is that even though he had numerous children living in the immediate area, he declared that he had "no other family." While it is possible that Ishmael was simply lying in order to create the impression of greater poverty, several factors mitigate against this explanation. First, the application was made in the presence of local officials whose own honesty was under close scrutiny in the wake of the earlier pension scandal.[73] Second, these Nicholas County officials would almost certainly have known about Benjamin Ishmael's large family, either from personal contact or from local records, especially tax lists.

By stating that he had "no other family," Benjamin Ishmael may have meant that only his wife currently lived with him, a use of the phrase that appears in other pension applications as well.[74] It is also possible that Ishmael, like many impoverished veterans, incorrectly assumed that the pension act was administered along the lines of traditional poor relief. For this reason, he and many other applicants emphasized that they did not have any family members who could financially support them. In fact, however, the personal assets of the applicant and not the ability of family members to provide support was what determined eligibility.

A total of twenty thousand veterans applied for pensions under the amended act of 1820.[75] Benjamin Ishmael resembled his fellow applicants in a number of important ways. Like him, 88.6 percent had been privates during the war, 62 percent now claimed to be infirm, 61 percent were non-landowning farmers or laborers, two-thirds were unable to sign their names, and a large plurality had enlisted in 1775–76 and had served between thirteen and thirty-six months. Benjamin Ishmael's $116 in assets put him slightly below the national applicant average of $129 in court-assessed wealth but slightly above the $102 average of applicants from the west, including Kentucky.

At the same time, however, Benjamin Ishmael differed from the majority of applicants in certain important respects. Strikingly, only 11.9 percent of veterans were seventy-five years or older, and the overall median age of applicants was sixty-five. Indeed, Benjamin Ishmael appears to have been older than all of the other applicants from Nicholas County, in most cases by two decades.[76] A majority of the pension applicants had enlisted before the age of twenty-six (7.8 percent were between eight and fifteen years old when they joined) and only 17.8 percent had been older than twenty-eight. Benjamin Ishmael, as we have seen, appears to have been around forty when he enlisted. Close to half of all applicants came from the Northeast and another 31.5 percent lived in the Mid-Atlantic region, while only 8.1 percent were from the West. Three-quarters of all applicants had less than $100 in assets, and 13.4 percent reported no assets at all. Like Benjamin Ishmael, 11.3 percent had between $101 and $200. Finally, despite their poverty, only 16.8 percent of applicants reported receiving assistance from family, friends (as in Ishmael's case), or their community, as opposed to 83.2 percent who did not.

This time around, Ishmael was granted a pension. His claim was supported by the sworn testimony of two former comrades-in-arms, Hugh Drennon, a neighbor in Nicholas County, and John Rannels, a resident of Ohio.[77] Both men testified that in 1776 they had served with Benjamin Ishmael in Captain Abraham Smith's company in the Sixth Regiment of the Pennsylvania Line. In his testimony, Drennon noted that Ishmael had "faithfully continued in the actual service of the country for the period he enlisted for . . . when he was honorably discharged from said services."

Benjamin Ishmael was officially awarded a pension by the War Department on January 15, 1823. Unfortunately, the good news arrived a few months too late. The old patriot and pioneer had passed away on July 10, 1822. Although Ishmael did not live long enough to benefit from his pension, the government paid his survivors a lump sum of several hundred dollars, prorated to October 1, 1818, the date when he first applied. In death, if not in life, Benjamin Ishmael had succeeded in providing a nest egg for his wife and children.

In the following decades, numerous descendants of the family patriarch would continue to keep the Ishmael name and memory alive in Nicholas and the surrounding counties. One of these descendants, Benjamin Ishmael's oldest son, James, acquired one hundred acres of land in Nicholas County in 1819. He and his wife, Mary McFerrin, established a farm and raised nine children together until James's death in 1830. The couple's three oldest children, Margaret, William, and Benjamin, left Kentucky and eventually settled in Illinois. In 1832, the couple's third oldest son, John Samuel McFerrin Ishmael (1811–1885) married a woman named Elizabeth Lynn (b. 1810). They remained in Nicholas County and had twelve children before Elizabeth died in 1851.

Almost three decades later, John Samuel, who was both a farmer and a Methodist minister, and his son Timothy Lynn Ishmael (1846–1906) built a small church on land abutting their farm. Dedicated in November 1878 and opened for services on May 1, 1879, this Methodist church became known throughout the county as Ishmael Chapel.[78]

Today, more than two hundred years after Benjamin Ishmael first set foot in what would become Nicholas County, Kentucky, his descendants still live not far from where he settled. Indeed, Carl Ishmael, a great-grandson of John Samuel, currently owns the family farm next to Ishmael Chapel, which is still standing. This makes the Ishmaels the only family to have owned land continuously in that part of Nicholas County—sometimes called the "Ishmael section"—since the beginning of the nineteenth century.[79] Thus, in perhaps the greatest of the many ironies connected to the Tribe of Ishmael, a family that was supposed to be genetically predisposed to wandering has actually turned out to be remarkable for the opposite reason: the deep roots that its members planted in a single place.

Had all of Benjamin Ishmael's many descendants remained in Kentucky, there would never have been a Tribe of Ishmael to "discover" in the slums of Indianapolis. In the years before and after Benjamin Ishmael's death, however, many of his children and grandchildren joined the waves of poor migrants from Kentucky, Tennessee, and other Upland Southern states who began to settle the new frontier of the upper Midwest.

One of these migrants, the man who would supposedly become known as "Granddaddy Ishmael" among members of the Tribe of Ishmael, was Benjamin's third son and fifth child, John. Tax lists reveal that John Ishmael was never able to acquire any land while he was a resident of Nicholas County and, at best, only owned a couple of mares. In 1809, John married a local woman named Elizabeth ("Betsy") Harbet, and a few years later he served as a private in Johnson's Mounted Regiment during the War of 1812. By 1820, John Ishmael was back in Nicholas County, and he and his wife were struggling to raise five children under the age of ten with another one on the way.[80]

Given his difficult financial circumstances and growing family, it is not surprising that sometime in the late 1820s—he appears on the Nicholas County tax lists for the last time in 1826—John Ishmael decided to leave Kentucky for what he hoped would be greener pastures. Federal census lists indicate that John Ishmael—it is unclear what happened to Betsy— first settled in 1830 right across the Kentucky border in Scioto County,

Ohio, and then moved on to Indiana, where he spent the next several decades with children who had also moved to the state.

In 1840, John Ishmael was living in Delaware County, Indiana, along with three of his sons, Fred (b. 1815), Henry (b. 1812), and James (b. 1809).[81] That year, the Ishmael brothers wed three sisters from Ohio. Fred married Mary Ann Smith in April, Henry married Sarah Smith in June, and James married Susan Smith in July.[82] Sometime in the next decade, John Ishmael moved to Tipton County along with his sons Thomas (b. 1823), James, and Henry. The federal census from 1850 lists John as living in the household of Henry, an illiterate tenant farmer, and his wife, Sarah. Of that couple's four children in 1850, two are listed as having been born in Indiana, one in Illinois, and another in Ohio, indicating that since their marriage ten years earlier, the couple had moved from place to place in search of better circumstances.[83]

By 1860, Henry and Sarah Ishmael had settled in rural Cain Township, Fountain County, Indiana, where they joined three of Henry's brothers, Thomas, Frances (b. 1820), and James, along with their respective families. In the federal census for that year, John Ishmael appears in the household of his oldest son, James, and James's wife, Susan.[84] Many years later, Susan would gain dubious fame as the elderly matriarch of the Tribe of Ishmael. At the time, however, she was a young mother trying to take care of seven children—including an eight-year-old named Sarah, who would later become known as the "Ishmael woman who walks like a man and talks bass" and had four husbands—and an aging father-in-law. Making ends meet must have been difficult since the census describes James Ishmael as a farm laborer with only $100 in personal assets and no real estate. It probably did not help their condition that Susan, James, and his father, John, were all unable to read or write. Significantly, however, the census does not list them, or any of the other Ishmaels living in Fountain County in 1860, under the heading "dumb, blind, insane, idiotic, pauper, or convict."

Like his older brother James, Frances Ishmael worked as a farm laborer, was illiterate (as was his wife), and possessed a meager personal estate of only $50. The couple had five children. Their oldest, Joshua (b. 1842), is listed separately as a servant in another household. The four younger children, Frances (b. 1853), Henry (b. 1855), Andrew (b. 1856), and Margaret (b. 1858) would later appear prominently in accounts of the Tribe of Ishmael in Indianapolis.

Thomas, the third Ishmael brother living in Fountain County, and his first wife, Rachel (b. 1821), had seven children. He owned the equivalent of $100, worked as a boot- and shoemaker, and, like many other Ishmaels of his generation, fought in the Civil War.[85] James Frank Wright would later describe Thomas Ishmael's "three corned log cabin" as "perhaps the queerest structure in the state," while Hugo Leaming crowned him the "third patriarch" of the Tribe of Ishmael. Whether Thomas was, in fact, a leader of his extended family is impossible to say, though he may have trained his brother Henry in his trade, since the latter—once a farmer—is also listed as a shoemaker in the 1860 census. Since the federal census of 1850, Thomas and Rachel Ishmael had had three more children. The four oldest children, ranging in age from sixteen to ten years old, are described as attending school in the last year. The youngest, a girl named Ruth, is listed as only a year old at the time of the 1860 census.

On the eve of the Civil War, therefore, John Ishmael and his descendants were still living within a stone's throw of one another in rural Indiana. The Ishmael brothers worked as farm laborers and shoemakers, had large families, and shared the responsibility of taking care of their elderly father. The closeness of their families was intensified by the fact that three Ishmael brothers had married a trio of sisters, making their children first cousins on both sides. It may have also been strengthened by their shared poverty. In this respect, the Ishmaels were hardly unique. At the time, many other residents of Fountain County were uneducated and impoverished laborers and craftsmen.

Yet, as in Nicholas County, Kentucky, some residents of Cain Township had managed to acquire fertile farmland and, with it, financial stability. For example, the 1860 census lists among those farmers owning land Isaac Shoemaker, a thirty-six-year-old farmer with land worth $2,000, and Terrick Cumpton, a forty-nine-year-old farmer with land worth $3,200 who was wealthy enough to maintain a live-in servant. Moreover, as Fountain County became more settled, merchants, businessmen, and professionals began to form a middle class. By 1850, according to a contemporary history, the county supported ten flour mills, twenty sawmills (for the extensive lumber in the area), one woolen factory, one brewery, one distillery, one foundry, fifteen preachers, ten lawyers, twenty-five doctors, and between fifty and sixty stores and groceries.[86]

Although they were members of the working poor, extant records suggest that the Ishmaels in Fountain County were able to scrape by before the Civil War. As illiterate laborers, the Ishmael brothers could not accumulate enough capital to purchase land of their own, but they appear to have had stable if humble roofs over their heads—probably on the farms where they worked—and food in their pots. This situation would change dramatically following the war, however, when the state of Indiana, like the nation as a whole, entered a severe economic depression. Agricultural areas like Fountain County were especially devastated for a combination of reasons, including a drop in bank loans tied to future crops, a dramatic cut in military purchases, and the opening of the area west of the Mississippi to farming, which caused agricultural prices to tumble.[87] The result was a large increase in farm foreclosures, the laying off of laborers, and a veritable flood of migration from rural areas to cities like Indianapolis. In short, the socioeconomic conditions necessary for the formation of the so-called Tribe of Ishmael were beginning to take shape.

The postwar economic depression, which was only worsened by the financial crisis of 1873, had a powerful and immediate impact on the Ishmaels living in rural Indiana. Thereafter, many members of the family would disappear forever from official records like the federal census. Displaced by farm foreclosures and a lack of stable work and shelter, many Ishmaels apparently took to the road during this period. Some members of the younger generation, such as Frances, Andrew, Henry, and Margaret, as well as some of the older generation, like Susan and Fred, began to settle in Indianapolis. Soon after arriving, these desperately poor men and women would come to the attention of the Township Trustee and, in 1878, they would be "discovered" by Oscar McCulloch.

It is unclear what happened to the family patriarch, John Ishmael, during this traumatic period. Those who later wrote about the Tribe of Ishmael presented different versions of his death. James Frank Wright claimed that John Ishmael had died sometime between 1845 and 1848 and was buried in Covington, Indiana. In light of census records that list John Ishmael as alive in 1860, this version was obviously incorrect. Nevertheless, it inspired Hugo Leaming to state unequivocally that John Ishmael had died while traveling on the road in 1846. More plausibly, Arthur Estabrook suggested that "Granddaddy Ishmael" had died in the Fountain County Poor Asylum sometime around 1870. If true, this would indicate that after taking care of their father for decades, John Ishmael's children could no longer support him in the midst of the economic depression. Or, perhaps, the octogenarian had volunteered to enter the poorhouse so as not to burden his already overextended children.

Despite its plausibility, however, there is no extant evidence to support this version, nor did Estabrook cite any proof in his account. There is, however, one more possibility that does have documentary support. The federal census from 1870 indicates that John Ishmael may have returned to Nicholas County, Kentucky, to live with his son Samuel (b. 1811) and his wife Sarah (b. 1821) on their farm. This would have made financial sense, since Samuel was much better off than his brothers in Indiana, with $2,000 in real estate and $1,000 in personal assets.[88]

The image of an elderly John Ishmael, compelled to leave his desperately poor children and grandchildren in Indiana and return to a state he had left nearly half a century before, is poignant. But nothing exemplifies the Ishmael family's tragic circumstances in Indiana following the Civil War better than the story of its youngest member, Amanda Ishmael. Born in 1860 to Henry and Sarah Ishmael, Amanda was only a small child when the economic depression devastated the Indiana countryside. In the absence of any documentation regarding their fate, it is possible that Henry and Sarah Ishmael both died within a short time of one another, leaving behind Amanda and her siblings as orphans.[89] Alternatively, Henry and Sarah may have been forced to make a decision that would have been painful for any family and, in particular, for one as close knit as the Ishmaels. Either way, by the fall of 1867, Amanda Ishmael had become an inmate of the Fountain County poorhouse.

However she ended up there, Amanda did not remain institutionalized for long. In the Fountain County list of indentures for 1847–84, we find the following record, dated September 20, 1867:

> Indenture of apprenticeship between Lewis R. Hetfield, overseer of the poor inmates of the County House of Fountain County, State of Indiana, on the part of Amanda Ishmael, an inmate of said House without parents or guardian and James Orr of the same county, witnesseth that said Lewis R. Hetfield for said Amanda Ishmael and as such overseer of the poor who is supposed to be about seven years of age hath and doth hereby bind said Amanda Ishmael as an apprentice unto James Orr until the fourth day of September, 1876, nine years from date hereof to work at the usual occupation required about a house. And that said James Orr covenants with said Lewis R. Hetfield who acts for said Amanda Ishmael that he will have her learn all that is usually required to be learned as a housekeeper etc., and to provide her, during the time she may be with him the said James Orr with all necessaries proper to her age and condition, and cause her to be sent to school three (3) months in each year during her continuance to reside with him and on the 4th day of September 1876, to give her good clothing.[90]

With this contract, Amanda Ishmael was handed over to James Orr for the next nine years to work as his housekeeper. Death records from

Fountain County indicate why James Orr needed someone to cook and clean for him. In June 1861, Orr's wife, Jane (née Miller), died at the age of thirty-six. Three years later, in July 1864, Orr's daughter, Mary, aged fourteen, also passed away. Apparently, Amanda Ishmael would be the sole "woman of the house," at the tender age of seven.

This stark document speaks to a different, even more brutal kind of poverty than the form experienced by Benjamin Ishmael, Amanda's great-grandfather, during the period in which he composed his last will and testament a half century before. Although he was always a poor man and may have even started out life as an indentured servant, Benjamin Ishmael had managed to keep his family intact and was even able to pass on a legacy—however humble—to his many children. Now, by contrast, Amanda had become a living symbol of the crisis that over-whelmed the Indiana branch of the Ishmael family following the Civil War. For the first time in their history, some of the Ishmaels were so poor that they could no longer look after their most vulnerable and needy members, whether old, as in the case of John, or young, as in the case of Amanda. It is significant in this regard that none of Amanda's relatives in Fountain County could apparently afford to take her in.

Unfortunately, Amanda Ishmael's sad story would be repeated over and over again in the years following the Civil War as thousands of poor and orphaned children became "bound servants" in Indiana and other Midwestern states. Without a doubt, the most famous of these children was Mary Alice Smith, a girl from Liberty, Indiana, whose experiences inspired James Whitcomb Riley's poem "Little Orphant Annie" (a printer's error changed the original "Allie" into "Annie"). At the age of nine, both of Mary Alice's parents died, and her uncle bound her out as a ser-vant in the home of Reuben and Elizabeth Riley, where she did house-work and helped to take care of the family's four children, including James. In his famous poem, Riley later described Mary Alice's arrival and her household duties:

> Little Orphant Annie's come to our house to stay,
> An' wash the cups an' saucers up, an' brush the crumbs away,
> An' shoo the chickens off the porch, an' dust the hearth, an' sweep,
> An' make the fire, an' bake the bread, an' earn her board-an'-keep.[91]

Amanda Ishmael's responsibilities—the "work at the usual occupa-tion required about a house," as her contract put it—must have resem-bled Mary Alice Smith's duties. However, unlike the real little orphan Allie, who quickly became a beloved fixture in the Riley household, we have no idea what kind of experience Amanda Ishmael had in James Orr's home or whether she served out the full nine years of her indenture. Concerning the remainder of her life, we possess only the broadest outlines. In 1881, Amanda Ishmael married a man named Charles Wesley Brady in Pawnee City, Nebraska, had six children, and died at the age of sixty-five in Topica, Illinois, in 1925.[92]

Like the story of Benjamin Ishmael, that of his great-granddaughter shatters many of the assumptions that underlies Oscar McCulloch's portrait of the Tribe of Ishmael. Amanda Ishmael was not a career criminal or a habitual wanderer, nor is there any evidence to suggest that she was "feebleminded." Instead, she was one of the youngest—and, therefore, most vulnerable—members of an already poor family that was devastated by factors far outside of its control. As illiterate members of the rural working poor, the Ishmaels of Indiana belonged to one of the most socially and economically disadvantaged classes of nineteenth-century America.

At the same time, the Ishmaels retained Upland Southern values like strong kinship ties, an independent spirit, and a suspicion of centralized authority. This complex socioeconomic background, rather than any genetic predisposition toward criminality, wandering, or feeblemindedness, explains the genesis of the behaviors that became associated with the so-called Tribe of Ishmael.

Contrary to the accounts by Oscar McCulloch and his successors, the Ishmaels did not arrive in the area of Indianapolis when it was still a Native American settlement (i.e., prior to 1822). John Ishmael was still in Nicholas County, Kentucky, during this period. Nor is there any evidence to suggest that the Ishmaels were ever welcomed with open arms by the native inhabitants because of their supposed "Indian" ways and "half-breed" ancestry. In fact, federal census records for Indianapolis do not list any Ishmaels in the city prior to 1870, when three individuals are mentioned. Most likely, the first member of the family to settle in Indianapolis was Fred Ishmael (by then married to Kate Thornton), who appears in *Logan's Indianapolis Directory* for 1868 under the heading "Frederick Ishmell, laborer."[93]

Even during the lean years following the Civil War, it appears that most members of the Ishmael family in Indiana either continued to live and work in rural communities throughout the state or, as Amanda Ishmael did when she gained her freedom, they migrated further west in search of better lives. A smaller number of Ishmaels settled in the city of Indianapolis, where they formed part of the rapidly growing underclass of displaced rural migrants. Most of these migrants eventually became part of the industrialized wage-labor economy that came to dominate Indianapolis and other American cities in the second half of the nineteenth century.

From the accounts of contemporary observers, it appears that many of the Ishmaels living in Indianapolis did not, at least not immediately, follow suit. Instead of joining the wage-labor economy, the Ishmaels and some of their fellow migrants—particularly those with Upland Southern roots—lived a kind of hybrid rural-urban existence. Rather than working in one of the city's new factories, stockyards, or industrial laundries, the assortment of people eventually labeled "Ishmaelites" retained their economic and social independence by adopting an itinerant lifestyle.

It is likely that some members of the "tribe" would have entered the wage-labor economy had they had the opportunity. But like thousands of poor, unskilled workers in Indianapolis, they were unable to find employment during the lean years that followed the financial crisis of 1873. Lacking a safety net, the most fortunate of the city's poor residents managed to find shelter, however run-down, in the slums that emerged in Indianapolis during this period. The less fortunate were forced to join the swelling ranks of what had been known as the "strolling poor" in the eighteenth century and what we now call the "homeless."

During the mid-1870s, a distinctive pattern emerged among some of the itinerant and homeless people in Indianapolis. They would spend part of the year living in the city, where they earned money by hauling ashes, skimming grease, and in some cases, begging or committing petty crimes to supplement their meager incomes. The rest of the year they would spend traveling the countryside, visiting kin throughout the Upper Midwest and doing seasonal labor on farms. It is this group of people, including some members of the Ishmael family itself, that eventually become known as the Tribe of Ishmael or the Ishmaelites. The rest, as they say, is history.

Afterword

There remains a final chapter of the Tribe of Ishmael's story to tell, one inspired by my contact with contemporary members of the Ishmael family itself. I did not discover these Ishmaels in a broken-down shack or in an isolated valley. In fact, I did not discover them at all. Unlike the downtrodden and hunted people described by Oscar McCulloch, Arthur Estabrook, or Hugo Leaming, the Ishmaels I encountered were not hidden on the margins of society. Rather, they were proudly and openly celebrating their family heritage via the twenty-first century's version of the public square: the Internet.

I came across the Ishmael family genealogical Web site by chance. To say I was surprised would be an understatement. It was at the beginning of my research, and I still believed that the Ishmaels, along with the other families belonging to their "tribe," had been driven underground or worse by the eugenics movement during the 1920s and 1930s. Upon scrolling through the numerous messages posted by family members, however, it became clear to me not only that the Ishmaels were alive and well but, it seemed, that none of them had any idea that their ancestors had once belonged to something called the Tribe of Ishmael. Rather than a cacogenic clan or a marginalized crypto-Muslim community, the Ishmaels on the Web site appeared to be comfortable middle-class Americans who got together for annual family picnics.

Besides the jarring disjunction between the published accounts of the Tribe of Ishmael and the image presented by the family today, two things jumped out at me from the Ishmael Web site. The first was that many contributors had questions about where the Ishmael family and its unusual surname had originated. One person openly asked whether any Ishmaels were currently Jewish or Muslim (a question that received no affirmative responses). Among the suggestions posted by family members were that the Ishmaels were originally French or German Jews, that they were Pennsylvania Dutch, or that they were Irish or English. The most popular and, as we have already seen, most likely theory was that the Ishmaels had originally come from Wales. The second thing that struck me was the large number of messages that discussed their family patriarch, Benjamin Ishmael. From the biographical information and long list of descendants posted on the site—including many mentioned by McCulloch and Estabrook in their accounts—it became clear that this was none other than the Benjamin Ishmael who was the supposed founder of the Tribe of Ishmael.

The existence of the Ishmael genealogical Web site completely undermined the eugenicists' portrait of a hopelessly cacogenic family whose inferior germ plasm would doom its members to a future of poverty, crime, and degradation unless they were prevented from reproducing. Nor did the national emergency supposedly posed by the Ishmael family during the 1920s ever materialize. Instead, seventy years after the eugenics movement singled out the family at the Chicago world's fair to represent the dangers of bad breeding, the Ishmaels were proudly trying to reconstruct their ancestors' stories.

There was a powerful irony in the fact that the Ishmaels themselves were creating the same kind of elaborate family trees that Oscar McCulloch and his successors had once constructed. Rather than trying to prove the family's degeneracy, however, the point of the Ishmaels' own genealogical research was to celebrate their family history. On the Web site, contributors swapped stories about colorful family members from the past, like their patriarch, Benjamin Ishmael, and "Fiddling" Jack Ishmael, who owned a gold mine in Calaveras County, California, with Samuel Clemens (better known as Mark Twain). They also mentioned members of the clergy, businesspeople, academics, physicians, law enforcement agents, and other professionals who belonged to more recent generations of the family. If contributors to the Web site knew of the Tribe of Ishmael, they certainly weren't discussing it. Then again, I thought, maybe they just didn't want to air the family's dirty laundry in a public forum.

In order to see whether memories of the tribe had in fact survived among current members of the family, I decided to get in touch with them. As delicately as I could, I explained the history of the Tribe of Ishmael and asked whether the subject rang a bell. Among the people I eventually made contact with, it did not. I could not help but wonder, however, whether at least some of the Ishmaels who did not respond to my inquiries actually knew about the history of the Tribe of Ishmael and, for that very reason, were suspicious of my intentions and refused to talk. Perhaps, as in Arthur Estabrook's day, they simply did not want their family to become the subject of further exploitation or surveillance.

As I conducted more research over the next few years, I would think a great deal about this issue. I tried to keep in mind that Oscar McCulloch, Arthur Estabrook, and Hugo Leaming had all possessed good intentions—at least in their own eyes—when they wrote about the Tribe of Ishmael. Unlike my predecessors, I sought to avoid making tendentious claims about the Ishmaels, and, conversely, I tried to document their history with information from a wide variety of sources, including the family itself. But I also knew that like all reconstructions of the past, my own narrative, even if turned out to be illuminating, would also be incomplete. At least, I hoped, it would treat the Ishmael family with respect, something that had so often been absent from previous accounts.

The responses I eventually received from members of the Ishmael family when I told them about the Tribe of Ishmael's various incarnations, ranged from the amused to the angry. Ultimately, several members of the family shared their extensive genealogical information with me. While this book's narrative does not represent the Ishmaels' own version of their history—only a member of the family could produce that—it does reflect the influence of some of their research. Indeed, it would not have been possible for me to tell the story that I have if the Ishmaels themselves had not first devoted so much time and effort to documenting the lives of their ancestors.

Today, the American government no longer supports draconian social policies such as mass sterilization, antimiscegenation laws, involuntary institutionalization, and restricted immigration on the basis of eugenics. Yet more and more people have become involved in what a biologist colleague of mine calls "boutique eugenics." On the basis of startling advances in genetics, many prospective parents now seek to influence the makeup of their unborn children. Indeed, eugenics is making a dramatic comeback, albeit in a form that empowers individuals, rather than the state. In this brave new world, the story of the Tribe of Ishmael serves as a powerful reminder of the socially destructive role that eugenics once played in an earlier phase of American history and what it may yet become if we are not careful.

Within this context, contemporary Ishmaels' efforts to preserve their own past constitutes a powerful refutation of the eugenics movement and its attempts to demonize and eliminate their family. In the years since eugenicists put the Ishmaels on display at the Chicago world's fair of 1933, state-sponsored eugenics has been discredited in the United States. By contrast, the Ishmael family has continued to grow, and many of its members now take great pride in exploring their heritage. Ironically, from our perspective at the beginning of the twenty-first century, it is the eugenicists themselves, not the Ishmaels, the Jukes, the Win, or any of the other supposedly cacogenic groups, who appear to us like an antisocial tribe that once threatened the fabric of the United States.

Notes

1. For a good discussion of the Century of Progress Exposition and a photograph of the Indian Village and the General Motors Tower, see Robert Rydell, *World of Fairs: The Century-of-Progress Expositions* (Chicago: University of Chicago Press, 1993), 92–105. On the history of ethnological villages at world's fairs, including the Columbian Exposition of 1893, see Robert Rydell, *All the World's a Fair: Visions of Empire at American International Expositions, 1876–1916* (Chicago: University of Chicago Press, 1984).

2. The eugenicists' preference for "live" displays is clear from their activities throughout the 1920s and 1930s. Beginning with the Kansas State Fair of 1920, the eugenics movement organized "Fitter Families" exhibits in fairs around the country. As part of these exhibits, eugenics workers chose contestants from among the fairgoers whose physiological and psychological traits were then evaluated and recorded. Although the eugenics movement did not have an official exhibit at the New York World's Fair of 1939, Robert Rydell has noted that eugenicist principles "undergirded" the "Typical American Families" display, which was jointly underwritten by the Ford Motor Company, the Federal Housing Administration (FHA), and the Johns Manville Company (a manufacturer of asbestos shingles). Prior to the fair, families were invited to send in essays explaining why they were typical and filled out a questionnaire that included "racial origin" as one of the categories. Not surprisingly, the winners of the contest were native-born whites; they received a free trip to the fair in a new Ford automobile and were housed on the fairgrounds in structures built by the FHA with asbestos materials provided by Manville. On the "Fitter Families" movement, see Rydell, *World of Fairs,* 38–54; on the New York World's Fair of 1939, ibid., 56–57.

For the most thorough bibliography on the eugenics movement in the United States, see Paul Lombardo and Gregory Dorr, "Eugenics Bibliography," at www.healthsystem.virginia.edu/internet/bio-ethics/bibliographylombardo.cfm. Three of the most important general histories remain Mark Haller, *Eugenics: Hereditarian Attitudes in American Thought* (New Brunswick, N.J.: Rutgers University Press, 1963); Daniel Kevles, *In the Name of Eugenics: Genetics and the Uses of Human Heredity* (New York: Knopf, 1985); and Kenneth Ludmer, *Genetics and American Society: A Historical Approach* (Baltimore: Johns Hopkins University Press, 1972). More recent works that explore different aspects of the eugenics movement and its impact on American public policy include (but are hardly limited to) Laura Briggs, *Reproducing Empire: Race, Sex, Science, and U.S. Imperialism in Puerto Rico* (Berkeley: University of California Press, 2002); Daylanne English, *Eugenics in American Modernism and the Harlem Renaissance* (Chapel Hill: University of North Carolina Press, 2003); Wendy Kline, *Building a Better Race: Gender, Sexuality, and Eugenics from the Turn of the Century to the Baby Boom* (Berkeley: University of California Press, 2005); Nancy Ordover, *American Eugenics: Race, Queer Anatomy, and the Science of Nationalism* (Minneapolis: University of Minnesota Press, 2003); Alexandra Stern, *Eugenic Nation: Faults and Frontiers of Better Breeding in Modern America* (Berkeley: University of California Press, 2005).

3. Quotes are from Harry Laughlin, "The Eugenics Exhibit at Chicago: A Description of the Wall-Panel Survey of Eugenics Exhibited in the Hall of Science, Century of Progress Exposition, Chicago, 1933–34," *Journal of Heredity* 26, no. 4 (1935): 155–162.

4. On the Social Gospel movement in the United States, see Walter Rauschenbusch, *A Theology for the Social Gospel* (New York: Macmillan, 1917). See also Paul Allen Carter, *The Decline and Revival of the Social Gospel: Social and Political Liberalism in American Protestant Churches, 1920–1940* (Ithaca, N.Y.: Cornell University Press, 1956); Susan Curtis, *A Consuming Faith: The Social Gospel and Modern American Culture* (Columbia: University of Missouri Press, 2001); Charles Howard Hopkins, *The Rise of the Social Gospel in American Protestantism, 1865–1915* (New Haven: Yale University Press, 1940); C. Howard Hopkins and Ronald White, Jr., *The Social Gospel: Religion and Reform in Changing America* (Philadelphia: Temple University Press, 1975); Ralph Luker, *The Social Gospel in Black and White: American Racial Reform, 1885–1912* (Chapel Hill: University of North Carolina Press, 1998).

5. Theodore Allen, *The Invention of the White Race* (London and New York: Verso, 1994). Also see Rydell, *World of Fairs*, 55.

6. Noel Ignatiev, *How the Irish Became White* (New York: Routledge, 1996); David Roediger, *The Wages of Whiteness: Race and the Making of the American Working Class* (London and New York: Verso, 1999).

7. Michael Katz, *The Undeserving Poor: From the War on Poverty to the War on Welfare* (New York: Pantheon Books, 1989), 13.

8. The quote is from William Moraley, an indentured servant who arrived in the colonies in the 1720s; see *The Infortunate: The Voyage and Adventures of William Moraley, an Indentured Servant,* ed. Susan Klepp and Billy G. Smith (University Park: Pennsylvania State University Press, 2005): 53. For different interpretations of its significance, see James Lemon, *The Best Poor Man's*

Country: A Geographical Study of Early Southeastern Pennsylvania (Baltimore: Johns Hopkins University Press, 1972); Billy G. Smith, "'The Best Poor Man's Country'?" in *Down and Out in Early America,* ed. Billy G. Smith (University Park: Pennsylvania University Press, 2004).

9. Jacob Riis, *How the Other Half Lives* (New York: Charles Scribner's Sons, 1890; reprint, New York: Penguin, 1997), 183–184.

10. Horatio Alger, *Ragged Dick, or Street Life in New York* (Boston: A.K. Loring, 1868), 19.

11. On the broader phenomenon of failure in nineteenth-century America, see Scott Sandage, *Born Losers: A History of Failure in America* (Cambridge: Harvard University Press, 2005).

12. Ashley Montague, *Human Heredity* (Cleveland: World Publishing Co., 1959), 288.

13. For the expression "tribal twenties," see John Higham, *Strangers in the Land: Patterns of American Nativism, 1860–1925* (New Brunswick, N.J.: Rutgers University Press, 1955).

14. Albert Edward Wiggam, *The Next Age of Man* (Indianapolis: Bobbs-Merrill Company, 1927), 28–29.

15. Christine Rosen, *Preaching Eugenics: Religious Leaders and the American Eugenics Movement* (New York: Oxford University Press, 2004),130.

16. See Paul Lombardo, "Miscegenation, Eugenics, and Racism: Historical Footnotes to *Loving v. Virginia,*" *Davis Law Review* 21 (1988): 422–452.

17. Edward J. Larson, *Sex, Race, and Science: Eugenics in the Deep South* (Baltimore: Johns Hopkins University Press, 1995), 153–154.

18. Hugo Leaming, "The Ben Ishmael Tribe: A Fugitive 'Nation' of the Old Northwest," in *The Ethnic Frontier: Group Survival in Chicago and the Midwest,* ed. Melvin Holli and Peter Jones (Grand Rapids, Mich.: Wm. B. Eerdmans Publishing Co., 1977), 98–141, at 122.

19. Ibid., 141.

20. See, for example, Ron Sakolsky and James Koehnline, eds., *Gone to Croatan: Origins of North American Dropout Culture* (Brooklyn, N.Y.: Autonomedia Dropout Press, 1993); Peter Lamborn Wilson, *Sacred Drift: Essays on the Margins of Islam* (San Francisco: City Lights Books, 1993); and on the Internet James Erwin, "Footnotes to History: The Nations You Didn't Learn About in High School," www.buckyogi.com/footnotes/. On the basis of Leaming's work, Michael Gomez writes in *Black Crescent: The Experience and Legacy of African Muslims in the Americas* (New York: Cambridge University Press, 2005), "there is a more discernable Islamic influence among the latter [i.e., the Tribe of Ishmael]. Perhaps what is more important is that there is a linkage between the Ishmaelites and the movement of Noble Drew Ali, thereby possibly representing at least one uninterrupted chain of transmission of Islamic influence from the eighteenth century into the twentieth" (186). Gomez later adds, "It is with the Ishmaelites of Kentucky, Indiana, and Illinois, however, that the Islamic dimension is reified" (196). And he refers to the Tribe of Ishmael as "a group with its own unique relationship to Islam. . . . In fact, members of the Ishmaelite diaspora from Indiana, arriving in places such as Detroit, encountered the Moorish Science movement and joined" (200). Gomez discusses the

Ishmaelites alongside other groups in the Americas with purportedly Islamic roots (e.g., the Melungeons).

21. www.muslim.org; see archive for Jan. 1, 1999.

22. Ibid., archive for Aug. 20, 1999.

23. Elof Axel Carlson, *The Unfit: A History of a Bad Idea* (Cold Spring Harbor, N.Y.: Cold Spring Harbor Laboratory Press, 2001), 177.

24. Edwin Black, *War against the Weak: Eugenics and America's Campaign to Create a Master Race* (New York: Four Walls Eight Windows, 2003), 53.

25. Vijay Prashad, *The Karma of Brown Folk* (Minneapolis: University of Minnesota Press, 2000), 20.

26. On this subject, see the recent book by Michael Oren, *Power, Faith, and Fantasy: America in the Middle East, 1776 to the Present* (New York: W. W. Norton and Company, 2007). Oren's work appeared after I had finished writing this book.

27. Katz, *Undeserving Poor*, 16.

28. Oscar Lewis, "The Culture of Poverty," in *On Understanding Poverty*, ed. Daniel P. Moynihan (New York: Basic Books, 1968), 188.

29. Oscar Lewis, *La Vida: A Puerto Rican Family in the Culture of Poverty— San Juan and New York* (New York: Random House, 1966), xxlv–xlvii.

30. On the Moynihan report, see Katz, *Undeserving Poor*, 44–52.

31. Gunnar Myrdal, *Challenge to Affluence* (New York: Pantheon Books, 1963), 10. For an analysis of Myrdal's use of this concept and its genealogy and significance in general, see Herbert Gans, *The War against the Poor: The Underclass and Antipoverty Policy* (New York: Basic Books, 1995), 27–28.

32. "The American Underclass: Destitute and Desperate in the Land of Plenty," *Time*, Aug. 29, 1977, 14–27.

33. Gans, *War against the Poor*, 36.

34. On the concept of "race rebels," see Robin Kelley, *Race Rebels: Culture, Politics, and the Black Working Class* (New York: Free Press, 1996).

35. In his work *Off the Books: The Underground Economy of the Urban Poor* (Cambridge: Harvard University Press, 2006), Sudhir Venkatesh explores the interstitial economic activities of residents of a poor African American neighborhood on Chicago's South Side. In many ways, his portrait of this contemporary community evokes parallels with the Indianapolis slum residents who became stigmatized as the Tribe of Ishmael. As Venkatesh explains (389, n. 1), the phrase "shady world" was coined by the sociologists St. Clair Drake and Horace Cayton in their book *Black Metropolis: A Study of Negro Life in a Northern City* (Chicago: University of Chicago Press, 1993; orig. pub. 1945).

36. Thomas Paine, "Agrarian Justice." Although the pamphlet was published in 1797, Paine notes in the author's preface that he actually wrote it in the winter of 1795–96.

1. HOW OSCAR MCCULLOCH DISCOVERED THE ISHMAELITES

1. Much of the biographical portrait in this chapter is based on Genevieve Weeks, *Oscar Carleton McCulloch, 1843–1891: Preacher and Practitioner of Applied Christianity* (Indianapolis: Indianapolis Historical Society, 1976), and

Stephen Ray Hall, "Oscar McCulloch and Indiana Eugenics" (Ph.D. diss., Virginia Commonwealth University, 1993).

2. Edward Leary, *Indianapolis: The Story of a City* (Indianapolis: Bobbs-Merrill Company, 1971), 129.

3. For a description of this event, see William Doherty, "John Caven," in *The Encyclopedia of Indianapolis,* ed. David Bodenhamer and Robert Barrows (Bloomington: Indiana University Press, 1994), 392.

4. Hester Anne Hale, *Indianapolis: The First Century* (Indianapolis: Marion County/Indianapolis Historical Society, 1987), 113.

5. For these demographic statistics, see Gregory Rose, "Hoosier Origins: The Nativity of Indiana's United States–Born Population in 1850," *Indiana Magazine of History* 81 (Sept. 1985): 201–232; Gregory Rose, "Upland Southerners: The County Origins of Southern Migrants to Indiana by 1850," *Indiana Magazine of History* 82 (Sept. 1986): 242–263; Gregory Rose, "Migration Patterns" and "Upland Southerners," in *Encyclopedia of Indianapolis,* ed. Bodenhamer and Barrows, 1005–1007, 1375–1377.

6. The joke and statistics appear in Andrew Cayton, *Frontier Indiana* (Bloomington: Indiana University Press, 1996), 272.

7. Jacob Piatt Dunn, *Greater Indianapolis: The History, the Industries, the Institutions, and the People of a City of Homes* (Chicago: Lewis Publishing Co., 1910), 1: 250–253; Hale, *Indianapolis,* 113.

8. Berry Sulgrove, *History of Indianapolis and Marion County* (Philadelphia: L.H. Everts and Co., 1884), 88.

9. W.R. Holloway, *Indianapolis: A Historical and Statistical Sketch of the Railroad City* (Indianapolis: Indianapolis Journal Print, 1870), 248.

10. Sulgrove, *History of Indianapolis,* 92.

11. Howard Johnson, *A Home in the Woods: Pioneer Life in Indiana, 1821–1907; Oliver Johnson's Reminiscences* (Bloomington: Indiana University Press, 1951), 118.

12. Sulgrove, *History of Indianapolis,* 92. See also Holloway, *Indianapolis,* 55.

13. Johnson, *Home in the Woods,* 118.

14. Quoted in Cayton, *Frontier Indiana,* 291.

15. Ibid., 293.

16. Sulgrove, *History of Indianapolis,* 90.

17. Johnson, *Home in the Woods,* 119.

18. George Cottman, "Old Time Slums of Indianapolis," *Indiana Magazine of History* 7 (1911): 173.

19. Ibid.

20. Sulgrove, *History of Indianapolis,* 90.

21. Hale, *Indianapolis* 114.

22. Piatt Dunn, *Greater Indianapolis,* 252.

23. Cottman, "Old Time Slums," 171.

24. McCulloch's fourteen-volume diary (for 1877–91) is in the Rev. Oscar C. McCulloch Papers, L363, Indiana State Library, Indiana Division (hereafter cited as McCulloch Papers). In quoting the diary, I have reproduced his sometimes idiosyncratic spelling, punctuation, and grammar.

25. In the State of Indiana counties are divided into townships. Marion County consists of a number of townships, including Center Township, where Indianapolis is located. Each township has a chief administrative officer known as a trustee, who provides poor relief and other functions.

26. The Charity Organization Society copied this Township Trustee report into the case files of several members of the Ishmael family. See, for example, George Ishmael's file, Indiana Historical Society, Family Service Association Records, Series 7: BV 1215, no. 1431.

27. On the discovery, see Weeks, *McCulloch,* 169–171; Hall, "McCulloch and Eugenics," 97–99.

28. On the use of the phrase "Tribe of Ishmael" to refer to Muslims in early sources on Islam, see Michael Cook and Patricia Crone *Hagarism: The Making of the Islamic World, Hagarenes and the Tribe of Ishmael* (Cambridge: Cambridge University Press, 1977).

29. See Rashi on Genesis 16:12.

30. Letter 18, Headquarters of Fifth Iowa Infantry, Boonville, Missouri, 9/22/1861, see www.rootsweb.com/~iabuchan/history/136.htm.

31. Weeks discusses McCulloch's interest in the "Eastern Question"; *McCulloch,* 40. Robert Arthur Arnold, *Through Persia by Caravan* (New York: Harper and Brothers, 1877); Frederick Burnaby, *Ride to Khiva* (New York: Harper and Brothers, 1877); Edward Freeman, *The Turks in Europe* (New York: Harper and Brothers, 1877).

32. Edwin Godkin, "The Eastern Question," *North American Review* 124 (1877): 106–126.

33. I have been unable to locate the bibliographic information for this work.

34. Arnold, *Persia by Caravan,* 491.

35. On this conflict, see Henry Castor *The Tripolitan War, 1801–1805: America Meets the Menace of the Barbary Pirates* (New York: F. Watts, 1971).

36. On this topic, see Timothy Marr, "Imagining Ishmael: Studies of Islamic Orientalism in America from the Puritans to Melville" (Ph.D. diss., Yale University Press, 1997).

37. For the nickname "Grasshopper Gypsies" applied to the Ishmaelites of Indiana, see James Frank Wright, "The Tribe of Ishmael," 28; unpublished manuscript in the Indiana State Archives, Commission on Public Records. I examine this manuscript at length in chapter 3.

38. David Millard, *A Journal of Travels in Egypt, Arabia Petrea, and the Holy Land* (New York: Lamport, Blakemann and Law, 1853). On this phenomenon, see Terry Brooks Hammons, "'A Wild Ass of a Man': American Images of Arabs to 1948" (Ph.D. diss., University of Oklahoma, 1978).

39. Letter from C. C. Royce to Warren Keifer of Springfield, Ohio, August 4, 1880, as quoted in *The History of Clark County, Ohio* (Chicago: W. H. Beers & Co.), 223.

40. Fuad Sha'ban, *Islam and Arabs in Early American Thought: The Roots of Orientalism in America* (Durham, N.C.: Acorn Press, 1991), 189.

41. Mark Twain, *The Innocents Abroad* (New York: Harper and Brothers, 1911), 2: 199. On Twain's Near Eastern musings, see Richard Fleck, "The

Complexities of Mark Twain's Near Eastern Stereotyping," *Mark Twain Journal* 21 (summer 1982): 13–15; Marwan Obeidat, *American Literature and Orientalism* (Berlin: K. Schwarz, 1998), 119–123.

42. In his dissertation "Imagining Ishmael," 183–224, Timothy Marr devotes an entire chapter, called "'Turkey Is in Our Midst': Imagining the Mormon Church as an American 'Islam,' 1830–1912," to exploring this fascinating topic. Most of my information concerning nineteenth-century efforts to "Islamicize" Mormonism is based on this fine piece of work.

43. Ballard Dunn, *How to Solve the Mormon Problem: Three Letters* (New York: American News Company, 1877), 3–4.

44. Marr, "Imagining Ishmael," 203.

45. Catharine Waite, *The Mormon Prophet and His Harem* (Cambridge, Mass.: Riverside Press, 1866), 35.

46. Marr, "Imagining Ishmael," 222–223.

47. Freeeman, *The Turks in Europe*, 77.

48. Nicole Hahn Rafter, *White Trash: The Eugenics Family Studies 1877–1919* (Boston: Northeastern University Press, 1988), 28.

49. Richard Dugdale, *"The Jukes": A Study in Crime, Pauperism, Disease, and Heredity; Also, Further Studies of Criminals* (New York: G. P. Putnam's Sons, 1877).

50. See Weeks, *McCulloch*, 165–218, for McCulloch's involvement in Indianapolis charity organizations. Hall discusses McCulloch and the Indianapolis Benevolent Society; "McCulloch and Eugenics," 116–125.

51. Oscar McCulloch, "Fifty Years of the Indianapolis Benevolent Society," in *Year-Book of Charities, 1885–1886* (Indianapolis: Carlon & Hollenbeck, 1886), 17.

52. On these laws, see Katz, *Undeserving Poor*, 11–12.

53. Weeks, *McCulloch*, 173.

54. Hall, "McCulloch and Eugenics," 118–121.

55. On this development, see Higham, *Strangers in the Land*, 32–33.

56. Matthew Frye Jacobson, *Whiteness of a Different Color: European Immigrants and the Alchemy of Race* (Cambridge: Harvard University Press, 1998), 71.

57. As cited in Hall, "McCulloch and Eugenics," 122–124.

58. As cited in Weeks, *McCulloch*, 175.

59. See Hopkins, *Rise of the Social Gospel*.

60. On McCulloch and the Social Gospel, see Weeks, *McCulloch*, 130–156.

61. Ibid., 182.

62. Statistics for poor relief given for Center Township, Marion County (i.e., Indianapolis) are taken from Arthur Estabrook, *The Tribe of Ishmael* (unpublished manuscript, 1922), 8. Series 2, Box 1, Folder 7, in Arthur Estabrook Papers, 1910–1943, M.E. Grenander Department of Special Collections and Archives, University Libraries, State University of New York at Albany (hereafter referred to as the Estabrook Papers).

63. As cited in Hall, "McCulloch and Eugenics," 121.

64. On this phase of McCulloch's career, see Hall, "McCulloch and Eugenics," 125–164; Weeks, *McCulloch*, 183–218.

65. On the broader phenomenon, see Frank Watson, *The Charity Organization Movement in the United States* (New York: Macmillan Co., 1922).

66. As cited in Weeks, *McCulloch,* 187.

67. Hall, "McCulloch and Eugenics," 214–215.

68. Letter to Editor, *Indianapolis Journal,* Nov. 15, 1884, as cited in Weeks, *McCulloch,* 201.

69. Weeks, *McCulloch,* 103–113.

70. As cited in Hall, "McCulloch and Eugenics," 100.

71. Ibid., 104–105.

72. As David Mayall has written, the "1880s were perhaps the heyday of the Gypsy as subject, with articles published in a wide array of newspapers and journals"; *Gypsy-Travellers in Nineteenth-Century Society* (New York: Cambridge University Press, 1988), 9.

73. Marlene Sway, *Familiar Strangers: Gypsy Life in America* (Urbana: University of Illinois Press, 1988), 37–39, mentions evidence that Roma were already present in America during the colonial period, though significant numbers only began arriving in the 1880s and 1890s.

74. Jane Darlington, *Marion County, Indiana, Birth Records, July 1882-September, 1907* (Zionsville, Ind.: Biosynergetics, Inc., 1987).

75. As cited in Mayall, *Gypsy-Travellers,* 114.

76. See Kline, *Building a Better Race,* p. 13.

77. Weeks, *McCulloch,* 154.

78. Ibid., 143.

79. Ibid.

80. Hall, "McCulloch and Eugenics," 235.

81. Ibid., 236.

82. Ibid.

83. Weeks, *McCulloch,* 202.

84. As Peter Hall has noted, "During the mid-1880s, throughout the cities and above all throughout London, there was a spirit of cataclysmic, even violent, change in the air"; *Cities of Tomorrow: An Intellectual History of Urban Planning and Design in the Twentieth Century* (Oxford: Blackwell Publishing, 2002), 25.

85. Andrew Mearns, *The Bitter Cry of Outcast London* (London: Clarke, 1883), 5.

86. Quotes are from Charles Booth, "The Inhabitants of Tower Hamlets (School Board Division), Their Condition and Occupations," *Journal of the Royal Statistical Society* 50 (1887): 326–391; and "Conditions and Occupations of the People in East London and Hackney, 1887," *Journal of the Royal Statistical Society* 51 (1888): 276–33, as cited in Hall, *Cities of Tomorrow,* 28–31.

87. The review appeared in the *Indianapolis News,* December 24, 1890. See Weeks, *McCulloch,* 81–82. General William Booth, *In Darkest England* (New York: Funk and Wagnalls, 1890); Riis, *How the Other Half Lives*; Henry Morton Stanley, *In Darkest Africa* (New York: Charles Scribner's Sons, 1890).

88. Booth, *In Darkest England,* 18.

89. On this topic, see Daniel Pick, *Faces of Degeneration: A European Disorder, c.1848–c.1918* (New York: Cambridge University Press, 1989).

90. This confirms Pick's view that "the 'aggression' of evolutionary discourse may have had as much to do with perceived 'terrors', 'primitiveness' and fragmentation 'at home' as in the colonies"; ibid., 38.

91. Cited in ibid., 12.

92. Ibid., 109.

93. Hall, "McCulloch and Eugenics," 138.

94. "Extract from Report of the Standing Committee on the Organization of Charity," *Yearbook of Charities 1888–1889;* Address Made at Sixteenth Annual Conference of Charities and Corrections, San Francisco, September 10–18, 1889.

95. In this regard, I would modify Rafter's claim that "*none* of the works [i.e., the family studies] trace bad immigrant or urban families"; *White Trash* 13, italics in original. In a note, she adds that "McCulloch's 'Tribe of Ishmael' (1888) does not really provide an exception because although the Ishmaels 'gypsied' around the margins of cities, they were in no way integrated into urban life" (13, n. 16). In fact, however, the problem with the Ishmaels is that they were very much integrated into the life of the city, just not in the way approved of by social reformers like Oscar McCulloch.

2. IN DARKEST INDIANAPOLIS

1. Oscar McCulloch, "The Tribe of Ishmael: A Study in Social Degradation," Conference of Charities and Correction, *Proceedings* (1888), 154–159. Reprint: (Indianapolis: Charity Organization Society, 1889), 1–7.

2. Bruce Aldridge, "The Tribe of Ishmael Came and Multiplied," *Indianapolis Magazine,* July 1972, 37.

3. Ray Lankester, *Degeneration: A Chapter in Darwinism* (London: Macmillan Co., 1880), 59.

4. McCulloch, "The Tribe of Ishmael," 1.

5. Ibid.

6. William Melish, *The History of the Imperial Council Ancient Arabic Order Nobles of the Mystic Shrine for North America, Second Edition, 1872–1921* (Cincinnati: Abingdon Press, 1921), 36–38.

7. Ibid., 14, 25–26.

8. Ibid., 280.

9. Zeynep Celik, "Speaking Back to Orientalist Discourse at the World's Columbian Exposition," in *Noble Dreams, Wicked Pleasures: Orientalism in America, 1870–1930,* ed. Holly Edwards (Princeton: Princeton University Press, 2000), 77–99.

10. On Webb, see Richard Brent Turner, *Islam in the African-American Experience* (Bloomington: Indiana University Press, 1997), 63–66.

11. Washington Irving, *Mahomet and His Successors,* ed. Henry Pochmann and E.N. Feltskog (Madison: University of Wisconsin Press, 1970), 9–10. See Obeidat, *American Literature and Orientalism;* Sha'ban, *Islam and Arabs in Early American Thought.*

12. *Journals of Ralph Waldo Emerson,* ed. Edward Waldo Emerson and Waldo Emerson Forbes (Boston and New York: Houghton Mifflin Co., 1909–1914), 1: 327–328, 479.

13. Marr, "Imagining Ishmael," 225.

14. Riis, *How the Other Half Lives*, 147.

15. As cited in Roland Freeman, *The Arabbers of Baltimore* (Centreville, Md.: Tidewater Publishers, 1989), 3.

16. *Punch*, July–December 1851.

17. *Harper's Weekly*, September 19, 1868; italics added.

18. Freeman, *The Arabbers*, 8.

19. Edward Said, *Orientalism* (New York: Vintage Books, 1979), 207.

20. McCulloch, "Tribe of Ishmael," 5.

21. Ibid.

22. Ibid., 2–3.

23. Ibid., 5.

24. John H.B. Nowland, *Early Reminiscences of Indianapolis, with Short Biographical Sketches of Its Early Citizens, and of a Few of the Prominent Business Men of the Present Day* (Indianapolis: Sentinel Book and Job Printing House, 1870), p. 273, mentions that the first homicide in the city occurred before 1840.

25. For these and other examples of hereditarian views of alcohol, see Haller, *Eugenics*, 14, 19, 31.

26. McCulloch, "Tribe of Ishmael," 6.

27. Ibid., 5.

28. Charles Davenport, *The Feebly Inhibited: Nomadism, or the Wandering Impulse, with Special Reference to Heredity* (Washington, D.C.: The Carnegie Institution of Washington, 1915), 7, 11, 11 n. 1.

29. McCulloch, "Tribe of Ishmael," 5.

30. On this subject, see Hale, *Indianapolis*, 52.

31. Roediger, *The Wages of Whiteness*, 19.

32. Ibid., 21.

33. Jane Helleiner, *Irish Travellers: Racism and the Politics of Culture* (Toronto: University of Toronto Press, 2000), 35. Also see Mary McCann, Joseph Ruane, and Séamas Ó Síocháin, *Irish Travellers: Culture and Ethnicity* (Belfast: The Institute of Irish Studies, The Queen's University of Belfast, 1994). On the broader phenomenon of marginal communities in urban contexts, see David Sibley, *Geographies of Exclusion: Outsiders in Urban Societies* (Oxford: Blackwell, 1981).

34. Helleiner, *Irish Travellers*, 33.

35. McCulloch, "Tribe of Ishmael," 5.

36. Helleiner, *Irish Travellers*, 33.

37. Ibid., 111.

38. Ibid., 68–69.

39. Leaming refers to "Tinkers" (i.e., Travellers) as a possible component of the Tribe of Ishmael; "The Ben Ishmael Tribe," 106.

40. Jared Harper, "'Gypsy' Research in the South," in *The Not so Solid South: Anthropological Studies in a Regional Subculture*, ed. J. Kenneth Morland (Athens: University of Georgia Press, 1971), 16–24.

41. Charity Organization Society Case file for Ed Maiden and his family. Family Service Association Records, Series 7, date of entry, 3-26-90

(Manuscripts Collections Department, William Henry Smith Memorial Library, Indiana Historical Society). I discuss the case files of the Charity Organization Society in greater detail in chapter 4.

42. John Hartigan, Jr., *Racial Situations: Class Predicaments of Whiteness in Detroit* (Princeton: Princeton University Press, 1999), 32.

43. On the invention of the concepts *hillbilly* and *Appalachia* in general, see Anthony Harkins, *Hillbilly: A Cultural History of an American Icon* (New York: Oxford, 2003); John O'Brien, *At Home in the Heart of Appalachia* (New York: Knopf, 2001); Henry Shapiro, *Appalachia on Our Mind: The Southern Mountains and Mountaineers in the American Consciousness, 1870–1920* (Chapel Hill: University of North Carolina Press, 1978). For an impassioned take on this subject by an author who explicitly identifies himself as "white trash," see Jim Goad, *The Redneck Manifesto: How Hillbillies, Hicks, and White Trash Became America's Scapegoats* (New York: Simon and Schuster, 1997).

44. Hal Bruno, "Chicago's Hillbilly Ghetto," *The Reporter*, June 4, 1964, 28–31.

45. Lewis Killian, "The Adjustment of Southern White Migrants to Northern Urban Norms," *Social Forces* 16 (1937): 67.

46. Respectively, Grace Leybourne," Urban Adjustments of Migrants from the Southern Appalachian Plateaus," *Social Forces* 16 (1937): 245; Hartigan, *Racial Situations*, 88.

47. Bruno, "Chicago's Hillbilly Ghetto," 28–29, 30.

48. James Maxwell, "Down from the Hills and into the Slums," *The Reporter*, December 13, 1956, 27.

49. Ibid., 28.

50. Leybourne, "Urban Adjustments of Migrants," 241.

51. McCulloch, "Tribe of Ishmael," 6.

52. John Seeley et al., *Commmunity Chest: A Case Study in Philanthropy* (Toronto: University of Toronto Press, 1957), 495, n. 31. On this phenomenon, in general, see Michael Patrick and Evelyn Goodrich Trickel, *Orphan Trains to Missouri* (Columbia: University of Missouri Press, 1997).

53. Weeks, *McCulloch*, 210.

54. McCulloch, "Tribe of Ishmael," 5.

55. Oscar McCulloch, "State and National Registration of the Dependant, the Defective and the Delinquent Classes," *Proceedings of the National Conference of Charities and Correction*, 1891.

3. HOW THE OTHER HALF LIVES

1. McCulloch cited the help of "Mr. [James] Frank Wright, detailed by the county commissioners to assist in the prosecution of this investigation"; "The Tribe of Ishmael," 2. For biographical information on Wright, see his obituary in the *Indianapolis Star*, July 31, 1927, part 2, 22.

2. James Frank Wright, "The Tribe of Ishmael," unpublished manuscript in Indiana State Archives, Commission on Public Records. In 1917, Wright lent his original notes to Arthur Estabrook, who used them extensively in his own work

on the Tribe of Ishmael. According to the cover of the extant manuscript, Estabrook returned a typed version of Frank's notes to Amos Butler, the head of the Board of State Charities of Indiana, in 1922. This manuscript was later donated to the Indiana State Archives in 1935 by Laura Greely, the chief clerk of the State Board of Charities. Although the manuscript lacks page numbers, I have added them for the purpose of reference.

3. Ibid., 65, 68.

4. Ibid., 124.

5. Ibid., 114.

6. Ibid., 2.

7. Sulgrove, *History of Indianapolis,* 88.

8. Bruno, "Chicago's Hillbilly Ghetto," 29.

9. Dunn, *Greater Indianapolis,* 1: 240.

10. Ibid.

11. Leaming, "The Ben Ishmael Tribe," 141.

12. Case files compiled by the Charity Organization Society (COS) were preserved by the Family Service Association, which maintained their confidentiality for seventy-five years from the date of collection. Although more than a century has passed, the Family Service of Central Indiana, which now controls use of the documents, does not allow researchers to publish direct quotes from the files. However, I have included the relevant case file numbers so that others who are interested can examine the files, as I did. On the history of these case files, see Karen Larson and Betsy Caldwell, "The Family Service Association of Indianapolis Records, 1879–1971," Collection Guide, Indiana Historical Society. The case files themselves are in Family Service Association Records, Collection no. M0102, Series 7: Records, 1879–1923, BV1196–BV1231; hereafter cited as Family Service Association Records.

13. Hall, "McCulloch and Eugenics," 129, quotes McCulloch's article, "Three Months Work," *Indianapolis Journal,* May 1, 1880.

14. Hall, "McCulloch and Eugenics," 110.

15. Wright, "Tribe of Ishmael," 1.

16. Johnson, *A Home in the Woods,* 75.

17. Wright, "Tribe of Ishmael," 1.

18. Ibid., 3.

19. Ibid., 4.

20. Ibid., 5.

21. Ibid., 7.

22. Ibid., 8.

23. Kate Thornton's COS case file appears in the Family Service Association Records, Series 7: BV 1209, no. 657.

24. Wright, "Tribe of Ishmael," 11–13.

25. Wright's speech appears in Thurman Rice, "The 'Tribe of Ishmael' Study," *One Hundred Years of Medicine: Indianapolis, 1820–1920: Monthly Bulletin: Indiana State Board of Health* 45 (1952): 236.

26. Wright, "Tribe of Ishmael," 18–20.

27. Ibid.

28. Ibid.

29. McCulloch, "The Tribe of Ishmael," 4.

30. *Indianapolis News,* Oct. 14, 1881, 3. Thanks to Alison Clement for pointing out this article to me.

31. Wright, "Tribe of Ishmael," 10. See Henry Ishmael's COS case file, Family Service Association Records, Series 7: BV 1221 no. 1349.

32. Andy Ishmael and Sarah Williams COS case file, Family Service Association Records, Series 7: BV 1197 no. 529; BV 1221 no. 1260.

33. Wright, "Tribe of Ishmael," 51.

34. George Williams and Maggie Ishmael COS case file, Family Service Association Records, Series 7: BV 1198 no. 693.

35. Thomas Williams, COS case file, Family Service Association Records, Series 7: BV 1196 no. 491; BV 1998 no. 14.

36. Wright, "Tribe of Ishmael," 48–50.

37. Ibid., 51–53.

38. Ibid., 13.

39. Ibid., 56, 110, 50.

40. Ibid., 93, 105, 103, 74.

41. Ibid.,121, 129.

42. Leaming, "The Ben Ishmael Tribe," 108.

43. Wright, "Tribe of Ishmael," 51.

44. Ibid., 52.

45. Ibid.

46. Ibid., 8.

47. Ibid., 14, 25. Isaiah Eads COS case file, Family Service Association Records, Series 7: BV 1209 no. 858.

48. Wright, "Tribe of Ishmael," 23, 27.

49. Ibid., 32, 31.

50. See ibid., 33–37.

51. United States Federal Census, "Blacks and Mulattoes," Marion County, Indiana, 1860.

52. Leaming, "The Ben Ishmael Tribe," 108.

53. Stacey Nicholas, "John Freeman Fugitive Slave Case (of 1853)," in *The Encyclopedia of Indianapolis,* ed. David Bodenhamer and Robert Barrows (Bloomington: Indiana University Press, 1994).

54. Leaming, "The Ben Ishmael Tribe," 114.

55. Wright, "Tribe of Ishmael," 37.

56. Ibid., 15–16.

57. Ibid., 9.

58. As cited in Rice, "The 'Tribe of Ishmael' Study," 236.

59. Indiana Historical Society, Family Service Association Records, Series 7: BV 1215 no. 1431.

60. Wright, "Tribe of Ishmael," 39–40.

61. Ibid., 40.

62. Ibid., 107–108.

63. Ibid., 112.

64. Leaming, "The Ben Ishmael Tribe," 103.

65. Wright, "Tribe of Ishmael," 113.

66. Ibid., 54.
67. Ibid., 97.
68. Ibid., 86.
69. Ibid., 87.
70. Ibid., 44.
71. Ibid., 12.
72. Leaming, "The Ben Ishmael Tribe," 122.

4. THE ISHMAELITES AND THE MENACE OF THE
FEEBLEMINDED

1. Harry Laughlin, "Eugenics in America," address delivered at Burlington House, London, Jan. 29, 1924. Reprinted in *Eugenics Review* 17 (April 1925): 28.

2. Ibid.

3. Arthur Estabrook and Charles Davenport, *The Nam: A Study in Cacogenics* (Cold Spring Harbor, N.Y.: Eugenics Record Office, 1912), 1, 2.

4. Arthur Estabrook to Charles Davenport, Jan. 17, 1912, Charles Davenport Papers, American Philosophical Society, B: D27, no. 2; hereafter cited as Davenport Papers.

5. Mark Haller notes: "Estabrook's conclusion . . . that 'one half of the Jukes were and are feeble-minded' and further that 'all of the Juke criminals were feeble-minded' [was] a startling conclusion, all the more startling since his own figures in the body of the report do not bear it out"; *Eugenics*, 108.

6. Ibid.

7. Ibid., 63.

8. Arthur Estabrook, *The Jukes in 1915* (Washington, D.C.: Carnegie Institution of Washington, 1916), iii.

9. Stephen Jay Gould, *The Mismeasure of Man* (New York: W. W. Norton and Company, 1996), 201.

10. Gertrude Hall to Arthur Estabrook, Jan. 30, 1917, Estabrook Papers, Box 1, Series 1, Folder 1.

11. John Hurty, "Practical Eugenics in Indiana," *Ohio State Medical Journal* 8, no. 2 (1912): 60.

12. As cited in Haller, *Eugenics*, 49.

13. Thurman Rice, "The Beginnings of Organized Charity in Indianapolis," *One Hundred Years of Medicine: Indianapolis, 1820–1920: Monthly Bulletin: Indiana State Board of Health* 44 (1952): 212. On Rice, see Nancy Ordover, *American Eugenics*, 227, n. 61; Lucretia Ann Saunders, "Thurman Brooks Rice," in *The Encyclopedia of Indianapolis*, ed. Bodenhamer and Barrows, 1193.

14. On Kate Parker's connection to McCulloch and the Tribe of Ishmael, see McCulloch, "The Tribe of Ishmael," 2.

15. Kate Parker to Carleton McCulloch, May 7, 1914, McCulloch Papers, L363.

16. Rafter, *White Trash*, 21.

17. As cited in Gould, *Mismeasure of Man*, 195.

18. *Eugenical News* 2 (June, 1917): 44. For a discussion of the number of female field-workers, see Frances Hassencahl, "Harry H. Laughlin, 'Expert Eugenics Agent' for the House Committee on Immigration and Naturalization, 1921–1931" (Ph.D. diss., Case Western University, 1970), 79–80.

19. On Estabrook's involvement in this project, see Arthur Estabrook, "The Work of the Indiana Committee on Mental Defectives," lecture delivered on May 18, 1922, at the National Association for the Study of the Feebleminded in St. Louis. In the Indiana State Archives (Indianapolis), Commission on Public Records, Board of State Charities Collection 14-x-1, 035274.

20. Arthur Estabrook to Charles Davenport, Nov. 17, 1915, Davenport Papers, B: D27, no. 2.

21. Arthur Estabrook to Charles Davenport, Feb. 16, 1916, Davenport Papers, B: D27, no. 2.

22. Ibid.

23. Arthur Estabrook to Lewellys Barker, March 31, 1916, Davenport Papers, B: D27, no. 2.

24. Arthur Estabrook to Charles Davenport, Feb. 7, 1920, Davenport Papers, B: D27, no. 2.

25. Arthur Estabrook to Charles Davenport, Aug. 19, 1921, Davenport Papers, B: D27, no. 2.

26. Arthur Estabrook, "The Tribe of Ishmael," *Eugenical News* 6 (July–August 1921): 50–51.

27. As cited in Haller, *Eugenics*, 26.

28. Kline, *Building a Better Race*, 21.

29. Gould, *Mismeasure of Man*, 191.

30. Ibid., 193, 186.

31. Ibid., 204.

32. Indiana State Archives, Board of State Charities Collection.

33. Estabrook's lecture was titled "The Tribe of Ishmael" and was essentially the same as the article of the same title in *Eugenical News*; *Eugenics, Genetics and the Family: Scientific Papers of the Second International Congress of Eugenics* (Baltimore, Williams and Wilkins Company, 1923), 1: 398–404; quotes at 404, 401, 399. Follow-up discussion was recorded under the title "The Tribe of Ishmael—A Study in Cacogenics," 431–433.

34. As cited in Gould, *Mismeasure of Man*, 195.

35. Estabrook in *Eugenics, Genetics and the Family*, 399.

36. Ibid., 404.

37. Follow-up in *Eugenics, Genetics and the Family*, 432.

38. Arthur Estabrook to Charles Davenport, Aug. 11, 1922, Davenport Papers, B: D27, no. 2.

39. Estabrook, "Tribe of Ishmael," unpublished manuscript in the Estabrook Papers.

40. Ibid., 10, 32–33.

41. Ibid., 28.

42. Ibid., 31.

43. Ibid., 51.

44. Ibid., 31.

45. Ibid., 51, 167.

46. Jared Harper, "'Gypsy' Research in the South," in *The Not so Solid South: Anthropological Studies in a Regional Subculture,* ed. J. Kenneth Morland (Athens: University of Georgia Press, 1971), 18, 19.

47. Estabrook, "Tribe of Ishmael," unpublished manuscript, 249, 236. Subsequent page references to this source are given in parentheses in the text.

48. A. C. Rogers and Maud A. Merrill, *Dwellers in the Vale of Siddem: A True Story of the Social Aspect of Feeble-Mindedness* (Boston: Richard A. Budger, 1919).

49. See Paul Lombardo, "Three Generations, No Imbeciles: New Light on *Buck v. Bell,*" *New York University Law Review* 60, no. 1 (1985): 50–62.

50. For a brief chronology of the case, see Heller, *Eugenics,* 138–139.

51. Arthur Estabrook and Ivan McDougle, *Mongrel Virginians: The Win Tribe* (Baltimore: Williams and Wilkins, 1926), 201–202.

52. Ivan McDougle to Arthur Estabrook, May 3, 1924. Estabrook Papers, Box 1, Series 1, Folder 3.

53. Estabrook and McDougle, *Mongrel Viriginians,* 202.

54. See the extensive correspondence between Estabrook and W. A. Plecker, the Registrar of Vital Statistics for the Commonwealth of Virginia Bureau of Vital Statistics and State Board of Health. Estabrook Papers, Box 1, Series 1, Folders 3–4.

5. THE TRIBAL TWENTIES

1. Hassencahl, "Harry H. Laughlin," 64–65.

2. Harry Laughlin, "Eugenics in America," reprinted in *Eugenics Review,* April, 1925.

3. "Biological Aspects of Immigration," Hearings Before the Committee on Immigration and Naturalization, House of Representatives, 66th Congress, 2nd Session, April 16–17, 1920 (Washington: Government Printing Office, 1921), 4.

4. David Starr Jordan, *Foot-Notes to Evolution: A Series of Popular Addresses on The Evolution of Life* (New York: D. Appleton and Company, 1898), 310–311.

5. Jacobson, *Whiteness of a Different Color,* 84.

6. Gould, *Mismeasure of Man,* 262.

7. Higham, *Strangers in the Land.*

8. Jacobson, *Whiteness of a Different Color,* 83.

9. Madison Grant, *The Passing of the Great Race: The Racial Basis of European History* (New York: Charles Scribner's Sons, 1916), 167.

10. Lothrop Stoddard, *The Rising Tide of Color: Against White World-Supremacy* (New York: Charles Scribner's Sons, 1920), 5.

11. Ibid., xxiii, xxii.

12. Ibid, xxxi.

13. Ibid., 102.

14. Lothrop Stoddard, *The New World of Islam* (New York: Charles Scribner's Sons, 1921), 355.

15. Ibid., 301.

16. Helen McCready Kearney, "American Images of the Middle East, 1824–1924: A Century of Antipathy" (Ph.D. diss., University of Rochester, 1975), 299.

17. Alixa Naff, *Becoming American: The Early Arab Immigrant Experience* (Carbondale: Southern Illinois University Press, 1985, 253.

18. Ibid.

19. For the Halladjian and Dow cases, see Jacobson, *Whiteness of a Different Color*, 234–235.

20. Naff, *Becoming American*, 111.

21. On the concept of "brown face" performances by whites during this period, see Prashad, *The Karma of Brown Folk*, 30.

22. Kearney, "American Images of the Middle East," 326.

23. Noble Drew Ali, *The Holy Koran of the Moorish Science Temple of America* (Chicago: n.p., 1927). For a relatively early view of this work, see Frank Simpson, "The Moorish Science Temple and Its 'Koran,'" *Moslem World* 37 (1947): 56–61. Also see Gomez, *Black Crescent*, 203–275.

24. For biographical information on Noble Drew Ali, see Nathaniel Deutsch, "'The Asiatic Black Man': An African American Orientalism?" *Journal of Asian American Studies* 4 (2001): 193–208; Gomez, *Black Crescent*, 203ff.; Aminah Beverly McCloud, *African American Islam* (New York: Routledge, 1995), 11–17; Susan Nance, "Mystery of the Moorish Science Temple: Southern Blacks and American Alternative Spirituality in 1920s Chicago," *Religion and American Culture: A Journal of Interpretation* 12 (2002): 123–166; Turner, *Islam in the African-American Experience*, 90–98; Wilson, *Sacred Drift*, 16.

25. On these concepts, see Yvonne Yazbeck Haddad and Jane Idleman Smith, *Mission to America: Five Islamic Sectarian Communities in North America* (Gainesville: University Press of Florida, 1993), 82–83.

26. Ali, *Holy Koran*, chapter 45, 56–57.

27. On the Theosophical and Romantic Orientalist roots of Ali's *Holy Koran*, see Deutsch, "'Asiatic Black Man,'" 201; Nance, "Mystery of the Moorish Science Temple," 127–134.

28. On the Shriners and the Moorish Science Temple, see Gomez, *Black Crescent*, 241–250.

29. On Fard, see Claude Andrew Clegg III, *An Original Man: The Life and Times of Elijah Muhammad* (New York: St. Martin's Press, 1997), 20–35; Karl Evanzz, *The Messenger: The Rise and Fall of Elijah Muhammad* (New York: Pantheon, 1999), 73–92; Matthias Gardell, *Louis Farrakhan and the Nation of Islam* (Durham, N.C.: Duke University Press, 1996), 50–58; Gomez, *Black Crescent*, 276–330.

30. Elijah Muhammad, *Message to the Blackman in America* (Newport News, Va.: United Brothers Communications Systems, 1992), 20.

31. Ibid., 17.

32. Turner, *Islam*, 165.

33. Muhammad, *Message to the Blackman*, 164.

34. Ibid., 4.

35. See Deutsch, "'Asiatic Black Man,'" 197.

36. As cited in Evannz, *The Messenger*, 144.

37. As cited in David Remnick, *King of the World: Muhammad Ali and the Rise of an American Hero* (New York: Alfred A. Knopf, 1998), 287.

38. Jack Olsen, *Black Is Best: The Riddle of Cassius Clay* (New York: Dell, 1967), 120.

39. On this phenomenon, see Vijay Prashad, *Everybody Was Kung Fu Fighting: Afro-Asian Connections and the Myth of Cultural Purity* (Boston: Beacon Press, 2001), 28–34.

40. Leonard Shihlien Hsu, ed., *Sun Yat-Sen: His Political and Social Ideals* (Los Angeles: University of Southern California Press, 1933), 170.

41. Lajpat Rai, "An Asiatic View of the Japanese Question," *Outlook* 114 (1916): 386.

42. "Negro Editor Preaches War for Equality," *New York Tribune*, Dec. 2, 1918, 4. On the context for these quotes, see Ernest Allen Jr., "When Japan Was 'Champion of the Darker Races': Satokata Takahashi and the Flowering of Black Messianic Nationalism," *Black Scholar* 24 (1994): 28–29.

43. Allen, "When Japan Was 'Champion,'" 33–34.

44. Turner, *Islam*, 84, 87.

45. Ibid., 89.

46. Kearney, "American Images of the Middle East," 300.

47. Turner, *Islam*, 124. On the Ahmadiyah, also see Gomez, *Black Crescent*, 252–254, 274, 278.

48. Turner, *Islam*, 129.

49. Ibid.

50. On this phenomenon, see Prashad, *The Karma of Brown Folk*, 38.

51. Stoddard, *Rising Tide of Color*, 102.

52. Muhammad, *Message to the Blackman*, 33, 31.

53. NOI Lessons, "Lost-Found Lesson No. 1," 1970, Answer 7, as cited in Clegg, *An Original Man*, 298.

54. Elijah Muhammad, *The Fall of America* (Chicago: Muhammad's Temple of Islam, 1973), 150.

55. Molefi Kete Asante, *Afrocentricity* (Trenton, N.J.: Africa World Press, 1988), 2, 5, 14.

56. Judith Stein, *The World of Marcus Garvey* (Baton Rouge: Louisiana State University Press, 1986), 5; Turner, *Islam*, 160; E. Essien-Udom, *Black Nationalism: A Search for Identity in America* (Chicago: University of Chicago Press, 1962), 346.

57. *Birth Control Review* 16 (June 1932): 163.

58. The July–August 1932 issue of *Birth Control Review* published supportive letters to the editor from representatives of the NAACP, Urban League, and other black organizations.

59. Elmer Carter, "Eugenics for the Negro," *Birth Control Review* 16: 169.

60. M. O. Bousfield, "Negro Public Health Work Needs Birth Control," *Birth Control Review* 16: 170; Walter Tarpenning, "God's Chillun," *Birth Control Review* 16: 171–172.

61. W. E. B. DuBois, "Black Folk and Birth Control," *Birth Control Review* 16 (June 1932): 167.

62. Matthew Pratt Guterl, *The Color of Race in America, 1900–1940* (Cambridge: Harvard University Press, 2001), 144.

63. Muhammad, *Message to the Blackman*, 102.

64. Ibid., 107.

65. Ibid., 112.

66. Ibid., 116.

67. Ibid.

6. LOST-FOUND NATION

1. Hassencahl, "Harry H. Laughlin," 351.

2. Black, *War against the Weak*, 395.

3. Hugo Leaming, "The Ben Ishmael Tribe," 133. The links between the American eugenics movement and the Nazi regime in Germany have been explored by Stefan Kuhl, *The Nazi Connection: Eugenics, American Racism, and German National Socialism* (New York: Oxford University Press, 1994). Also see Paul Lombardo, "The American Breed: Nazi Eugenics and the Origin of the Pioneer Fund," *Albany Law Review* 65 (May 2002): 743–830.

4. Black, *War against the Weak*, 425.

5. Robert Horton, "Tribe of Ishmael," in *The Encyclopedia of Indianapolis*, ed. Bodenhamer and Barrows, 1342.

6. Rice, "The 'Tribe of Ishmael' Study," 236–237.

7. Aldridge, "The Tribe of Ishmael Came and Multiplied," 38.

8. Most of this biographical information was based on interviews with people who knew Hugo Leaming, as well as on his Minister's Record Sheet, which the Unitarian Universalist Association of Congregations, in Boston, Mass., generously shared with me; and Graham Hodges, "Editor's Introduction," in Hugo Prosper Leaming, *Hidden Americans: Maroons of Virginia and the Carolinas* (New York: Garland Publishing, Inc., 1995), vii–xi.

9. Author interview with Marjorie Newlin Leaming, former wife of Hugo Leaming, Feb. 21, 2003.

10. Author interview with Dale Chapman, longtime friend of Hugo Leaming, May 12, 2002.

11. Hugo Prosper Leaming, "Hidden Americans: Maroons of Virginia and the Carolinas" (Ph.D. diss., University of Illinois at Chicago Circle, 1975), 7, 660–661.

12. Ibid. On the phrase the "other America," see Michael Harrington, *The Other America: Poverty in the United States* (New York: Macmillan, 1962).

13. Leaming, "Hidden Americans," 386 n. 88.

14. Leaming, "The Ben Ishmael Tribe," 127.

15. Ibid., 137.

16. Turner, *Islam*, 197.

17. For information on these and other African Muslims in America, see Allan Austin, *African Muslims in Antebellum America: Transatlantic Stories and Spiritual Struggles* (New York: Routledge, 1997); Sylviane Diouf, *Servants of Allah: African Muslims Enslaved in the Americas* (New York: New York University Press, 1998); Michael Gomez, *Black Crescent*, esp. 128–184, and

"Muslims in Early America," *Journal of Southern History* 60 (1994): 671–709.

18. Savannah Unit of the Georgia Writers Project of the Works Projects Administration, *Drums and Shadows: Survival Studies among the Georgia Coastal Negroes* (Athens: University of Georgia Press, 1986; orig. pub. 1940).

19. Austin, *African Muslims*, 106.

20. Morroe Berger, "The Black Muslims," *Horizon* 6 (winter 1964): 54.

21. Philip Curtin, ed., *Africa Remembered: Narratives by West Africans from the Era of the Slave Trade* (Madison: University of Wisconsin Press, 1967).

22. Alex Haley, *Roots* (Garden City, N.Y.: Doubleday, 1976).

23. Terry Alford, *Prince among Slaves* (New York: Harcourt Brace Jovanovich, 1977).

24. Leaming, "The Ben Ishmael Tribe," 386–387 n. 96.

25. Gomez, *Black Crescent*, 143–184.

26. These legends are collected in Ronald Baker, *From Needmore to Prosperity: Hoosier Place Names in Folklore and History* (Bloomington: Indiana University Press, 1995), 214.

27. On such marketing, see Holly Edwards, "A Million and One Nights: Orientalism in America, 1870–1930," in *Noble Dreams, Wicked Pleasures*, ed. Edwards, 43.

28. Naff, *Becoming American*, 128.

29. Leaming, "The Ben Ishmael Tribe," 135.

30. "Trace Ancestry to Mighty Sampson," *Chicago Defender*, June 1, 1927, as cited in Nance, "Mystery of the Moorish Science Temple," 162 n. 96.

31. Author interviews with Dale Chapman and Marjorie Newlin Leaming.

32. Hodges, "Editor's Introduction," in Leaming, *Hidden American*, p. ix.

33. Sakolsky and Koehnline, eds., *Gone to Croatan*, p. 11.

7. THE ISHMAELS: AN AMERICAN STORY

1. Gary Nash, "Poverty and Politics in Early American History," in *Down and Out in Early America,* ed. Billy G. Smith (University Park: Pennsylvania University Press, 2004), 8.

2. See John Rowlands and Sheila Rowlands, *Welsh Family History: A Guide to Research* (Birmingham, Eng,: Federation of Family History Societies Ltd, 1998), 59–75.

3. On the early Welsh community in Pennsylvania, see Charles Browning, *Welsh Settlement of Pennsylvania* (Philadelphia: W. J. Campbell, 1912).

4. See Charles Boyer, ed., *Ship Passenger Lists: Pennsylvania and Delaware (1641–1825)* (Newhall, Calif.: Boyer, 1980).

5. Antrim Township, Cumberland County, Pennsylvania, Tax List, 1769. In Cumberland County Historical Society Collection, Carlisle, Pa.

6. See *Pennsylvania Archives* (Philadelphia: Joseph Severns, 1851–1935), series 6, vol. 2, 9. On these soldiers, see Gregory Knouff, "Soldiers and Violence on the Pennsylvania Frontier," in *Beyond Philadelphia: The American Revolution in the Pennsylvania Hinterland,* ed. John Frantz and William Pencak (University Park: Pennsylvania University Press, 1998).

7. A man named Robert Ishmael, who died while serving in the Revolutionary War, may have been another brother.

8. This and many other details of Benjamin Ishmael's military service are found in his 1818 Federal Pension application, along with his revised application from 1822. See Benjamin Ishmael, Federal Pension file, S 35460, National Archives Trust Fund Board, Washington, D.C.

9. On the organization of this unit on Jan. 9, 1776, see Robert Crist, "Cumberland County," in *Beyond Philadelphia*, ed. Franz and Pencak, 125. Also see John Trussell, Jr., *The Pennsylvania Line: Regimental Organization and Operations, 1776–1783* (Harrisburg: Pennsylvania Historical and Museum Commission, 1977), 93–101.

10. On the "rage militaire" that swept the colonies in this period, see Charles Royster, *A Revolutionary People at War: The Continental Army and American Character, 1775–1783* (Chapel Hill: University of North Carolina Press, 1979), 25–54. Royster quotes a letter from Philadelphia dated 1775 that mentions "the Rage Militaire, as the French call a passion for arms, has taken possession of the whole Continent" (25). On this issue, also see Robert Middlekauff, "Why Men Fought in the American Revolution," *Huntington Library Quarterly* 43 (1980): 135–148, reprinted in Peter Onuf, ed., *Patriots, Redcoats, and Loyalists* (New York and London: Garland Publishing, Inc., 1991), 1–16.

11. John Shy, *A People Numerous and Armed: Reflections on the Military Struggle for American Independence* (Ann Arbor: University of Michigan Press, 1990), 178. On the Tories and their fate in this area, see Crist, "Cumberland County," 126–129.

12. Robert Cooper, *Courage in a Good Cause; or The Lawful and Courageous Use of the Sword . . .* (Lancaster, Pa.: n.p., 1775), 23—25; quoted in Royster, *A Revolutionary People at War,* 27–28, 225.

13. Chaplain William Linn, as quoted in Royster, *A Revolutionary People at War,* 156.

14. Robert McConnell Hatch, *Thrust for Canada: The American Attempt on Quebec in 1775–1776* (Boston: Houghton Mifflin Company, 1979), 215, 216, 217.

15. Charles Henry Jones, *History of the Campaign for the Conquest of Canada in 1776* (Philadelphia: Porter and Coates, 1882), 76–77.

16. Ibid., 80–81.

17. Benjamin Ishmael, Federal Pension file, S 35460.

18. Gregory Knouff, *The Soldiers' Revolution: Pennsylvanians in Arms and the Forging of Early American Identity* (University Park: Pennsylvania State University Press, 2004), 71.

19. Ibid., xxiii; and see 63, 173.

20. Royster, *A Revolutionary People at War,* 373.

21. Mark Lender, "The Enlisted Line: The Continental Soldiers of New Jersey" (Ph.D. diss., Rutgers University, 1975), 302; John Sellers, "The Common Soldier in the American Revolution," in *Military History of the American Revolution: Proceedings of the Sixth Military History Symposium, United States Air Force Academy, 10–11 October 1974,* ed. Stanley Underdal

(Washington, D.C.: Office of Air Force History, Headquarters USAF, 1976), 165. For a discussion of these views, see Royster, *A Revolutionary People at War,* 373–378.

22. Knouff, *The Soldiers' Revolution;* Middlekauff, "Why Men Fought"; John Resch, *Suffering Soldiers: Revolutionary War Veterans, Moral Sentiment, and Political Culture in the Early Republic* (Amherst: University of Massachusetts Press, 1999); Royster, *A Revolutionary People at War.*

23. Benjamin Ishmael, Federal Pension file, S 35460. In his 1818 pension application, Benjamin Ishmael claimed to be eighty-two years old, meaning that he would have been forty-two years old in 1778. In his revised 1822 application, however, Ishmael is listed as then eighty-three years old, meaning that he would have been thirty-nine years old in 1778. During this period, it was not uncommon for different documents to mention slightly different ages for the same individual.

24. Crist, "Cumberland County," 129.

25. John Carothers to Thomas Wharton, April 24, 1778, as cited in Knouff, *The Soldiers' Revolution,* 72.

26. William Irvine to Anthony Wayne, July 6, 1781, as quoted in Crist, "Cumberland County," 127.

27. Washington Township, Cumberland County, Pennsylvania, Tax Lists, 1780, in Cumberland County Historical Society Collection.

28. Karl Geiser, *Redemptioners and Indentured Servants in the Colony and Commonwealth of Pennsylvania* (New Haven, Conn.: Tuttle, Morehouse, and Taylor Co., 1901), 91.

29. For this estimate, see Carter Goodrich, "Indenture," in *Encyclopaedia of the Social Sciences* (New York: Macmillan Co., 1930–1935), 7: 646; Abbot Emerson Smith, *Colonists in Bondage: White Servitude and Convict Labor in America, 1607–1776* (Chapel Hill: University of North Carolina Press, 1947), 336; and more recently, David Galenson, *White Servitude in Colonial America: An Economic Analysis* (New York: Cambridge University Press, 1981), 17. On the small percentage of servants (5 to 7 percent of the total number) for whom records have survived, see Galenson, 16–17.

30. See Sharon Salinger, *"To Serve Well and Faithfully": Labor and Indentured Servants in Pennsylvania 1682–1800* (New York: Cambridge University Press, 1987).

31. Cheesman Herrick, *White Servitude in Pennsylvania: Indentured and Redemption Labor in Colony and Commonwealth* (Philadelphia: John Joseph McVey, 1926); reprint (New York: Negro Universities Press, 1969), 252–253.

32. Knouff, *The Soldiers' Revolution,* 47–48. Concerning this, Knouff comments: "During the period of increased need for soldiers in 1776, servants and apprentices, too, flocked to the army for economic and other reasons. . . . While the promise of better economic status was one element of why apprentices and servants enlisted, liberty from servitude, risky as it could be, was often another."

33. Washington Township, Cumberland County, Pennsylvania, Tax Lists, 1783, Cumberland County Historical Society Collection.

34. On this phenomenon, see Paul G. E. Clemens and Lucy Simler, "Rural Labor and the Farm Household in Chester County, Pennsylvania, 1750–1820,"

in *Work and Labor in Early America,* ed. Stephen Innes (Chapel Hill: University of North Carolina Press, 1988), 106–143; Lucy Simler, "Tenancy in Colonial Pennsylvania: The Case of Chester County," *William and Mary Quarterly* 3d Ser., 43 (1986): 542–569.

35. My thanks to the staff of the Cumberland County Historical Society, who suggested this possibility to me in a personal communication.

36. See Merri Lou Scribner Schaumann, ed., *Indictments: 1750–1800, Cumberland County, Pennsylvania* (Dover, Pa.: M. L. S. Schaumann, 1989).

37. Nash, "Poverty and Politics," 27. On the Whiskey Rebellion in Cumberland County, see Thomas Slaughter, *The Whiskey Rebellion: Frontier Epilogue to the American Revolution* (New York: Oxford University Press, 1988), 206–208.

38. These and other quotes in praise of Kentucky from this period are in John Mack Faragher, *Daniel Boone: The Life and Legend of an American Pioneer* (New York: Henry Holt and Company, 1992), 70.

39. Billy G. Smith, "'The Best Poor Man's Country'?" in *Down and Out in Early America,* ed. Smith, xii. On xiii, Smith explains that "most scholars have misunderstood William Moraley's account of 'the best poor man's country.' He used the expression to praise Mid-Atlantic inhabitants for their generous hospitality to impecunious travelers rather than to paint a rosy portrait of early North America. Instead, he criticized the exploitation of and limited economic opportunities available to people without property." For a different view, see James Lemon, *The Best Poor Man's Country: A Geographical Study of Early Southeastern Pennsylvania* (Baltimore: Johns Hopkins University Press, 1972).

40. Gordon Wood, *The Radicalism of the American Revolution* (New York: Alfred A. Knopf, 1991), 4, as cited in Smith, "'The Best Poor Man's Country'?," xiii.

41. Nash, "Poverty and Politics," 1, has noted that the historian Gordon Wood even went so far as to claim, "Poverty and economic deprivation were not present in colonial America."

42. Jackson Turner Main, *The Social Structure of Revolutionary America* (Princeton: Princeton University Press, 1965), 6, 11, 286.

43. *Carlisle Gazette,* Feb. 15, 1786, as cited in Main, *The Social Structure of Revolutionary America,* 236–237.

44. As cited in Nash, "Poverty and Politics," 28.

45. Ibid., 5, where Nash notes that "lifelong landlessness expanded markedly in the eighteenth century."

46. On this phenomenon, see Douglas Jones, "The Strolling Poor: Transiency in Eighteenth-Century Massachusetts," *Journal of Social History* 8 (1975): 28–54; Nash, "Poverty and Politics," 4.

47. Nash, "Poverty and Politics," 26.

48. Faragher, *Daniel Boone,* 272.

49. William Henry Perrin, ed., *History of Bourbon, Scott, Harrison and Nicholas Counties, Kentucky* (Chicago: O. L. Baskin and Co., 1882), 36.

50. Arthur Estabrook to Lewellys Barker, March 31, 1916, Davenport Papers, B: D27, no. 2.

51. John Filson, *Life and Adventures of Colonel Daniel Boon, The First White Settler of the State of Kentucky* (Brooklyn: C. Wilder, 1823). Filson first published *The Adventures of Colonel Daniel Boon* in an appendix to his *Discovery, Settlement, and Present State of Kentucke* (Wilmington, Del.: James Adams, 1784).

52. Faragher, *Daniel Boone,* xii–xiv.

53. Perrin, *History of Bourbon,* 329, 39.

54. Ibid., 333–334.

55. These statistics are from the Nicholas County, Kentucky, Tax Books, 1800. I examined the microfilmed copy in the Family History Library, Church of Jesus Christ of the Latter Day Saints, Salt Lake City, US/CAN Film 8185.

56. Ibid., for 1801–6.

57. Fleming County, Kentucky, Tax Books, 1810. Family History Library, US/CAN Film 7969.

58. Ibid., for 1811–14.

59. Benjamin's oldest son, James Ishmael, is listed in the Nicholas County tax rolls for 1819 as owning 100 acres of third-rate land on the Licking River watercourse. Although the county is different, it may in fact be the same land, since the final border between Nicholas and Fleming counties was only demarcated in 1823.

60. Will of Benjamin Ishmael, in Will Book B, p. 148, Nicholas County Court House, Kentucky.

61. *Annals of Congress,* 15th Congress, 1st session, 1817–1818, 2518–2519, as cited in John Resch, "Federal Welfare for Revolutionary War Veterans," *Social Service Review* 56 (June 1982): 171. Also see Resch, *Suffering Soldiers,* 118. Much of the discussion in the following pages is indebted to Resch's excellent book as well as observations made to me in personal communications.

62. Resch, *Suffering Soldiers,* 9.

63. On the phrase "suffering soldier" and its significance, see Resch, *Suffering Soldiers.*

64. Resch, "Federal Welfare for Revolutionary War Veterans," 172.

65. Resch, *Suffering Soldiers,* 147.

66. Ibid., 137.

67. Ibid., 101.

68. See Benjamin Ishmael, Federal Pension file, S 35460.

69. Resch, "Federal Welfare for Revolutionary War Veterans," 172.

70. Resch, *Suffering Soldiers,* 129. Resch has observed that the "program nearly bankrupted the government" (142).

71. Ibid., 153.

72. Benjamin Ishmael, Federal Pension file, S 35460.

73. As Resch notes, "public watchfulness, as a result of the 1819 pension scandal, discouraged falsehoods"; *Suffering Soldiers,* 222.

74. Ibid., 161.

75. For the statistics in the following paragraphs, see ibid, 210–231; Resch, "Federal Welfare for Revolutionary War Veterans," 173–181.

76. Joan Weissinger Conley, ed., *History of Nicholas County* (Carlisle, Ky.: Nicholas County Historical Society, Inc., 1976), 211–221, lists all of the pension applicants from Nicholas County.

77. Apparently, Benjamin Ishmael's family had continued to pursue the pension following his death, since John Rannels testified on his behalf in November 1822, that is, several months after Ishmael passed away.

78. Conley, *History of Nicholas County,* 133.

79. Ibid.

80. 1820 Federal Census, Nicholas County, Kentucky.

81. 1840 Federal Census, Delaware County, Indiana.

82. List of Indiana Marriages Before 1850, Genealogy Division Database, Indiana State Library.

83. 1850 Federal Census, Tipton County, Indiana.

84. 1860 Federal Census, Fountain County, Indiana.

85. Thomas Ishmael served in the 58th Regiment of the Indiana Infantry and other units from 1861 to 1865.

86. For the early history of Fountain County, see Hiram Beckwith, *History of Fountain County: Together with Historic Notes on the Wabash Valley, Gleaned from Early Authors, Old Maps and Manuscripts* (Chicago: H. H. Hill and N. Iddings, 1881).

87. On this phenomenon, see Thomas Wessel, "Agricultural Depression and the West, 1870–1900," *European Contributions to American Studies* 16 (1989): 72–80.

88. The 1870 Federal Census for Precinct 4 of Nicholas County, Kentucky, lists a John W. Ishmael in the household of Samuel and Sarah Ishmael.

89. Unfortunately, I have thus far been unable to trace the fate of Henry and Sarah Ishmael after 1860.

90. Fountain County, Indiana, Indentures, Book 1, 1847–1884, 113; Genealogical Section, Indiana State Library.

91. James Whitcomb Riley, "Little Orphant Annie," *Complete Works* (Indianapolis: Bobbs-Merrill, 1916), 5: 1169–72.

92. Today, some of Amanda's descendants are involved in reconstructing her life story. My thanks to Nancy Robinson, in particular, for sharing her genealogical information with me.

93. *Logan's Indianapolis Directory* (Indianapolis: Logan and Co., 1868).

Selected Bibliography

ARCHIVAL SOURCES

Cumberland County Historical Society Collection, Carlisle, Pa.

Charles Davenport Papers. American Philosophical Society, Philadelphia.

Arthur Estabrook Papers, 1910–1943. M. E. Grenander Department of Special Collections and Archives, University Libraries, State University of New York at Albany.

Family Service Association Records, Collection no. M0102, Series 7: Records, 1879–1923, BV1196–BV1231. Manuscripts Collections Department, William Henry Smith Memorial Library, Indiana Historical Society, Indianapolis.

Indiana State Archives. Commission on Public Records, Indianapolis.

Indiana State Library, Indiana Division, Indianapolis.

Harry H. Laughlin Papers. Pickler Memorial Library, Truman State University, Kirksville, Mo.

Reverend Oscar C. McCulloch Papers. Indiana State Library, Indiana Division, Indianapolis.

Unitarian-Universalist Association, Inactive Minister Files, 1825–1999. Andover-Harvard Theological Library, Harvard Divinity School, Cambridge, Mass.

SECONDARY SOURCES

Aldridge, Bruce. "The Tribe of Ishmael Came and Multiplied." *Indianapolis Magazine,* July 1972, 23, 36–38.

Alford, Terry. *Prince Among Slaves.* New York: Harcourt Brace Jovanovich, 1977.

Alger, Horatio. *Ragged Dick, or Street Life in New York.* Boston: A. K. Loring, 1868.

Ali, Noble Drew. *The Holy Koran of the Moorish Science Temple of America.* Chicago: n.p., 1927.

Allen, Ernest. Jr. "When Japan Was 'Champion of the Darker Races': Satokata Takahashi and the Flowering of Black Messianic Nationalism." *Black Scholar* 24 (1994): 23–46.

Allen, Theodore. *The Invention of the White Race.* London and New York: Verso, 1994.

Arnold, Robert. *Through Persia by Caravan.* New York: Harper and Brothers, 1877.

Asante, Molefi Kete. *Afrocentricity.* Trenton: Africa World Press, 1988.

Austin, Allan. *African Muslims in Antebellum America: Transatlantic Stories and Spiritual Struggles.* New York: Routledge, 1997.

Baker, Ronald. *From Needmore to Prosperity: Hoosier Place Names in Folklore and History.* Bloomington: Indiana University Press, 1995.

Beckwith, Hiram. *History of Fountain County: Together with Historic Notes on the Wabash Valley, Gleaned from Early Authors, Old Maps and Manuscripts.* Chicago: H.H. Hill and N. Iddings, 1881.

Berger, Morroe. "The Black Muslims." *Horizon* 6 (Winter 1964): 48–65.

Black, Edwin. *War against the Weak: Eugenics and America's Campaign to Create a Master Race.* New York: Four Walls Eight Windows, 2003.

Bodenhamer, David, and Robert Barrows, eds. *The Encyclopedia of Indianapolis.* Bloomington: Indiana University Press, 1994.

Boyer, Charles, ed. *Ship Passenger Lists: Pennsylvania and Delaware (1641–1825).* Newhall, Calif.: Boyer, 1980.

Briggs, Laura. *Reproducing Empire: Race, Sex, Science, and U.S. Imperialism in Puerto Rico.* Berkeley: University of California Press, 2002.

Browning, Charles. *Welsh Settlement of Pennsylvania.* Philadelphia: W. J. Campbell, 1912.

Bruno, Hal. "Chicago's Hillbilly Ghetto." *The Reporter,* June 4, 1964, 28–31.

Burnaby, Frederick. *Ride to Khiva.* New York: Harper and Brothers, 1877.

Carlson, Elof Axel. *The Unfit: A History of a Bad Idea.* Cold Spring Harbor, N.Y.: Cold Spring Harbor Laboratory Press, 2001.

Carter, Paul Allen. *The Decline and Revival of the Social Gospel: Social and Political Liberalism in American Protestant Churches, 1920–1940.* Ithaca, N.Y.: Cornell University Press, 1956.

Castor, Henry. *The Tripolitan War, 1801–1805: America Meets the Menace of the Barbary Pirates.* New York: F. Watts, 1971.

Cayton, Andrew. *Frontier Indiana.* Bloomington: Indiana University Press, 1996.

Clegg, Claude Andrew, III. *An Original Man: The Life and Times of Elijah Muhammad.* New York: St. Martin's Press, 1997.

Clemens, Paul, and Lucy Simler. "Rural Labor and the Farm Household in Chester County, Pennsylvania, 1750–1820." In *Work and Labor in Early America,* edited by Stephen Innes. Chapel Hill: University of North Carolina Press, 1988.

Conley, Joan Weissinger, ed. *History of Nicholas County.* Carlisle, Ky.: Nicholas County Historical Society, Inc., 1976.

Cook, Michael, and Patricia Crone. *Hagarism: The Making of the Islamic World, Hagarenes and the Tribe of Ishmael.* Cambridge: Cambridge University Press, 1977.

Cottman, George. "Old Time Slums of Indianapolis." *Indiana Magazine of History* 7 (1911): 170–173.

Crist, Robert. "Cumberland County." In *Beyond Philadelphia: The American Revolution in the Pennsylvania Hinterland,* edited by John Frantz and William Pencak. University Park: Pennsylvania University Press, 1998.

Curtin, Philip, ed. *Africa Remembered: Narratives by West Africans from the Era of the Slave Trade.* Madison: University of Wisconsin Press, 1967.

Curtis, Susan. *A Consuming Faith: The Social Gospel and Modern American Culture.* Columbia: University of Missouri Press, 2001.

Davenport, Charles. *The Feebly Inhibited: Nomadism, or the Wandering Impulse, with Special Reference to Heredity.* Washington, D.C.: The Carnegie Institution of Washington, 1915.

Deutsch, Nathaniel. "'The Asiatic Black Man': An African American Orientalism?" *Journal of Asian American Studies* 4 (2001): 193–208.

Diouf, Sylviane. *Servants of Allah: African Muslims Enslaved in the Americas.* New York: New York University Press, 1998.

Drake, St. Clair, and Horace Cayton. *Black Metropolis: A Study of Negro Life in a Northern City.* Chicago: University of Chicago Press, 1993; orig. pub. 1945.

Dugdale, Richard. *"The Jukes": A Study in Crime, Pauperism, Disease, and Heredity; Also, Further Studies of Criminals.* New York: G. P. Putnam's Sons, 1877.

Edwards, Holly, ed. *Noble Dreams, Wicked Pleasures: Orientalism in America, 1870–1930.* Princeton: Princeton University Press, 2000.

English, Daylanne. *Eugenics in American Modernism and the Harlem Renaissance.* Chapel Hill: University of North Carolina Press, 2003.

Erwin, James. "Footnotes to History: The Nations You Didn't Learn About in High School." www.buckyogi.com/footnotes/

Essien–Udom, E. *Black Nationalism: A Search for Identity in America.* Chicago: University of Chicago Press, 1962.

Estabrook, Arthur. *Mongrel Virginians: The Win Tribe.* Baltimore: Williams and Wilkins, 1926.

———. "The Tribe of Ishmael," *Eugenical News* 6 (July–August, 1921): 50–51.

———. "The Tribe of Ishmael." Unpublished manuscript, 1922. Arthur Estabrook Papers, 1910–1943, M. E. Grenander Department of Special Collections and Archives, State University of New York at Albany Libraries, APAP-069, Box 1, Series 2, Folder 7.

Estabrook, Arthur, and Charles Davenport. *The Nam: A Study in Cacogenics.* Cold Spring Harbor, NY: Eugenics Record Office, 1912.

Estabrook, Arthur, and Ivan McDougle. *The Jukes in 1915:* Washington D.C.: Carnegie Institution of Washington, 1916.

Evanzz, Karl. *The Messenger: The Rise and Fall of Elijah Muhammad.* New York: Pantheon, 1999.

Faragher, John Mack. *Daniel Boone: The Life and Legend of an American Pioneer.* New York: Henry Holt and Company, 1992.

Filson, John. *Life and Adventures of Colonel Daniel Boon, The First White Settler of the State of Kentucky.* Brooklyn: C. Wilder, 1823.

Fleck, Richard. "The Complexities of Mark Twain's Near Eastern Stereotypying." *Mark Twain Journal* 21 (summer 1982): 13–15.

Freeman, Edward. *The Turks in Europe.* New York: Harper and Brothers, 1877.

Freeman, Roland. *The Arabbers of Baltimore.* Centreville, Md.: Tidewater Publishers, 1989.

Galenson, David. *White Servitude in Colonial America: An Economic Analysis.* New York: Cambridge University Press, 1981.

Gans, Herbert. *The War Against the Poor: The Underclass and Antipoverty Policy.* New York: Basic Books, 1995.

Gardell, Matthias. *Louis Farrakhan and the Nation of Islam.* Durham, N.C.: Duke University Press, 1996.

Geiser, Karl. *Redemptioners and Indentured Servants in the Colony and Commonwealth of Pennsylvania.* New Haven: Tuttle, Morehouse, and Taylor Co., 1901.

Goad, Jim. *The Redneck Manifesto: How Hillbillies, Hicks, and White Trash Became America's Scapegoats.* New York: Simon & Schuster, 1997.

Godkin, Edwin. "The Eastern Question," *North American Review* 124 (1877): 106–126.

Gomez, Michael. *Black Crescent: The Experience and Legacy of African Muslims in the Americas.* New York: Cambridge University Press, 2005.

———. "Muslims in Early America." *Journal of Southern History* 60 (1994): 128–184.

Gould, Stephen Jay. *The Mismeasure of Man.* New York: W. W. Norton and Company, 1996.

Grant, Madison. *The Passing of the Great Race: The Racial Basis of European History.* New York: Charles Scribner's Sons, 1916.

Guterl, Matthew Pratt. *The Color of Race in America, 1900–1940.* Cambridge: Harvard University Press, 2001.

Haddad, Yvonne Yazbeck, and Jane Idleman Smith. *Mission to America: Five Islamic Sectarian Communities in North America.* Gainesville: University Press of Florida, 1993.

Hale, Hester Anne. *Indianapolis: The First Century.* Indianapolis: Marion County/Indianapolis Historical Society, 1987.

Haley, Alex. *Roots.* Garden City, N.Y.: Doubleday, 1976.

Hall, Peter. *Cities of Tomorrow: An Intellectual History of Urban Planning and Design in the Twentieth Century.* Oxford: Blackwell Publishing, 2002.

Hall, Stephen Ray. "Oscar McCulloch and Indiana Eugenics." Ph.D. dissertation, Virginia Commonwealth University, 1993.

Haller, Mark. *Eugenics: Hereditarian Attitudes in American Thought.* New Brunswick, N.J.: Rutgers University Press, 1963.

Hammons, Terry Brooks. "'A Wild Ass of a Man': American Images of Arabs to 1948." Ph.D. dissertation, University of Oklahoma, 1978.

Harkins, Anthony. *Hillbilly: A Cultural History of an American Icon.* New York: Oxford, 2003.

Harper, Jared. "'Gypsy' Research in the South." In *The Not So Solid South: Anthropological Studies in a Regional Subculture,* edited by J. Kenneth Morland. Athens: University of Georgia Press, 1971.

Harrington, Michael. *The Other America: Poverty in the United States*. New York: Macmillan, 1962.

Hartigan, John, Jr. *Racial Situations: Class Predicaments of Whiteness in Detroit*. Princeton: Princeton University Press, 1999.

Hassencahl, Frances. "Harry H. Laughlin, 'Expert Eugenics Agent' for the House Committee on Immigration and Naturalization, 1921–1931." Ph.D. dissertation, Case Western University, 1970.

Hatch, Robert McConnell. *Thrust for Canada: The American Attempt on Quebec in 1775–1776*. Boston: Houghton Mifflin Company, 1979.

Helleiner, Jane. *Irish Travellers: Racism and the Politics of Culture*. Toronto: University of Toronto Press, 2000.

Herrick, Cheesman. *White Servitude in Pennsylvania: Indentured and Redemption Labor in Colony and Commonwealth*. Philadelphia: John Joseph McVey, 1926.

Higham, John. *Strangers in the Land: Patterns of American Nativism, 1860–1925*. New Brunswick, N.J.: Rutgers University Press, 1955.

Holloway, W. R. *Indianapolis: A Historical and Statistical Sketch of the Railroad City*. Indianapolis: Indianapolis Journal Print, 1870.

Hopkins, Charles Howard. *The Rise of the Social Gospel in American Protestantism, 1865–1915*. New Haven: Yale University Press, 1940.

Hopkins, C. Howard, and Ronald White, Jr. *The Social Gospel: Religion and Reform in Changing America*. Philadelphia: Temple University Press, 1975.

Horton, Robert. "Tribe of Ishmael." In *The Encyclopedia of Indianapolis*, edited by David Bodenhamer and Robert Barrows. Bloomington: Indiana University Press, 1994.

Hsu, Leonard Shihlien, ed. *Sun Yat-Sen: His Political and Social Ideals*. Los Angeles: University of Southern California Press, 1933.

Ignatiev, Noel. *How the Irish Became White*. New York: Routledge, 1996.

Jacobson, Matthew Freye. *Whiteness of a Different Color: European Immigrants and the Alchemy of Race*. Cambridge: Harvard University Press, 1998.

Johnson, Howard. *A Home in the Woods: Pioneer Life in Indiana, 1821–1907; Oliver Johnson's Reminiscences*. Bloomington: Indiana University Press, 1951.

Jones, Charles Henry. *History of the Campaign for the Conquest of Canada in 1776*. Philadelphia: Porter and Coates, 1882.

Jones, Douglas. "The Strolling Poor: Transiency in Eighteenth-Century Massachusetts." *Journal of Social History* 8 (1975): 28–54.

Jordan, David Starr. *Foot-Notes to Evolution: A Series of Popular Addresses on The Evolution of Life*. New York: D. Appleton and Company, 1898.

Katz, Michael. *The Undeserving Poor: From the War on Poverty to the War on Welfare*. New York: Pantheon Books, 1989.

Kearney, Helen McCready. "American Images of the Middle East, 1824–1924: A Century of Antipathy." Ph.D. dissertation, University of Rochester, 1975.

Kelley, Robin. *Race Rebels: Culture, Politics, and the Black Working Class*. New York: Free Press, 1996.

Kevles, Daniel. *In the Name of Eugenics: Genetics and the Uses of Human Heredity*. New York: Knopf, 1985.

Killian, Lewis. "The Adjustment of Southern White Migrants to Northern Urban Norms." *Social Forces* 16 (1937): 66–69.

Kline, Wendy. *Building a Better Race: Gender, Sexuality, and Eugenics from the Turn of the Century to the Baby Boom.* Berkeley: University of California Press, 2005.

Knouff, Gregory. "Soldiers and Violence on the Pennsylvania Frontier." In *Beyond Philadelphia: The American Revolution in the Pennsylvania Hinterland,* edited by John Frantz and William Pencak. University Park: Pennsylvania University Press, 1998.

———. *The Soldiers' Revolution: Pennsylvanians in Arms and the Forging of Early American Identity.* University Park: Pennsylvania State University Press, 2004.

Kuhl, Stefan. *The Nazi Connection: Eugenics, American Racism, and German National Socialism.* New York: Oxford University Press, 1994.

Lankester, Ray. *Degeneration: A Chapter in Darwinism.* London: Macmillan and Co., 1880.

Larson, Edward. *Sex, Race, and Science: Eugenics in the Deep South.* Baltimore: Johns Hopkins University Press, 1995.

Laughlin, Harry. "Eugenics in America." *Eugenics Review* 17 (April 1925): 28–35.

———. "The Eugenics Exhibit at Chicago: A Description of the Wall-Panel Survey of Eugenics Exhibited in the Hall of Science, Century of Progress Exposition, Chicago, 1933–34." *Journal of Heredity* 26 (1935): 155–162.

Leaming, Hugo. "The Ben Ishmael Tribe: A Fugitive 'Nation' of the Old Northwest." In *The Ethnic Frontier: Group Survival in Chicago and the Midwest,* edited by Melvin Holli and Peter Jones. Grand Rapids, Mich.: Wm. B. Eerdmans Publishing Co., 1977.

———. "Hidden Americans: Maroons of Virginia and the Carolinas." Ph.D. dissertation, University of Illinois at Chicago Circle, 1975.

———. *Hidden Americans: Maroons of Virginia and the Carolinas.* New York: Garland Publishing, Inc., 1995.

Leary, Edward. *Indianapolis: The Story of a City.* Indianapolis: Bobbs-Merrill Company, 1971.

Lemon, James. *The Best Poor Man's Country: A Geographical Study of Early Southeastern Pennsylvania.* Baltimore: Johns Hopkins University Press, 1972.

Lender, Mark. "The Enlisted Line: The Continental Soldiers of New Jersey." Ph.D. dissertation, Rutgers University, 1975.

Lewis, Oscar. "The Culture of Poverty." In *On Understanding Poverty,* edited by Daniel P. Moynihan. New York: Basic Books, 1968.

———. *La Vida: A Puerto Rican Family in the Culture of Poverty—San Juan and New York.* New York: Random House, 1966.

Leybourne, Grace. "Urban Adjustments of Migrants from the Southern Appalachian Plateaus." *Social Forces* 16 (1937): 238–246.

Logan's Indianapolis Directory. Indianapolis: Logan and Co., 1868.

Lombardo, Paul. "The American Breed: Nazi Eugenics and the Origin of the Pioneer Fund." *Albany Law Review* 65 (May 2002): 743–830.

———. "Miscegenation, Eugenics, and Racism: Historical Footnotes to *Loving v. Virginia.*" *Davis Law Review* 21 (1988): 422–452.

————. "Three Generations, No Imbeciles: New Light on *Buck v. Bell.*" *New York University Law Review* 60, no. 1 (1985): 50–62.

Ludmer, Kenneth. *Genetics and American Society: A Historical Approach.* Baltimore: Johns Hopkins University Press, 1972.

Luker, Ralph. *The Social Gospel in Black and White: American Racial Reform, 1885–1912.* Chapel Hill: University of North Carolina Press, 1998.

Main, Jackson Turner. *The Social Structure of Revolutionary America.* Princeton: Princeton University Press, 1965.

Marr, Timothy. "Imagining Ishmael: Studies of Islamic Orientalism in America from the Puritans to Melville." Ph.D. dissertation, Yale University, 1997.

Maxwell, James. "Down from the Hills and into the Slums." *The Reporter,* December 13, 1956, 27–29.

Mayall, David. *Gypsy-Travellers in Nineteenth-Century Society.* New York: Cambridge University Press, 1988.

McCann, Mary, Joseph Ruane, and Séamas Ó Síocháin. *Irish Travellers: Culture and Ethnicity.* Belfast: The Institute of Irish Studies, The Queen's University of Belfast, 1994.

McCloud, Aminah Beverly. *African American Islam.* New York: Routledge, 1995.

McCulloch, Oscar. "Fifty Years of the Indianapolis Benevolent Society." In *Year-Book of Charities, 1885–1886.* Indianapolis: Carlon and Hollenbeck, 1886.

————. Personal diary (1877–1891). Reverend Oscar C. McCulloch Papers, Indiana State Library, Indiana Division, Indianapolis.

————. "State and National Registration of the Dependant, the Defective and the Delinquent Classes" In *Proceedings of the National Conference of Charities and Correction* (1891).

————. "The Tribe of Ishmael: A Study in Social Degradation," *Proceedings of the Conference of Charities and Correction* (1888), 154–159. Reprint: Indianapolis: Charity Organization Society, 1889.

Mearns, Andrew, *The Bitter Cry of Outcast London.* London: Clarke, 1883.

Melish, William. *The History of the Imperial Council Ancient Arabic Order Nobles of the Mystic Shrine for North America, Second Edition, 1872–1921.* Cincinnati: Abingdon Press, 1921.

Middlekauff, Robert. "Why Men Fought in the American Revolution." *Huntington Library Quarterly* 43 (1980): 138–148. Reprinted in Peter Onuf, ed. *Patriots, Redcoats, and Loyalists:* New York and London: Garland Publishing, Inc., 1991.

Millard, David. *A Journal of Travels in Egypt, Arabia Petrea, and the Holy Land.* New York: Lamport, Blakemann and Law, 1853.

Montague, Ashley. *Human Heredity.* Cleveland: World Publishing Co., 1959.

Muhammad, Elijah. *The Fall of America.* Chicago: Muhammad's Temple of Islam, 1973.

————. *Message to the Blackman in America.* Newport News, Va.: United Brothers Communications Systems, 1992.

Myrdal, Gunnar. *Challenge to Affluence.* New York: Pantheon Books, 1963.

Naff, Alixa. *Becoming American: The Early Arab Immigrant Experience.* Carbondale: Southern Illinois University Press, 1985.

Nance, Susan. "Mystery of the Moorish Science Temple: Southern Blacks and American Alternative Spirituality in 1920s Chicago." *Religion and American Culture: A Journal of Interpretation* 12 (2002): 123–166.

Nash, Gary. "Poverty and Politics in Early American History." In *Down and Out in Early America,* edited by Billy G. Smith. University Park: Pennsylvania University Press, 2004.

Nicholas, Stacey. "John Freeman Fugitive Slave Case (of 1853)." In *The Encyclopedia of Indianapolis,* edited by David Bodenhamer and Robert Barrows. Bloomington: Indiana University Press, 1994.

Nowland, John. *Early Reminiscences of Indianapolis, with Short Biographical Sketches of Its Early Citizens, and of a Few of the Prominent Business Men of the Present Day.* Indianapolis: Sentinel Book and Job Printing House, 1870.

Obeidat, Marwan. *American Literature and Orientalism.* Berlin: K. Schwarz, 1998.

O'Brien, John. *At Home in the Heart of Appalachia.* New York: Knopf, 2001.

Olsen, Jack. *Black Is Best: The Riddle of Cassius Clay.* New York: Dell, 1967.

Ordover, Nancy. *American Eugenics: Race, Queer Anatomy, and the Science of Nationalism.* Minneapolis: University of Minnesota Press, 2003.

Oren, Michael. *Power, Faith, and Fantasy: America in the Middle East, 1776 to the Present.* New York: W. W. Norton and Company, 2007.

Patrick, Michael, and Evelyn Goodrich Trickel. *Orphan Trains to Missouri.* Columbia: University of Missouri Press, 1997.

Perrin, William Henry, ed. *History of Bourbon, Scott, Harrison and Nicholas Counties, Kentucky.* Chicago: O. L. Baskin and Co., 1882.

Piatt Dunn, Jacob. *Greater Indianapolis: The History, the Industries, the Institutions, and the People of a City of Homes.* Chicago: The Lewis Publishing Co., 1910.

Pick, Daniel. *Faces of Degeneration: A European Disorder, c.1848–c.1918.* New York: Cambridge University Press, 1989.

Prashad, Vijay. *Everybody Was Kung Fu Fighting: Afro-Asian Connections and the Myth of Cultural Purity.* Boston: Beacon Press, 2001.

———. *The Karma of Brown Folk.* Minneapolis: University of Minnesota Press, 2000.

Rafter, Nicole Hahn. *White Trash: The Eugenics Family Studies 1877–1919.* Boston: Northeastern University Press, 1988.

Rauschenbusch, Walter. *A Theology for the Social Gospel.* New York: Macmillan, 1917.

Remnick, David. *King of the World: Muhammad Ali and the Rise of an American Hero.* New York: Alfred A. Knopf, 1998.

Resch, John. "Federal Welfare for Revolutionary War Veterans." *Social Service Review* 56 (June 1982): 171–195.

———. *Suffering Soldiers: Revolutionary War Veterans, Moral Sentiment, and Political Culture in the Early Republic.* Amherst: University of Massachusetts Press, 1999.

Rice, Thurman. "The Beginnings of Organized Charity in Indianapolis." *One Hundred Years of Medicine: Indianapolis, 1820–1920: Monthly Bulletin: Indiana State Board of Health* 44 (1952).

———. "The 'Tribe of Ishmael' Study." *One Hundred Years of Medicine: Indianapolis, 1820–1920: Monthly Bulletin: Indiana State Board of Health* 45 (1952).

Riis, Jacob. *How the Other Half Lives.* New York: Charles Scribner's Sons, 1890. Reprint, New York: Penguin, 1997.

Riley, James Whitcomb. "Little Orphant Annie," in *Complete Works,* vol. 5, Indianapolis: Bobbs-Merrill Company, 1916.

Roediger, David. *The Wages of Whiteness: Race and the Making of the American Working Class.* London and New York: Verso, 1999.

Rose, Gregory. "Hoosier Origins: The Nativity of Indiana's United States–Born Population in 1850." *Indiana Magazine of History* 81 (September 1985): 201–232.

———. "Upland Southerners: The County Origins of Southern Migrants to Indiana by 1850." *Indiana Magazine of History* 82 (September 1986): 242–263.

Rosen, Christine. *Preaching Eugenics: Religious Leaders and the American Eugenics Movement.* New York: Oxford University Press, 2004.

Rowlands, John, and Sheila Rowlands. *Welsh Family History: A Guide to Research.* Birmingham, Eng.: The Federation of Family History Societies Ltd., 1998.

Royster, Charles. *A Revolutionary People at War: The Continental Army and American Character, 1775–1783.* Chapel Hill: University of North Carolina Press, 1979.

Rydell, Robert. *All the World's a Fair: Visions of Empire at American International Expositions, 1876–1916.* Chicago: University of Chicago Press, 1984.

———. *World of Fairs: The Century-of-Progress Expositions.* Chicago: University of Chicago Press, 1993.

Said, Edward. *Orientalism.* New York: Vintage Books, 1979.

Sakolsky, Ron, and James Koehnline, eds. *Gone to Croatan: Origins of North American Dropout Culture.* Brooklyn: Autonomedia Dropout Press, 1993.

Salinger, Sharon. *"To Serve Well and Faithfully": Labor and Indentured Servants in Pennsylvania 1682–1800.* New York: Cambridge University Press, 1987.

Sandage, Scott. *Born Losers: A History of Failure in America.* Cambridge: Harvard University Press, 2005.

Saunders, Lucretia Ann. "Thurman Brooks Rice." In *The Encyclopedia of Indianapolis,* edited by David Bodenhamer and Robert Barrows. Bloomington, Indianapolis: Indiana University Press, 1994.

Savannah Unit of the Georgia Writers Project of the Works Projects Administration. *Drums and Shadows: Survival Studies Among the Georgia Coastal Negroes.* Athens: University of Georgia Press, 1986; orig. pub. 1940.

Schaumann, Merri Lou Scriber, ed. *Indictments: 1750–1800, Cumberland County, Pennsylvania.* Dover, Pa.: M. L. S. Schaumann, 1989.

Seeley, John, et al. *Commmunity Chest: A Case Study in Philanthropy.* Toronto: University of Toronto Press, 1957.

Sellers, John. "The Common Soldier in the American Revolution." In *Military History of the American Revolution: Proceedings of the Sixth Military*

History Symposium, United States Air Force Academy, 10–11 October 1974, edited by Stanley Underdal. Washington, D.C.: Office of Air Force History, Headquarters USAF, 1976.

Sha'ban, Fuad. *Islam and Arabs in Early American Thought: The Roots of Orientalism in America.* Durham, N.C.: The Acorn Press, 1991.

Shapiro, Henry. *Appalachia on Our Mind: The Southern Mountains and Mountaineers in the American Consciousness, 1870–1920.* Chapel Hill: University of North Carolina Press, 1978.

Shy, John. *A People Numerous and Armed: Reflections on the Military Struggle for American Independence.* Ann Arbor: University of Michigan Press, 1990.

Sibley, David. *Geographies of Exclusion: Outsiders in Urban Societies.* Oxford: Blackwell, 1981.

Simler, Lucy. "Tenancy in Colonial Pennsylvania: The Case of Chester County." *William and Mary Quarterly* 3d Series, 43 (1986): 542–569.

Simpson, Frank. "The Moorish Science Temple and Its 'Koran.'" *Moslem World* 37 (1947): 56–61.

Slaughter, Thomas. *The Whiskey Rebellion: Frontier Epilogue to the American Revolution.* New York: Oxford University Press, 1988.

Smith, Abbot Emerson. *Colonists in Bondage: White Servitude and Convict Labor in America, 1607–1776.* Chapel Hill: University of North Carolina Press, 1947.

Smith, Billy G., ed. *Down and Out in Early America.* University Park: Pennsylvania State University Press, 2004.

Stein, Judith. *The World of Marcus Garvey.* Baton Rouge: Louisiana State University Press, 1986.

Stern, Alexandra. *Eugenic Nation: Faults and Frontiers of Better Breeding in Modern America.* Berkeley: University of California Press, 2005.

Stoddard, Lothrop. *The New World of Islam.* New York: Charles Scribner's Sons, 1921.

———. *The Rising Tide of Color: Against White World-Supremacy.* New York: Charles Scribner's Sons, 1920.

Sulgrove, Berry. *History of Indianapolis and Marion County.* Philadelphia: L. H. Everts and Co., 1884.

Sway, Marlene. *Familiar Strangers: Gypsy Life in America.* Urbana: University of Illinois Press, 1988.

Trussell, John, Jr. *The Pennsylvania Line: Regimental Organization and Operations, 1776–1783.* Harrisburg: Pennsylvania Historical and Museum Commission, 1977.

Turner, Richard Brent. *Islam in the African-American Experience.* Bloomington: Indiana University Press, 1997.

Twain, Mark. *The Innocents Abroad.* New York: Harper and Brothers, 1911.

Venkatesh, Sudhir. *Off the Books: The Underground Economy of the Urban Poor.* Cambridge: Harvard University Press, 2006.

Waite, Catharine. *The Mormon Prophet and His Harem.* Cambridge, Mass.: Riverside Press, 1866.

Watson, Frank. *The Charity Organization Movement in the United States.* New York: Macmillan Co., 1922.

Weeks, Genevieve. *Oscar Carleton McCulloch, 1843–1891: Preacher and Practitioner of Applied Christianity.* Indianapolis: Indianapolis Historical Society, 1976.

Wessel, Thomas. "Agricultural Depression and the West, 1870–1900." *European Contributions to American Studies* 16 (1989): 72–80.

Wiggam, Albert Edward. *The Next Age of Man.* Indianapolis: Bobbs-Merrill Company, 1927.

Wilson, Peter Lamborn. *Sacred Drift: Essays on the Margins of Islam.* San Francisco: City Lights Books, 1993.

Wood, Gordon. *The Radicalism of the American Revolution.* New York: Alfred A. Knopf, 1991.

Wright, James Frank. "The Tribe of Ishmael." Unpublished manuscript, Indiana State Archives, Commission on Public Records.

Index

Abd ar-Rahman, Ibraham, 164, 165
African American Islam: Asiatic identification by, 144–49; black racial purity and, 151–54; competing historical tendencies in, 169–70; emergence during 1920s and, 140–42; Ishmaelites and, 11–15, 162, 168–69, 208–8n20; rise to prominence of, 163–66; themes in history of, 14–15
African American people: black nationalist movement and, 148–49; in 1870s Indianapolis, 22, 25; Muslim slaves and, 13, 164–66, 172. *See also* African American Islam
The African Times and Orient Review, 146
Ahmadiyah movement, 146–47
Aid to Families with Dependent Children (AFDC), 100
alcohol abuse: Estabrook and, 123; McCulloch and, 59; Wright's portrayal and, 86, 93, 95–96. *See also* drinking in rural culture
Alford, Terry: *A Prince among Slaves,* 165
Alger, Horatio, 6–7, 181–82
Ali, Ben. *See* Bilali
Ali, Duse Mohammed, 146
Ali, Muhammad (born Cassius Clay), 13, 144, 163
Ali, Noble Drew, 140–42, 144, 147, 207–8n20; *Holy Koran (Seven Circle Koran),* 141–42
Ali ben Said, Muhammad. *See* Ben Said, Muhammad Ali

Allen, Theodore, 5
Allen, Woody, 17
American Dream mythology, 18
American Eugenics Society, 156
American nativism. *See* Tribal Twenties
American Orientalism: Estabrook and, 162; history of, 13–14; McCulloch and, 162; Midwestern town names and, 167; negative stereotypes and, 5, 8, 43–44, 51, 55–56, 139; Orientalist films and, 138–39, 162; romantic portrayals and, 51–55, 138–39; writings on Islam and, 30–31
American "underclass," 16–17
antimiscegenation legislation, 8–9, 75, 128–29, 156
Arabber (slang term), 55–56
Arnold, Robert, 31
Asiatic threat, 134–38, 139. *See also* African American Islam; Islam
authority, suspicion of: Ishmaelites and, 107–8, 203; Upland Southern migrants and, 199

Bagby brothers, 25
Baltimore, Maryland, 55–56
Bara, Theda, 138
Barbary Pirate War, 31
Barbour, Lucian, 92–93
Barker, Lewellys, 108
Bartlett, Caroline, 94
Battle of Blue Licks, 183
begging, 27, 37, 78, 82, 83, 84, 122
Bell, Alexander Graham, 102, 114
Ben Ali. *See* Bilali (Ben Ali)

Text: 10/13 Sabon
Display: Sabon
Compositor: International Typesetting and Composition
Indexer: Marcia Carlson
Printer and binder: Sheridan Books, Inc.